The Cheapskate's Guide to

PARIS

The Cheapskate's Guide to

PARIS

Hotels, Food, Shopping, Day Trips, and More

REVISED AND UPDATED

CONNIE EMERSON

CITADEL PRESS
Kensington Publishing Corp.
www.kensingtonbooks.com

CITADEL PRESS books are published by

Kensington Publishing Corp.
850 Third Avenue
New York, NY 10022

First Kensington printing August 2001

10 9 8 7 6 5 4 3 2 1

Printed in the United States of America

Library of Congress Control Number: 2001092632

ISBN 0-8065-2215-1

Contents

*places where dinner costs much less. We'll take you down
the gastronomic path from boulangeries, brasseries, and
bistros to supermarkets and swanky restaurants, pointing
out bargains along the way.*

Someone once said, "A little knowledge is a dangerous thing." But when it comes to Paris, a little knowledge is vital if you want to save money. And since the more you know the more bargains you'll find, this chapter shows you how to get the information needed to find them.

Acknowledgments

It takes a lot of people to write a book, not just the one whose name is on the cover. I can't acknowledge some of them by name—the Basque taxi driver in Biarritz, the science professor at Parc la Villette, the school children on a field trip. To the others, whose names I know—Laura Colby, Pat Crawley, Joy Crowley, George Emerson, Ralph Emerson H. III, Judy Fitzgerald, Jean Pierre Haase, Mary Jean Jecklin, Susan Manlin Katzmann, Renata Polt, Louise Prevost, Earlene and George Ridge, Celia and Tom Scully—my deep appreciation. Thanks, too, to my editor, Allan J. Wilson, as well as the other people at Citadel Press who worked on the project. And, as always, a huge thank you to my husband, Ralph, for his encouragement and support.

Introduction

Paris is the stuff of travel dreams. Even stay-at-homes long to experience April in Paris, Paris in the spring, or Paris at any time at all. Much of the "City of Light's" charisma comes from its romantic mystique, which began as far back as the fourteenth century, when one visitor observed that "to be in Paris, is to be."

Since that time, an ever-increasing number of people have become enamored with the city and the legends—part reality, part myth—that have grown up around her. From the fictional Jean Valjean in *Les Miserables* to the operatic Mimi and Rodolfo in their *La Boheme* garret; from the paintings of Toulouse-Lautrec's can-can girls at the Moulin Rouge to accounts of the laissez-faire life of Americans like F. Scott Fitzgerald and Ernest Hemingway, we've snatched pieces of Parisian life. Although we wonder if the city can possibly live up to its image, we hold fast to the dream.

Now you've decided to turn your version of that dream into reality. You're concerned, though, that the trip will cost a small fortune. Worry no more. The last time *I* saw Paris, in all corners of the city it was possible to find bargains: reasonably priced dinners in those intimate cafes with a single red rose on each table; charmingly French hotel rooms at discounted rates; free sights, activities, and entertainment—more than you could possible squeeze into one vacation.

To be sure, there are very expensive hotels. And comparatively speaking, rack rates (rates that are published) for almost any room in Paris will be higher than a comparable one in most other major cities of the world. Notice, though, that we're talking about the *published* rates—not what you actually have to pay. It's just as possible to find good deals on Paris hotels as elsewhere—they'll just be good deals that cost somewhat more.

It's the same with food. You *can* spend $300 (and more) on dinner for two. But you certainly don't have to. In the majority of places to eat, complete dinners start between $20 and $30, and sometimes good-sized lunches are even less. By knowing where to go, you can cut dining costs still further. I've spent many days in Paris in which my total food cost was between $10 and $20. And I ate very well.

As far as attractions are concerned, you can have a great time without spending much money. More than a hundred museums, monuments, and important buildings—architectural treasures dating back to the twelfth century as well as impressive contemporary structures—are only some of the places to visit. While some charge admission fees, others are free.

Many of these important places are linked to the city's history, often violent and filled with intrigue, but never dull. As far as we know, the first Parisians were members of a Celtic tribe called the Parisii, who lived on the Île de la Cité. In 52 B.C. the Romans, who had until that time thought that only southern Gaul had value, extended the scope of their conquests to Paris. They renamed the area Lutetia, rebuilt structures on the island in the Roman style, and extended the settlement to the left bank, where evidence of their occupation survives today. Barbarian raids, however, forced the Romans to retrench and regroup. They built a wall around the Île de la Cité, where they prospered—more or less peacefully—until Clovis, chief of the Franks, defeated the Romans in 486 at the battle of Soissons.

The city then went into a decline and didn't revive until the tenth century, with the rise of Hugh Capet and the succeeding

Capetian kings. Although by the twelfth century Paris was on its way to becoming one of the world's leading cities, most of it was an appalling mess. The city's commercial center, on the right bank of the Seine, was a warren of narrow streets lined with buildings of wood and rubble. Standards of sanitation, like those of other Medieval cities, were deplorable. No provision was made for the collection of garbage, so refuse was thrown in the streets. A son of King Louis VI was killed when a hog, rooting in the offal in the rue St-Jacques, charged between the legs of his horse which threw him to the ground.

Amidst all this, however, grand buildings of stone and mortar—the Cathedral of Notre Dame, the Palais de Justice, the Louvre—began to be constructed. Also in the twelfth century, the University of Paris was founded, and a hundred years later the city had become the metropolis of northern Europe, with a population of about 240,000.

Then came the Hundred Years War (1337–1453), and in 1358 the first of the rebellions against the Crown. From that time, through the late Medieval period and into the Renaissance, French kings grew increasingly prone to living in the country in magnificent chateaus while centralizing their power in Paris. Throughout the next centuries, as in the past, progress was interrupted by a series of wars and the internal unrest that resulted from them. In 1598, at about the time of the end of the Wars of Religion, Henri IV began the transformation of Paris from a sixteenth-century Medieval city into the classical showplace it was to become, completing the Hôtel de Ville (city hall), which had been started by Francois I, and the great gallery of the Louvre.

Henri VI and his chief minister, the Duke of Sully, followed by Louis XIII and Cardinal Richelieu, his chief minister, developed France economically and eradicated any traces of feudal authority by concentrating power in the central ruling figure—the king. Absolute monarchy in France reached its zenith during the reigns of the last three Louis. Louis XIV, who believed that he had been commissioned by God to reign, chose the sun as his official emblem to indicate that as the planets derived their glory and sustenance from the sun, the nation derived its from him.

Louis XV has been described by historians as an "indolent rake," and his grandson, Louis XVI, who succeeded him, as "weak in character and mentally dull." The latter has been accused of dragging the government to its lowest depths of extravagance and irresponsibility, yet it was during the reigns of these three (from 1643 to 1792, a total of 149 years), that many of Paris's most impressive buildings were erected. However, their collective building sprees were cut short in 1793, when Louis XVI was beheaded during the French Revolution.

Napoleon Bonaparte (1804–1814) was no less ardent about building campaigns than those that involved military conquest. But it was Napoleon III who, in 1852, began transforming Paris into Europe's most magnificent city. He put Baron Georges-Eugene Haussmann, a lawyer by training, in charge of the massive modernization project. During his 17 years as head of urban planning, Haussmann created a star of avenues radiating out from the Arc de Triomphe. Streets laid out in Medieval days were replaced by broad boulevards, city parks were created, and new sewer and water systems were installed.

Then, in 1870, France became involved in the Franco-Prussian war. Paris became a city under siege, and zoo animals were shot for food. When the war ended the following year, the country was thrown into political and economic chaos. It wasn't until almost 20 years later that Paris fully recovered and the Belle Epoche (the Beautiful Age) began. Art Nouveau was then the decorative style of choice, as the wealthy built mansions to reflect their prosperity.

Great scholars had gravitated to Paris since the founding of its university and the Sorbonne, but it was from the middle of the nineteenth century to the beginning of World War II that the city, as a center of art and literature, was at its height.

The years between World Wars I and II were also the glory days of the expatriate writers, whose views of Left Bank life became part of our American literary tradition.

Of all the events in its life, it was perhaps during the final days of the Nazi occupation that Paris was in its deepest crisis. General Von Cholitz had been commanded by Hitler to burn Paris to the ground. Fortunately, he didn't want history to remember him as the man who destroyed Paris, so he disobeyed the order.

I realize that to synopsize French history, with all its convolutions and contradictions, into a few pages is folly. But even a brief résumé of an extremely complicated two thousand years points to the fact that the rulers most maligned for their excesses—which included excessive expenditures on impressive buildings—are most responsible for the sights that are tourist treasures today. It also shows that the French have had a more turbulent history than almost any other country in Europe. When people speak of the French Revolution they're usually referring to only a few events during the uprising that lasted from 1789 until the coupe d'état by Napoleon Bonaparte in 1799. There have been other revolutions as well—the July Revolution of 1830, the February Revolution of 1848, the Paris Commune uprising of 1871, the student revolt of 1968, and though less violent, the workers' strikes of 1995.

That same revolutionary spirit guided the impressionists, the surrealists, and all other artists who ventured into new forms of expression. It propelled architects like Le Corbousier and Mansart, poets like Baudelaire, playwrights like Racine, philosophers like Descartes and Sartre, and the French fashion industry—all of which has combined to make Paris a dynamic place, with today's avant garde attractions mixed with those that were avant garde in their day. It's a city of extremes—very old and very new, classical and ultra-modern. And that goes for prices, too. Some pleasures are excessively expensive, others incredibly cheap.

Which brings us back to the purpose of this book—to help you find deals to make your Paris trip everything you hope it will be, without giving you the post-Paris blues when the credit card bills start coming in the mail. Each of the 13 chapters deals with a different aspect of travel—accommodations, dining, shopping, museums, sightseeing—in which bargains are available. You don't have to read them in any particular order; read those that apply to you, skip those that do not. In short, use the book as a starting point to find good deals that fit your personal travel style.

Just as you may enjoy nightclubbing more than I do, we also may have different ideas on what makes a bargain. While you may think admission to a chateau at half price is a value, I may prefer to save my money and walk around the grounds instead. Your idea of the perfect night out may be the Folies Bergère, while mine is listening to some great jazz piano. In short, we travelers don't all look at the world through the same glasses—rose colored or otherwise—so deals and discounts aren't going to have the same value to all of us. As a result, although I have earnestly tried not to let my own preferences and prejudices get in the way, I may have omitted a bargain or two merely because they didn't seem like bargains to me. Then, too, books have a finite number of pages, and Paris is a big city, with too many great hotels, restaurants, shops, and attractions to include in one volume. So a writer must make choices.

In the process of making mine, I've stuck to the premise that although it's exciting to get something for nothing, that's not always the way it works. In many of life's undertakings there are tradeoffs—you have to spend extra time looking for discount coupons, or walk to the back of a store to take advantage of an offer. So when this is the case, I've tried to balance the gain against any inconvenience.

Just about as good as getting something for nothing is getting it at a bargain. My philosophy has always been that it's foolish to pay $50 for something you can get for $25—that it's easier to save money than to earn it. So while parts of this book are about getting things for free, others are about getting a lot for very little. All of the book is dedicated to showing you how to obtain maximum value, whatever time and money you have to spend. It's also written with the hope that you'll have such a good time in Paris that you'll be planning a return trip on your flight home.

The Cheapskate's Guide to

PARIS

1

Pre-Paris Planning

Traveling to a foreign city you've never set eyes on can be a lot like going on a blind date, especially when the pleasures and problems you anticipate are derived from hearsay and hype (photos taken from the best angles). And like the blind date, chances of a trip to Paris being a success depend a lot upon the planning—based on the facts you have at hand—that you do in advance.

As with any trip, preplanning will also enable you to maximize both your time and money—and you'll have a better time in the bargain. This is especially true of foreign destinations, where language and cultural differences can be confusing when you're on the scene and don't have a clue how to get where you want to go.

That's not to say that you shouldn't travel to France because you don't know the language or understand the customs. But you should make an attempt to learn a few basic French phrases and find out about the courtesies of daily life.

Here's an example. Parisians have been described as haughty, arrogant, and disdainful of anyone who isn't one of them. But while we often think Parisians are rude, they think the same of us. And with reason. You see, we Americans are prone to begin conversations without first greeting the person we're talking to. In France, however, it's considered extremely impolite to approach a stranger on the street, a shopkeeper, or anyone, without greeting him or her with a *bonjour* ("good day") before saying anything else. It's also proper form to say *au revoir* upon leaving. You should also learn the French equivalents of our "please" and "thank you"—*s'il vous plaît* (seel voo PLAY) and *merci* (mehr-SEE). Not only is it polite, but you'll also have a better time if you try to say a few words. People naturally are more helpful and open when they know you're interested in them enough to try to communicate.

If you have time, take an adult education class. They're inexpensive and enjoyable. If you took French in high school or college, get a basic textbook and brush up on it. Even if you can't manage more than a couple of words, don't let that stop you. It's not necessary to speak French in order to have a good time.

Of course, it's more difficult to navigate efficiently when you don't know the language. And of course, you'll occasionally lose your bearings. But getting lost in Paris is actually fun, especially in the older districts, where each narrow street looks just like a Utrillo painting.

Destination Pros and Cons

There are other considerations, however, besides language to think about. Because Paris is relatively expensive, the decision to visit it isn't one most of us make on the spur of the moment. In choosing any destination, it's wise to analyze your expectations and the possibilities of their being met. Think about the aspects of travel that have made you happiest and what sorts of things have caused you to be less than pleased with journeys past. As far as travel is concerned, we all have preferences and prejudices, and it's a good idea to balance them, one against another, before we decide to take any trip.

I will readily admit that I have several Paris prejudices. I'm particularly sensitive to the *essence d'égout* that wafts from the sewer mains in the older parts of the city, and dodging the dog droppings on the sidewalks isn't my idea of a pleasant stroll. However, the compensations—watching sparrows bathe in a medieval churchyard puddle after the rain, walking along the Seine when the sun's last rays turn the buildings along its banks to spun gold, breakfasting on a *real* French pastry—more than make up for what I perceive as the city's deficiencies.

It's important, too, to take your stamina and physical condition into account. Paris is not an impossible destination for those unable to climb flights of steps easily or walk fairly long distances, but it is more expensive. Hotels equal in all other respects cost less if they don't have elevators.

By far the most economical transport—the Métro and bus service—requires negotiating stairways or walking long distances when making connections. Portal-to-portal taxi service will conserve your energy, but can easily cost more than $50 a day if you want to visit a number of attractions. The frequent lack of handrails, especially on the steps leading to the *bateaux-mouches* (sight-seeing boats on the Seine), is also a potential problem.

Another question to ask yourself is if your degree of concern about terrorist attacks is great enough to keep you from having a good time. Admittedly, Paris had its share of these attacks in the early '90s, but the violence has subsided over the past ten years. So when you look at the probabilities of your being involved, they are rather remote.

As far as crimes against individuals are concerned, you have less to worry about in Paris than in most major cities. As one U.S. citizen who has lived in Paris for years says, "Paris is just the opposite of most American cities. The central core is its safest part. The only way tourists could really get into trouble," she adds, "is by taking the wrong Métro line to its end just to see what's there. While many of the suburbs are very nice, some of them are loaded with housing projects where there's a great deal of racial tension."

Of course, as in any city, there are pickpockets at crowded tourist sites, and it's not a good idea to walk along deserted streets in questionable neighborhoods. (Stalingrad, Gare de

Lyon, and Oberkampf stations have a reputation for after-dark drug dealing.)

If you're concerned about possible medical emergencies, rest assured. Both the Hôpital Americain (American Hospital; 63, blvd Victor Hugo, Neuilly-sur-Seine; 46-41-25-25; Neuilly Métro station) and the Hôpital Brittanique (Hertford British Hospital; 3, rue Barbes, Levallois; 46-39-22-22; Levallois-Perett Métro station) offer 24-hour service.

Setting the Travel Wheels in Motion

Once you've decided that it makes sense for you to turn the Paris dream to reality, don't delay in starting to gather information. If you don't do regular business with a travel agent, ask friends and fellow workers for recommendations. A good travel agent can save you both time and money.

Of course, it's easier if you already have a travel agent— one who doesn't charge fees for services, and with whom you have done business previously. Agents are understandably reluctant to spend any appreciable amount of time helping plan a trip for a customer they haven't worked with—someone who may have the agent do all the research, then go elsewhere for the bookings.

If you're an unknown quantity, the agent will give you information from the computer, but it's unrealistic to expect him or her to invest time and expense making phone calls and searching through books and other sources to find accommodations or tours that exactly fit your specifications. By contrast, if you have a good working relationship with an agent, he or she will spend a great deal of time helping you plan your trip.

Ideally, the agent will give you some ideas, brochures, and general information when you begin planning. Most agents have access to a variety of publications, such as the *Official Airlines Guide (OAG)*, the *Official Hotel Guide*, and/or the *Star*

Guide, which is updated yearly and rates hotels with from two to five stars.

Combining your own research with the agent's input, you'll be able to make informed decisions that should save you money while fashioning a trip that's tailor-made to your travel measurements. The agent will finalize arrangements for you, receiving commissions from the suppliers.

Of course, it is possible to do all the planning and negotiating yourself. Although it's more difficult and time consuming, some travelers prefer to deal directly with the airlines and such—especially hotels. Whichever way you choose to go, gather together as many hotel brochures, tour guide photos, and as much rate information as you can. Even if you aren't a regular customer, most travel agents will let you look through the *Official Hotel Guide* and *Hotel and Travel Index,* which give rack (published) rates for hotels around the world. These are invaluable when you want to check the hotel rates charged in various packages against the rack rates. And judge the hotel photos with the knowledge that they're taken from the most flattering angles possible. If a photo doesn't look very appealing, chances are the room won't either.

While you're gathering info on airfares and accommodations, you'll want to send for general information and specifics about sight-seeing, activities, and the like (see chapter 13 for information sources). The more you know before you take off, the more money you'll save once you're on the scene. For instance, if you're going to do some business while in Paris that will require making a number of phone calls, you'll save money and time when you know about phone cards. They are called Telecartes and can be purchased for various amounts (the least expensive costs about $10) at *tabacs* (newsstands). When inserted in pay phones, these cards will enable you to make your calls for a fraction of what they'd cost if you dialed from your room, especially in the upscale hotels. When dialing direct to Paris from North America, dial 001 followed by 33 (the code for France), 1 (the Paris code), and the eight-digit Paris phone number. For example: 001-33-1-12-34-56-78. When calling the same number from another area code in France, dial 16-1 and the eight-digit phone number. You would dial only the eight-digit number when calling from Paris.

Before you phone home from your room, check to see what the hotel's international calling charges will be. Chances are they'll be exorbitant, even though your room was a bargain, especially if it falls into the first-class or deluxe category. Save money by going to a public phone booth and using your Telecarte to make the call.

You'll save both time and money obtaining good maps, including those of the subway (Métro) and bus routes, in advance of your trip. By studying them, you'll be able to plan each day's activities to save time that might otherwise have been spent backtracking or getting lost.

In addition to the maps available from the Office de Tourisme, you may want more detailed layouts of the various parts of the city. Although it costs from about $19 to $24 in France (the former price in the suburbs, the latter on the touristy rue de Rivoli), *Ponchet-Plan Net* is a great tool for getting acquainted with the way Paris is laid out. This book of maps contains a listing of every street in the city as well as maps that are large enough to be easily readable, with arrows indicating the direction of one-way streets. It also contains maps of the airports and outlying areas, a Métro map, and information on sports facilities, markets, and other places of interest, including the nearest Métro stations. It comes in two sizes, one pocket sized, the other 8½ by 12 inches. I prefer the larger book, since it's easier to read. But it's difficult to carry along on your explorations, so you need to locate your destinations in advance. Fortunately, the book is available online, at www.editions-ponchet.fr.

Another good map book is *Paris par Arrondissement,* which is available at several travel bookstores (see chapter 13). The regular edition costs $16.95; with thumb index, $19.95.

Whatever the Weather

If realization of your Paris dreams is dependent upon the weather—perhaps watching life from a sidewalk café table or spending sunny hours at the street markets—plan your trip for between the first of May and the middle of October. Forget about April in Paris. May is much more dependable for great spring weather, and cool air masses from the Russian steppes and Scandinavia can start pouring down in late October. Of course, if you're one of those lucky people who's not affected by weather and you don't mind cold winds, gloomy skies, and trees with no leaves, you'll save a lot of money. Both airfares and hotel rates are traditionally at their lowest—and often substantially so—during the winter months.

Most American tourists visit Paris in July and August. However, the chart below, which gives the high and low average temperatures by month, shows that other months are equally good weatherwise. Degress are Fahrenheit.

	JAN.	FEB.	MAR.	APR.	MAY	JUNE	JULY	AUG.	SEPT.	OCT.	NOV.	DEC.
HI	43	45	54	60	68	73	76	75	70	60	50	44
Low	34	34	39	43	49	55	58	58	53	46	40	36

It may come as a surprise, but you should know that Paris gets more rain than London. On average, there's at least some precipitation on 17 days during January, 16 in December, 15 in November, and 14 in February. However, the largest average amount of rainfall occurs in the May-through-September period (as well as during December), when there's an average 12 or 13 rainy days, with a total of 2.1 to 2.5 inches per month.

Choosing a Carrier

The commercial airlines currently flying regular schedules between North America and Paris are:

Air Canada	800/776-3000
Air France	800/237-2747
American Airlines	800/624-6262
British Airways (via London)	800/247-9297
Continental Airlines	800/344-1411
Delta	800/241-4141
Northwest Airlines	800/447-4747
United Airlines	800/241-6522
USAir	800/622-1015
Virgin Atlantic (via London)	800/862-8621

Air France and Continental fly to Orly Airport, south of the city, while the others use the newer Charles-de-Gaulle Airport, which is to the north.

Whether you pay full fare or half price for your ticket, and whether you sit in one of the plane's more desirable seats or one of its least, depend on two factors—your efforts and luck. And the former can greatly influence the latter.

By starting to plan well in advance of your departure date, you or your travel agent have time to shop around for the best fares. Study a diagram of the type of airplane you'll be taking (good travel agents and airline employees have access to the diagrams) so you can reserve one of the best seats in its class on the flight. When you've planned a trip far enough in advance, there's no reason you should have to pay the top ticket price or be squeezed in the middle of the center row.

Airfares for the North America–Paris route are almost always competitive with each other, but since there can be considerable variations in service and scheduling (and sometimes price), it's important to check around to see what's available. You'll almost always get your best fares in winter. Spring and fall air travel costs more but is usually cheaper than in summer. Like tickets for domestic flights, those to foreign destinations cost less if purchased in advance (usually 14 to 30 days). A minimum and maximum length of stay is also a condition that must be met. Midweek flights—Monday through Thursday—generally cost less than those on weekends.

Check airline ads announcing promotions in the weekly travel and entertainment sections of newspapers published in gateway cities closest to where you live. Sometimes they're advertised in weekday editions, too. Because they are limited in number and available for only a short time, fast action is necessary to get in on these bargains. On occasion, discounted tickets from selected U.S. cities to Paris are advertised by the airlines. Travelers living in the orbit of two or more international airports can often save by choosing one gateway rather than another.

Other Flight Information

In recent years, round-trip airfares to Paris have shown wide variations between the premium season and those for the period from November through May, but unlike unrestricted domestic fares, which have become increasingly higher, international air travel has maintained essentially the same price structure. Peak-season nonpromotional fares have been consistently in the $700 to $900 range, and the traditional low-season bargains have been available at pretty much the same low fares—in fact, at times some really super specials have been available.

This has, in great measure, been due to the Internet. When an airline has an unanticipated surplus of seats for a near-term date, low-price fares can be put on the net quickly and result in instant action.

In winter 2001, for instance, the Air France Web site offered New York or Boston to Paris six-night packages that started at $729 per person based on double occupancy. A package including airfare and six nights at Hôtel du Louvre cost $1,199—and the hotel's rack rate for double rooms is $287 to $350.

The savvy traveler would find out, though, that the same trip could be taken for less, because in the February 26, 2001, edition of the *New York Times,* air travel from New York's JFK to Paris was advertised for as low as $278, while Hôtel du Louvre rates were advertised on the Web for $260 a night. The Air France package ran $2,398 for two people, while the second combination cost only $2,116. Whenever you're figuring out the cost of air or accommodations on the Internet, be sure to determine whether taxes are included in the price.

Although there are dozens of Web sites with discounted travel for sale, not all of these deals are comparable, and not all sites are equally user friendly. Among those I have found easiest to use are www.expedia.com and www.travelocity.com. When I'm looking for a specific airline or hotel chain's Web site, but I don't know its exact address (URL), I use a search engine like Yahoo! or Google to find it for me.

In addition to the regularly scheduled commercial flights, several charter-flight operators fly between Paris and the United States and Canada. For some charters, you may have to purchase tickets far in advance, and stiff penalties in the event of cancellation are often required. Also, some charters are canceled if an insufficient number of passengers buy the service.

Charters seem to work best if the planes are contracted for by a group or organization that relies on its members to fill the flight and has a long track record of organizing them. Although some companies that provide planes are reliable, others aren't, so beware of doing business with those that aren't well established.

Consolidators (bucket shops) are another source of cut-rate tickets. Upon takeoff, empty seats on any commercial airplane constitute lost revenue. Airlines do everything they can to avoid these losses. When they anticipate light loads, they may advertise a limited number of tickets to the general public at cut-rate prices and sell blocks of tickets at greatly reduced rates to wholesalers, which in turn sell their unsold inventory to discounters. Airlines also sell these tickets directly to travel agencies that specialize in discounting.

Although you can often do as well when airlines have "sales," at other times, a reputable consolidator can be a source of savings.

If you've a choice between a discounted ticket on an airline with regular service and a charter flight, go with the former, even if the ticket is more expensive. When a regular airline flight is cancelled, you will be put on the airline's next available flight or ticketed on another airline that flies the same route. Charters and consolidators rarely have more than one flight a day to any particular overseas destination, so if the flight is cancelled, you won't be flying that day.

There's another risk as well. Like charter companies, consolidators can stop following through on their commitments; they may have continued to take payments from clients but stopped making payments to the airlines. If this happens and you have purchased consolidator tickets through a travel agency, you stand a good chance of getting your money refunded.

If you're dealing personally with the consolidator, pay with plastic. By sending a money order, or personal or certified check, you give up the important charge-back protection you enjoy when buying with a credit card. It's also easier to recoup your losses when you deal with a local consolidator, since you can file in small claims court if all else fails. Companies offering discounted Paris fares include:

TRAVAC, 989 6th Avenue, New York, NY 10018, and 2601 E. Jefferson Street, Orlando, FL 32803; 800/872-8800.
Council Charter, 205 E. 42nd Street, New York, NY 10017, 800/800-8222.

Cheap Tickets Inc., 345 Spear Street, San Francisco, CA
94105; 800/377-1000.
Travel Time Discounts, 1 Hallidie Plaza, No. 406, San Francisco, CA 94105; 415/677-0799.

Additional sources of cut-rate airline tickets—defying the
rule that booking flights early saves you money—are discount
travel clubs. Travel suppliers (wholesalers that buy blocks of
tickets from airlines, hotels, and the like) are sometimes left
with unsold inventory. They want to get money back on this
part of their investment, even if it's less than they receive nor-
mally—the anything's-better-than-nothing principle. Discount
travel clubs help the suppliers get rid of the inventory by
offering complete tour and cruise packages, seats on charter
flights, and, occasionally, seats on scheduled flights to their
members on a "last-minute" basis at a fraction of their regular prices—in most cases, from 15 to 60 percent off. "Last
minute," in reality, can be translated to mean a week or even
a month in advance. In exchange for yearly membership fees,
which generally run from $20 to $50, members are given
access to a toll-free hot-line number to call for information
on last-minute travel bargains. Some clubs also send newslet-
ters describing current offers to their subscribers. Among the
discount clubs now offering Paris tickets and tours are:

Last Minute Travel, 1249 Boylston Street, Boston, MA
02215; 800/527-8646.
Traveler's Advantage, 3033 S. Parker Road, Suite 1000,
Aurora, CO 80014; 800/548-1116.

Alternate Arrival Modes

There is the possibility, of course, that you will arrive in Paris
by rail from somewhere else in France, another country in
Europe, or from Great Britain via the channel tunnel (chun-

nel), ferry, or hovercraft. Whatever your method of transportation, some deals are better than others; it's just a matter of finding out about them. For instance, if you're traveling around Europe by rail, you'll want to tally up the cost of each leg of your journey to see whether a Eurailpass will save you money. Needless to say, the flexible passes that allow only a certain number of travel days during a specified period are much less expensive than passes that allow unlimited travel.

But if your trip involves extensive train travel around France, you'll definitely want to investigate the France Railpass, which allows travel on any three days during a month and costs $198 for first class, $160 for second. For two people traveling together, the Companion France Railpass costs 50 percent of the first- or second-class price for the *second* person's ticket. For $30 a day, up to six additional days in either class may be added. Even if you plan only one long excursion and a couple of day trips from Paris, you'll save with a pass. For senior discounts on train fares in France, see chapter 12.

Bedding Down

Accommodations will account for the biggest single expense of your Paris trip. An inexpensive room is considered one with a published rate of less than $150 a night. Moderately priced rooms are in the $150 to $250 price range. However, you won't be paying rack rates if you're a savvy traveler.

Paris definitely has seasons when rates are lower than at other times. Prices are generally at their lowest from November through March, except for those weeks in January and February when the couturier houses hold their showings of spring fashions. While airlines charge the most for their fares in June, July, and August (plus perhaps a few days at the end of May and the beginning of September), many hotel rooms cost less in August than in the other months from April through October. But regardless of peak season, it's possible to find bargains anytime you want to travel. Flexibility regarding days of the week isn't as important as in many other destinations, since some hotels cater to businesspeople, whereas others have a mostly tourist clientele. What's a slow part of the week at one hotel may well be the busiest at another. Since October is the month when conferences (conventions) are usually held throughout Europe, at that time you may find hotel space tight and rates high.

By spending some time weighing your options—pairing up hotels you want to stay in with the seasons they consider low or off peak, and by checking to see what promotions will be offered while you're in Paris, you can cut your accommodations bill in half. As far as planning-ahead time is concerned, three or four months is great; six is even better. Those extra weeks will let you pursue cost-cutting research that can save you hundreds of dollars.

Your planning will, of necessity, be influenced by the length of your Paris stay. The more time you have to spend, the more important your accommodations, and the less hurried—and more in depth—the pace of your explorations. If your Paris visit will be in conjunction with a trip to France or elsewhere in Europe, you'll be dealing with more variables than if the city is your only destination. For instance, several European tours offer extended-stay accommodations rates and open-ended arrangements on flights back to North America, while others do not. Staying in Paris at the start of your travels or at their end can sometimes make a difference as to whether you choose off-peak or winter rates.

Putting It All in a Package

People who aren't able to travel independently or who don't want to contend with all the decisions required for a Paris trip may want to consider a package tour. Among the leading companies that offer Paris tours are Jet Vacations (1775

Broadway, New York, NY 10019; 800/538-0999), which is a wholly owned subsidiary of Air France; DER Tour (9501 W. Devon Avenue, Rosemont, IL 60018; 800/538-0999); and Globus & Cosmos (5301 S. Federal Circle, Littleton, CO 80123; 800/851-0728, ext. 518).

If you decide that a package tour is your Paris travel answer, get brochures put out by several companies from your travel agent, then begin comparing what you get for the prices you pay. This can be more important than you might think, because often the extras on one tour aren't the things you enjoy doing, while those on another are.

Your International Monetary Fund

At some point in the planning process, you'll have to decide how much time and money you can afford to spend. When estimating your expenses, you should be aware that it's the law in France that taxes and service charges must be included in posted hotel and restaurant prices (any approximate prices quoted in this book include those amounts).

Although books tell you how to get by on low-budget amounts, it's more realistic to plan on spending from $125 to $200 per person, per day, exclusive of airfare and shopping. Nonetheless, budgets are such individual affairs that I don't want to get specific about what *you* can expect to spend— except to caution you to be realistic. It will cost much more if you fail to bring along sufficient funds, traveler's checks, or a major ATM card and have to get a cash advance on your credit card.

The French currency unit, the franc, is issued in bills (denominations of 20, 50, 100, and 500) and coins (1, 2, 5, 10, and 20). Each franc is composed of 100 centimes, so there are 5-, 10-, 20-, and 50-centime coins as well. Like any foreign currency, the value of the French franc (ff) varies in the relationship to the U.S. and Canadian dollars. The best way to determine its value is to check a current issue of the *Wall Street Journal* or a newspaper travel section.

Between the time that the first edition of this book was written in late 1995 and the updating of the current edition, the U.S. dollar rose dramatically—from about 5ff to 7.1 ff to the dollar. And the French inflationary rate has not kept pace with the increase. This means that with the same amount of dollars, travelers from the United States can buy more today than they could six years ago.

Due to such currency fluctuations, which occur almost daily, I have quoted prices in their U.S. dollar equivalents at the time the book was updated. Needless to say, the prices won't remain precisely the same, but they will give you a good idea of what things cost without your having to convert francs to dollars.

If you're arriving by plane and won't be met at the airport, you'll need francs to get into the city. This means you'll have to do some money exchanging either before you leave home or at the airport. In most cases, you'll get a better deal in the United States, because the airport rates are horrible—about 30 percent *less* than the official rate. In either case, change only as much as you anticipate you'll need. Remember that although banks aren't open on weekends, you can use most bank cards at automated teller machines (ATMs) located throughout the city. The BNP (Banque National Paris) has dozens of branches, each of which has an exterior ATM that takes Plus, Cirrus, and other major cards.

Most seasoned travelers agree that when you must have cash, you'll get the very best rates at an ATM. Despite the charges levied by your home bank and the bank where the machine is located, you'll come out ahead. Also, you'll save gobs of time if you don't have to stand in long foreign exchange lines at the bank—and saving time plus money is today's definition of value.

Better yet, plan to use a minimum of cash and rely on your charge card instead. (Of course, you'll want to take along some traveler's checks, just in case.) Naturally, this isn't an economically sound method if you have to pay off your charge-card bill plus interest in a series of monthly payments. Should you—perish the thought—be parted from your plastic, the following numbers are the ones to call in Paris. The lines are manned 24 hours a day.

American Express	47-08-31-21
Diners Club	47-62-75-75
MasterCard (Eurocard)	43-23-47-47
Visa (Carte Bleu)	42-77-11-90

If you must change money or traveler's checks, you'll get the best exchange rates at banks, which are generally open weekdays from 9 A.M. to 4:30 P.M. Traveler's checks bring a slightly higher rate than cash, because banks must ship the dollars they don't sell to their customers back to the United States, so dealing with cash costs them more than traveler's checks. Although the amount may be no more than one or two cents on a dollar, it becomes significant when you're exchanging $200 or $300.

Another financial word of advice: When you bring cash to France, carry it in bills of $20 and less. Because they have had problems with counterfeit $100 bills, banks often will not accept paper currency in that denomination. Also, whether you're exchanging currency or checks, be sure to ask if the service fee varies with the amount exchanged. You'll find that the same fee is charged whether you exchange any amount within a certain range—say $20 to $100—and higher fees (but not proportionately so) for amounts in a higher range. As a result, you'll want to avoid exchanging minimal amounts unless it's absolutely necessary.

In some countries, the few pennies you save by checking out the various exchange rates and fees aren't worth the effort. In France, however, where these vary greatly, your savings can amount to a substantial sum. Occasionally, you'll find money exchanges advertising that they cash all traveler's checks at no charge. In these cases, if the rate of exchange is competitive, you'll save anywhere from $3 to $5 on a $100 exchange. Usually, however, that rate is much lower than those at banks.

To get cash advances from charge cards is expensive—generally from about $5.95 to $9.95 for any amount up to $100; $95.95 to $99.95 for $1,000. Although it is sometimes possible to cash a personal check at the hotel where you're a guest, don't count on that being the policy.

Paris Packing With Panache

Traveling fully loaded costs money. You're forced to take taxis and to tip bell people more often, and your flexibility is limited. Say that on your second day in Paris, you find a better hotel room for less money. Having all that luggage brought down to the lobby, taking a cab six blocks, and getting your bags up to the nicer room may turn your savings into added expense.

By traveling light, you save not only money, but time as well: There's no waiting at the baggage carrousel. This is especially important when you must go through passport control, where the difference between being at the front of the line and the back can translate into half an hour or more. Some suitcases weigh almost as much empty as others do full, so carry only lightweight bags or backpacks, and pack only that which you absolutely must have.

Paris—fashion capital of the world—without a daily change of outfit, you ask? For Paris especially, as with any destination, you want to blend in with the crowd—not stick out as a tourist waiting to pay tourist prices. And for women at least, blending into the Paris scene means wearing a basic black dress or suit—wool in winter, lighter-weight fabrics in summer—accessorized with color. Therefore, women who pack only a couple of outfits—a simple black dress with accessories; a tailored pair of pants and jacket—can get by for two weeks or more. Men need only two pairs of pants, a sport coat, and three or four shirts.

If your customary dress is more casual and you don't plan to stay at the more traditional hotels, your jeans and turtle-necks will take up even less room. You will be identified as a tourist, though, since Parisians aren't nearly as fond of jeans as most of the rest of Europe.

What else you put into your luggage can minimize the time you spend packing and unpacking and avoid unnecessary expenses on your trip. Also in the time-saving department, placing items such as pantyhose and men's socks in gallon-sized plastic bags with zip closings makes them much easier to find.

An emergency supply of pain relievers, digestive tablets, needle and thread, safety pins, and moleskin to protect tender spots on your feet should go in another plastic bag. These items take up minimal space, and having them if the need arises will save you dollars as well as time.

If you plan to eat any picnic meals—in a park or your hotel room—bring along a stack of margarine tubs, plastic glasses, plastic cutlery, and a combination bottle and can opener. Wherever I travel, I always bring a 16-ounce bottle of spring-water in my carry-on luggage. Although it costs extra to drink bottled water for the entire trip, it's cheap insurance against the sort of intestinal upsets that changes in water can bring about.

Since clothes are lighter to carry on your body than in a bag, wear your heaviest clothes while traveling. Dress in three or four layers if you can, eliminating extra packing and ensuring comfort if your plane happens to be chilly. And speaking of being chilly, winter days in Paris can be cold and damp, so you may need a lined raincoat and a sweater underneath, or trousers and even long johns if you want to be comfortable traveling at that time of year. Women wearing skirts will want

Whatever else you pack, if you don't speak French, copy a short list of necessary French words and phrases to study on the plane ride and keep it in your pocket as a handy reference. The following should help you out in compiling your list.

French	Sounds Like	English
l'arrêt de bus	(lah-REH du bewss)	the bus stop
avez-vouz . . . ?	(ah-vay VOO)	do you have . . . ?
c'est	(seh)	it is
combien?	(kwang-bee-ANG)	how much?
correspondance	(koh-ress-pon-dahngss)	connection
déjeuner	(deh-zher-NEH)	lunch
dîner	(DE-neh)	dinner
entrée	(AHNG-treh)	entrance
grand, grande	(ghrahng)	large
interdit	(ahnn tehr DEE)	no trespassing
Je ne comprends pas	(zher neh kawng-prahng pas)	I don't understand
la laverie automatique	(lah lah-ve-REE oa-to-mah-TEEK)	self-service Laundromat
merci beaucoup	(mehr-SEE boh-COO)	thank you very much
non	(nawng)	no
oui	(uwee)	yes
petit, petite	(pu-TEE)	small
le petit déjeuner	(lu pu-TEE deh-zher-NEH)	breakfast
rue	(rhwoo)	street
s'il vous plaît	(see voo PLEH)	if you please
sortie	(sohr TEE)	exit
toilette	(twah-LETT)	bathroom

to put on either heavy tights, two pairs of pantyhose, or a combination thereof. Even in summer, there can be days and evenings when you'll need a sweater or light jacket and an umbrella along with sunglasses and sunscreen.

Most important of all are shoes—good, sensible walking shoes. Sturdy soles are also a must if you plan to do extensive walking on cobblestones. To be sure you have room for bring-home purchases, pack an extra carry-on in your luggage, and don't forget to bring an extra pair of glasses, if you wear them.

Like the French, you'll want to carry a string bag wherever you go (I line mine with a plastic bag). The bags are so commonly carried by men *and* women—usually for produce from the street markets—that they aren't attractive targets for pickpockets and purse snatchers.

There are all sorts of ways you can carry your money safely. Using snaps or Velcro as fasteners, I sew pockets inside the regular pockets of my traveling garments. I also use cotton pouches for passports and such under my clothes. Savvy men can use these simple pouches, too. One man I know wears a canvas fishing vest with its multiple pockets under a bulky sweater when he travels during cold weather; another keeps some folding money in his shoes.

Despite the advice I, or anyone, should give you, be assured that no rules for trip taking are carved in stone. But while there are no right or wrong ways to travel, there may be one way that's right for you. Do your best to discover it before you finish making plans and you'll have a true *bon voyage*.

CHAPTER

2

Finding the Right Room

Paris offers you a choice of more places to stay than almost anywhere else in the world—1,600 one- to four-star hotels, plus hundreds of others that aren't rated. Accommodations range from elegant suites to scruffy garrets; from neighborhood apartments to charming quarters in boutique hotels whose courtyards insulate them from city street hubbub—and every sort of room in between.

But since our North American hotel room expectations—especially *before* we have traveled abroad—are different from those of travelers from other countries, first-time visitors are sometimes disappointed with what they get for their money. Around the globe, we expect to find North American three-star amenities in midprice hostelries, and that is usually unrealistic. We are used to getting a great deal for our accommodations dollar—large rooms, big color TVs, enormous beds, plenty of space to move around in—even in parts of the country where rooms cost less than $50 a night.

You generally won't get those features in Paris rooms unless they're in the luxury class. For one thing, many hotels are conversions, having been built for another purpose. Some of the smaller ones were private residences, or a row of houses that were joined together. Therefore, it's fairly common to find hotels where no two rooms are alike. Some are larger; others have smaller windows. Maybe there are niches and nooks under the eaves. Quite often the locations of the connecting bathrooms defy any logic except that of expediency.

Many hotels are in very old buildings. The ceilings may be high, but the woodwork has been painted many times. Hallways may be narrower than we're used to, and elevators small.

Room size isn't considered as important in Europe as it is in North America. A room you pay $200 for in Paris is often half the size of the average hotel room in the United States or Canada. It may, however, contain a trouser press, an ironing board, a hair dryer, and other amenities that we Americans expect only in luxury hotels.

Generally speaking, the public areas in Paris hotels are far more splendid than the guest rooms, especially in modest hotels. Whenever you see hotel brochures that picture only the lobbies, restaurants, or bars, you can be quite sure that the rooms aren't nearly as photogenic.

Before I discuss hotels further, it's important to clarify one point. Not every building that's called a hotel is a place where travelers stay overnight. In the French language, an *hôtel* may be a hospital *(hotel-Dieu)*, a city hall *(hôtel de ville)*, or a large private home *(hôtel particulier)*. The Hôtel des Invalides, formerly a home for disabled war veterans, is one of the world's most important military museums and the burial place of Napoleon Bonaparte.

As to Paris hotels of the lodging variety, in addition to the one- to four-star and nonrated hotels, there are pensions, student rooms, and rental apartments or residence hotels, where rooms aren't available on a daily basis. Most of the luxury hotels are north of the Seine, many of them near the Champs-Elysées. A number of old mansions and palaces have been converted into boutique hotels in the Marais district, and Left Bank hotels often have a great deal of character. The lodging places in the Montparnasse area and at La Defense are essentially high-rise business hotels. And while there are lots of places to stay near Les Halles, along rue St-Denis, and in

Montmartre, many of them are sleazy and in areas that attract hookers and drug addicts.

As you begin to get involved in the hotel room selection process, take a few minutes to consider your interests, habits, physical condition, and sense of aesthetics in relation to the place where you stay. Answering the following questions will help you determine which options will give you the most psychic value for your money.

1. *Do you enjoy walking, and how far can you walk in a day without getting exhausted?* This is an extremely important consideration in Paris, since Métro and railroad strikes are fairly frequent. If you're used to walking miles, location won't be as important to you.

2. *When traveling, are you happier if you can take a short nap or have some quiet time at the hotel during the middle of the day?* This is also a factor when you're traveling with children who need naps or quiet time in order to be at their best.

3. *Do noises outside your hotel room—sirens, traffic, midnight revelers, and the like—keep you from getting a good night's sleep?* No room is a bargain if you don't get your Zs.

4. *Is a room's size important? What about its decor?* Some people don't seem to be influenced by these factors. Others—and I am one of them—are happiest when we enjoy our surroundings. Propped with pillows, watching a local TV program, or sitting at the desk writing postcards, we enjoy looking at the room around us.

5. *Is it important to have a variety of shops and restaurants nearby?* This should be a consideration for people who like to go window-shopping after the stores have closed, or don't care to travel far when they want to eat.

6. *Does having a restaurant on the premises matter?* Perhaps not important to most of us when the weather's fine, but vital when it's snowing or we're too tired to go farther than downstairs.

7. *Do you like to look out from your hotel window? What kinds of views please you most?* I remember one sunny Paris

morning when I spent half an hour watching people at the pavement café across the street—probably the highlight of that day.

8. *Do you enjoy sitting in hotel lobbies and taking in the general ambience?* This activity is especially gratifying if you're in a busy hotel with a lot going on.

9. *How do you feel about tub baths versus showers? Do you need twin beds or will a double bed do?* Rooms with showers generally cost less than those with tubs, and double-bed rooms are less expensive than those with twin beds.

10. *What amenities must a lodging place have in order to make you happy?* Which ones can you easily do without?

11. *Finally, do you look at the hotel room as an important part of a vacation, or is it low on your list of priorities?*

Equally important as what you look for in a hotel is its location. For some people, that means accessibility to public transportation; others want to stay within close distance of their favorite Paris activities. For example, if your passion is museums, you'll probably want to book lodgings in the 16th arrondissement. Paris's wealthiest area, the 16th features deluxe hotels and restaurants, grand homes, elegant shops, and about two dozen museums. It's also one of the quietest places to stay in what is generally a very noisy city. If you're the typical first-time Paris visitor interested in seeing *everything*, hotels near the Champs-Elysées, the Louvre, the Opéra, or in the heart of the Left Bank will allow you to walk to most of the traditional attractions as well as restaurants and shopping.

While I'm fairly relaxed about traveling without room reservations in most parts of Europe, the thought of Paris without a reservation for at least the first two nights of any stay gives me the shudders. And although it is important for even veteran travelers to have arranged for a place to lay their heads in advance, it's especially vital if you're making your first trip to the city. During mid-January and mid-February fashion-show time, hotels fill up and room rates rise. Other times during those months are usually the slowest of the year, but

January and February are also the months that have the worst weather. Occupancy rates are highest during May, June, and September. They're also up in October, traditional convention time in Europe.

Of course, I realize that there are people who actually enjoy living on the edge, who wouldn't be caught dead traveling with reservations. And they probably *won't* end up sleeping on the sidewalk. But they probably *will* spend much of their first day in the long lines at the accommodations referrals desk of the Office de Tourisme on the Champs-Elysées.

When you've analyzed your travel personality, your needs, and your budget, it's time—with the aid of a good map, brochures, and any other hotel information you may have gathered—to zero in on where you want to stay. Although it is possible to book a room the day before your journey, you'll be apt to get more for your money if you plan ahead, and the amount you save is often in proportion to the lead time you have. Since Paris hotel rates are as high as just about any in the world, those savings can mean big money.

Three basic methods can help you maximize your accommodations dollars: 1) buying your airfare and accommodations as a package, or a basic accommodations package from a tour company; 2) taking advantage of individual hotel or hotel chain promotions; and 3) finding a hotel that is a value even though its price isn't discounted, and then negotiating directly with the establishment for a better deal.

Air-and-accommodations package brochures used to be put out by virtually all the airlines that fly between North America and Paris. Not anymore, though. Travel agents, who spend most of their days booking flights and reserving rooms, say that fluctuating airfares have stopped the airlines from putting these packages together. You will find some brochures, though, especially those offered by British Air and Air France. The reduced number of air-and-accommodations packages, however, is made up for by an increasing number of airline and hotel specials announced via the Internet. By using information retrieved from a combination of sources—ads in newspaper travel sections, air-and-accommodations brochures procured at a travel agency, hotel rooms sold on a stand-alone basis by commercial tour companies, and specials advertised on the Internet, not to mention the individual airlines' and hotels' Web sites—you can put together money-saving packages of your own.

Buying an air-and-accommodations package means you must buy your flight ticket from a specific airline to be able to take advantage of the hotel rates that the carrier offers. Still, most packages are also available to travelers who wish to obtain their tickets using frequent flier coupons issued by the airline. If you plan to buy the entire air-and-accommodations package, don't worry too much about the airfare portion being competitive. One airline's prices on the various North America–Paris routes are usually almost the same as every other carrier's. The most practical of these packages are those that give you the choice of several hotels in various price ranges and locations.

Most of the hotels offered in packages are located in the parts of Paris that are most popular with tourists—Montmartre, the Left Bank, near the Arc de Triomphe, the Louvre, the Opéra, and the Eiffel Tower. Among the more expensive hotels (typical of package deals, the discount rate is greater for the places with pricier rooms) you'll find included in air-and-accommodations packages are:

Le Meridien Montparnasse (19e); rue du Commandant-Mouchotte; 44-36-44-36; rack rate $250–350.

Hôtel Lotti (a traditional upscale hotel located between the place Vendome and the Tuileries Gardens); 7, rue de Castiglione; 42-60-37-34; rack rate $380–520.

Hôtel George V; 31, av George V; 47-23-54-00; rack rate $325–625.

Demeure Hôtel Parc Victor Hugo; 55, av Raymond Poin-
caré; 44-05-66-66; rack rate $220–245.
Le Crillon; 10, place de la Concorde; 47-71-15-00; rack rate
$460–600.
Plaza Athenee; 25, av Montaigne; 47-23-78-33; rack rate
$380–540.
Hôtel du Louvre; place André Malraux; 44-58-38-38; rack
rate $300–385.
Hôtel Inter-Continental Paris; 3, rue Castiglione; 47-71-11-
11; rack rate $300–445.

You'll frequently see the names of several of the same
hotels listed in two or more airlines' package brochures. (If
you dislike staying at hotels that are popular with tour groups,
shy away from those mentioned in multiple brochures.) You
also may be able to find their names mentioned in discount
travel Web sites, or they may have their own Web sites on
which specials are announced. These multiple listings, however, make for great comparison-shopping.

Some of the airline, hotel, and tour company packages contain a few frills in addition to the basic airfare and hotel
room. They may include practical items like buffet breakfasts
and other complimentary meals or excursions like river
cruises.

When you're deciding on whether to buy the optional packages, you'll have to decide to what degree you want to make
your own choices while you're in Paris. Do you want to seek
out a restaurant that's popular with Parisians or go to one
that's obviously patronized by lots of tourists? You'll also have
to decide whether the extras are of value to you. If you're not
interested in museums, a museum pass will be a waste of
money. And walkers won't use the Métro enough to justify the
cost of a five-day pass.

Also, some "extras" are things you can actually obtain for
yourself. For instance, the 10 percent department store dis-

counts and fashion-show invitations are available to anyone
who picks up a Printemps or Galeries Lafayette brochure at a
tourism office or hotel—they're available everywhere.

Here's an example of how comparison-shopping works,
using a variety of resources. Say you want to go to Paris for
seven days, and you've seen Sofitel Paris Forum Rive Gauche
mentioned frequently. You look up the property in a hotel
guide, which tells you that the rack rate is $217 double. DER
Travel Services advertises rooms in the hotel starting at $85
per person per night, based on double occupancy. That's two
times $85 or $170. But as I'll point out in chapter 11, Sofitel's
Web page also advertises winter and summer sales. At these
times, room prices are 40 percent lower than the regular rate,
which would reduce the cost to $130 a night. By spending a
minimal amount of time researching, you can save hundreds
of dollars—in this case, if you were able to take advantage of
the lowest rate, you would pay $780 instead of $1,302 for a
six-night stay.

Or perhaps you decide on the Clarion St. James et Albany
(202, rue du Rivoli; 44-58-43-21; rack rate $226.80 double a
night). You find a special offer in a hotel directory that knocks
off $16. The price quoted by DER Tours is the same: $210.
Then you can go to the Internet and type in the hotel's name
at the Web site of your favorite search engine (Google found
nine Web sites with discounted rates for Clarion St. James et
Albany when I searched). Keep your searches going until
you've found the best rate for a lodging place that sounds
good to you.

Advertising Pays (You)

Brochures don't tell the whole air-and-accommodations story.
When airlines or hotels experience (or anticipate) unexpected
low load levels or occupancy rates, they want to do something
about it. Fast. So they put together bargain deals that usually

involve only certain airline routes and a limited number of hotels. After all, an empty seat on a U.S.–Paris flight or any room that goes empty in a Paris hotel represents revenue that cannot be recaptured. And the way to get the word out quickly about these bargains is to put advertisements in target-area newspapers. Although they're usually in Sunday paper travel sections, they may be in weekday editions as well. There are times, too, when these promotions are advertised nationwide. One such ad reduced the nightly rate at Hôtel Lutetia (45, blvd Raspail; 49-54-46-46) to $180 a night, which included buffet breakfast each day and one night's dinner vouchers for the two people sharing the room.

Since the offer was good during the first part of October— usually a high-season time of year—and fares on American Airlines were competitive, this was an excellent deal. What else made it one? The buffet breakfasts at the Lutetia include cheeses, meats, yogurt, cereal, fruit, several juices, American-style cooked breakfast dishes, a variety of rolls, and hot beverages. The hotel has a great Left Bank location just off the blvd St-Germain, and rack rates for a double room can go to $410 in high season.

You'll also occasionally find promotions advertised in magazines. However, magazine editorial copy and ads are usually in the works months in advance of publication. As a result, deals may be better (than those originally advertised in newspapers) at a later date when travel suppliers try to get rid of unsold airplane seats, hotel rooms, and tour packages.

Letter-Writing Campaigns

Another way to find out about hotel chain or individual hotel promotions is by writing directly to either the corporate headquarters or to the hotels. Don't expect travel agents to have this kind of information, and you have no assurance that the people manning the phones at a hotel's toll-free number have anything to tell you other than the rack rates in their computers.

Anyone with access to a word processor can whip out letters to a dozen hotels or more in half an hour, and for the cost of an airmail stamp to Europe can obtain information that well may save hundreds of dollars on a week's stay. Just give the dates you plan to be in Paris and ask for a hotel brochure, rate card, and information on any promotions or discounts that will be offered during the period. French hotel people are prompt in answering correspondence, so your replies should begin arriving within a week or 10 days.

When inquiring of any hotel, remember that many Paris hotels offer corporate rates. If you're associated with a business of any kind, you may be able to get a better rate because of it. Also, some of the lower-priced hotels do not accept charge cards; be sure to inquire in advance.

Upscale Price Slashing

Even if paying $400 to $500 a night for a hotel room doesn't faze you, it is silly to pay more than you have to. And it's the pricey hotels that are more apt than not to offer promotional packages with sizable savings.

Many of the top hotels seem to consider it embarrassing to admit they have vacant rooms—or at least they believe they'll ruin their reputations if the world finds out that their rooms aren't always in demand. So they advertise these savings discreetly, informing regular guests by mail, and answering inquiries from potential customers. By writing the upper-tier hotels, you may find that you can live in luxury for substantially less than the hotel's published rates. Hôtel Scribe, for example, where the rack rate is about $390 for a double room, has a weekend special of $290 per night for Friday, Saturday, and Sunday. The price includes buffet breakfast.

And at the Scribe, the bargains become greater as the prices go up. The rack rate for a duplex (sitting room plus mezzanine apartment) drops from about $740 to $500 a night when you stay eight or more nights. In other words, you can stay eight nights for $40 less than you can for six. On occasion, the hotel also offers event packages, such as the "Indian Film Festival." Since the Scribe also participates in air-and-accommodations packages, you would want to determine those per-night rates before deciding whether the hotel's promotions are the best value for you.

At some of the upscale hotels, rates during promotions aren't much lower than they are ordinarily, but you get more for your money. Take the elegant Prince de Galles (33, av George V; 47-23-55-11), for instance. Located about six blocks from the Arc de Triomphe and the Métro, it's a marvelous hotel with lovely guest rooms and faultless and friendly concierge services. In sum, staying at Prince de Galles is like visiting charming friends in their beautifully furnished private home. The only rub is that rack rates start at about $463 for a standard double room, and $515 for one in the superior class. However, with the "Luxury Weekend" package, you can stay for about $466 a night (two-night minimum) and get a $515 room, plus a few extras. These include buffet breakfasts (regularly $35 per person), which would amount to $140 for two people on the two mornings of their stay; a newspaper each morning; and turn-down service each night.

Room rates are occasionally discounted at Prince de Galles in other promotions as well. Special Christmas Eve and New Year's Eve packages can cut lodging costs by more than 25 percent, because they include free continental breakfasts.

More Ways to Save

Travel agency franchises, such as members of Travel Network, are also sources for reduced hotel room rates. Because of their large volume of collective clients, these organizations are able to buy blocks of rooms from hotels on a regular basis, and this, of course, is reflected in a lower price per unit. Discounts on Paris hotels in the Travel Network book, which lists the various properties, ranged from 4 to 36 percent.

One hotel in the book, Demeure Hôtel Baltimore (88 bis, av Kleber; 44-34-54-54) has a published rate of about $380. Various packages list it from $242 to $266, depending on the season. In July and August, promotions offered by the hotel provide dinner for two at a good restaurant with a stay of three nights, and with a six-night stay, the seventh night is free. The Baltimore, which is located just a few hundred feet from the Métro station, would be rated a three-star hotel in North America.

If you're willing to put out from $50 to $75, you may be able to save even more on hotel rooms, including those in the high price range. By joining one of the programs below you'll receive a hotel directory. Rooms in the hotels listed can be reserved for up to 50 percent off published rates. This is especially helpful for booking rooms in hotels that don't advertise promotions. Two companies offering these programs are:

Great American Traveler, Access, Box 27965, Salt Lake City, UT 84127; 800/331-8867 ($49.95 a year).

Privilege Card International, 3391 Peachtree Road NE, Suite 110, Atlanta, GA 30326; 800/236-9732.

A third company, Entertainment Publications (40 Oakview Street, Trumbull, CT 06611; 800/445-4137), sells directories for certain areas, such as the British Isles, France, and Europe, on a yearly discount basis. The directory for France, which includes Paris hotels and restaurants, costs $48.

Hotels on the edges of Paris often cost half as much as comparable properties in the heart of the city. They're not for visitors who want to be footsteps away from the Paris they've seen on TV travel programs, but people who are willing to commute to the city center for some of their sight-seeing will find that staying near the Peripherique will also cut down on dining costs and enable them to see a different slice of Parisian life. One of my very favorite Paris hotels, regardless of price, is

Holiday Inn La Villette (more about that in chapter 11), even though it's about 20 minutes away from the city center.

The Montparnasse area of Paris is another value-for-money hotel area. It's just far enough off the main tourist track to be less expensive, but still close enough that walkers can easily get to most Left Bank attractions and some on the Right Bank.

So far I've been talking about rooms in the moderate to luxury classes, since they're more nearly comparable to the $75 to $200 rooms North Americans are accustomed to. As I've said, Paris rooms that cost less than $150 are considered inexpensive. While I urge you to try to get moderate or first-class rooms for the "inexpensive" price, I realize that sometimes it can't be done. Therefore, I've included a number of hotels that are among the best of those I've discovered with rack rates of $180 or less (all prices include service charges and taxes, with the possible exception of a minor city tax). I'm not saying that you can't find a charming hotel with a lovely view and a great location for less. It's just that chances are the bath will be down the hall, or you'll have to climb a flight of stairs, or more. When you contact any of the following, be sure to ask about promotions and special rates.

Grand Hotel de Champagne (1er; 17, rue Jean Lantier; 42-36-60-00; Chatelet (Rivoli exit) or Pont Neuf Métro station). With hand-painted murals and a great deal of Gallic charm, this hotel has a largely European clientele. In a 16th-century building of hand-hewn stone, each room and suite has a different theme. Though the hotel is in the heart of the city, it's a quiet location, only a block from the river. Rack rate is $160 for a double room.

Hotel de l'Elysée (8e; 12, rue des Saussaies; 42-65-29-25; Champs-Elysées Clemenceau or Miromesnil Métro station). L'Elysée fits everyone's mental image of a French hotel, with canopied beds, wall sconces, fringed lamp shades, and pictures in gilded frames. The hotel's location is ideal for people who like to walk everywhere. Though it's in the high-rent district, its double rooms with showers start at $120.

Hôtel des Marronniers (6e; 21, rue Jacob; 43-25-30-60; St-Germain-des-Pres Métro station). This hotel, designated a national monument, is insulated from street noise by an enchanting courtyard at its entrance and a sunlit garden—complete with chestnut trees—behind. Although the guest rooms don't live up to the ground floor's promise, the location's great. Ask for a fourth-floor room on the garden side if you want great views of Paris rooftops. A double room with bath costs $140.

Hôtel Etoile Maillot (16e; 10, rue du Bois-de-Boulogne; 45-00-42-60; Argentine or Charles-de-Gaulle-Etoile Métro station) is a fashionable hotel in an extremely fashionable residential area. It's not far to the Métro station, so sight-seeing is only minutes away. Rack rates are about $130 for a room with shower and $154 for one with a bath.

Hôtel Eugenie (6e; 31, rue St-André-des-Arts; 43-26-29-03; St-Michel or Odeon Métro stations). Great value for money as far as Paris is concerned. Rooms are contemporary, with lots of extras like hair dryers and remote-control TV (though the screens are small). The hotel's location in the sixth arrondissement is only about two blocks from the Seine and six from Notre Dame. Double rooms cost about $118 for one bed and $130 for two.

Hôtel d'Angleterre (6e; 44, rue Jacob; 42-60-34-72; St-Germain-des-Pres Métro station). No cookie-cutter rooms in this hotel. Some of them are stunning. There's a neat interior patio, too, with lots of foliage. The neighborhood's also great for strolling around the building, which was once the British Embassy. Double-room prices start at about $120.

Hôtel des Saints-Pères (6e; 65, rue des Sts-Pères; 45-44-50-00; Sevres-Babylone Métro station). Almost all of the 40 guest rooms in this hotel open onto an interior court. The Left Bank location is on the same street as an interesting array of boutiques, antiques shops, and restaurants. Formerly a 17th-century private dwelling, the hotel's lobby is inviting, and the surroundings make it especially appealing.

Hôtel Abbatial St-Germain (5e; 46, blvd St-Germain; 46-34-02-12; St-Michel or Maubert Mutualité Métro station. If you want a great view, ask for one of the rooms on the upper floors with windows that look out on Notre Dame or the Pantheon. Double-room prices range from $116 to $150.

Hôtel Molière (1er; 21, rue Molière; 42-96-22-01; Palais-Royal or Pyramides Métro station). Recently redecorated, this hotel caters to an international clientele. Rooms have amenities such as mini bars (not often found in this price range) and satellite TV. The location—not far from the Louvre—is great for window-shoppers. Double rooms with a shower cost $94 to $116; with bath, $130 to $144.

Hôtel Lido (8e; 4, passage de la Madeleine; 42-66-27-37; Madeleine Métro station). This hotel is on a quiet corridor off the bustling place de la Madeleine. The quintessential small Parisian hotel, its lobby is elegantly appointed, and the guest rooms are charming. An excellent value for this part of the city, where most hotels cost much more. Single rooms are about $160; doubles, $186.

Hôtel Novanox (14e; 155, blvd du Montparnasse; 46-33-63-60; Vavin or Raspail Métro station). Stylishly decorated, this hotel is popular with models during the ready-to-wear collection showings. Only five years old, it has contemporary furniture that was specially designed for it. Rooms contain mini bars and safes (hair dryers are available upon request). Double rooms cost about $125.

Raspail Hôtel (14e; 15, rue Delambre; 43-35-34-50; Edgar Quinet Métro station. This hotel was restored in 1991 and has some marvelous art deco touches, such as its facade and staircase. The guest rooms, named for artists who frequented Montparnasse, have CNN, mini bars, safes, hair dryers, and air-conditioning. Room prices start at a little more than $100.

Hôtel Saint-Germain-des-Pres (6e; 36, rue Bonaparte; 43-26-00-19; St-Sulpice Métro station). In 1778, this hotel began life as a Masonic lodge where Benjamin Franklin, Captain

John Paul Jones, and Voltaire were members. Famous people kept coming after it became a hotel. Today, the clientele is not so notable, but the place still has a lot going for it, including a central, but sometimes hectic, Left Bank location.

Select Hôtel (5e; 1, place de la Sorbonne; 46-34-14-80; St-Michel or Luxembourg Métro station). Right next to the Sorbonne, this hotel features a great courtyard with tropical plants and singing birds. The many interesting architectural materials incorporated into its decor—granite, sandstone, and glass—combined with lots of green plants, make this a pleasant place to stay. It's close to Luxembourg Gardens, so plan on a Sunday stroll. Room prices start at about $106.

The Libertel group of hotels gets high marks as far as good value is concerned. There are 28 of these properties in Paris, of which several participate in air-and-accommodations packages. Formerly run-down establishments, they have all been renovated in the past few years by a clever Frenchwoman, Catherine Mamet, who has a great sense of style. The hotels are classified on the basis of location, facilities, and service into three categories, Libertel, Libertel tradition, and Libertel grand tradition. Rates at the least expensive properties start at about $78; at the most expensive, about $130.

Getting Precisely (or Almost) What You Want

Wherever you decide to stay, if you ask to reserve a room without being specific as to what you want, it's the luck of the draw. Most hotel personnel pay attention to special requests, however—they want their guests to be happy. So send along a wish list with your reservation.

Even if you don't make any requests, you still have an opportunity to improve your accommodations once you arrive. When you've greeted the person at reception (the front desk) with a *"bonjour"* and given your name, ask if the price you're paying is the best deal the hotel is offering at the time.

You may not get a better price, but if you're pleasant, you have a good chance of being given a better room.

If you aren't, make it a point to get to know the people at the front desk during your stay. Find out how your room compares with others that go for the same rate. If you determine that some of the rooms are better, ask to be put in one when there's a vacancy.

Alternative Accommodations

It's possible to rent apartments in Paris for only a couple of days or more. Most people who rent them say they aren't less expensive than hotel rooms, but they make big-time savings on dining possible and offer more space to move around. If you have Parisian friends to apartment hunt for you or North American friends to recommend places where they've stayed, getting a Paris rental apartment is a cinch.

When you're on your own, it isn't so easy. If possible, make your reservations through a company that's been recommended to you. Better yet, negotiate with apartment managers directly and save the commissions that the booking companies would get. The following companies handle Paris apartment rentals:

The French Experience, Inc.
370 Lexington Avenue
New York, NY 10017
212/986-1115

MDH, 713/942-940

PSR
Michigan Avenue, Suite 638
Chicago, IL 60611
312/587-7707

If you plan on staying for two weeks or more, you might check out ads for apartment rentals and house exchanges in newspaper travel pages or classified sections, such as that in the *New York Review of Books*. Travel publications such as *International Travel News* also have accommodations for rent in their classified section (see chapter 13). You might even consider renting a houseboat moored on the Seine. Although it will probably cost as much as a hotel room's rack rate, you may find that the experience is worth any added expense.

If you're a hostel fan, be sure to buy a Youth Hostel International (HI) card before you leave home. There's no age limit for people lodging at hostels, but a small surcharge is required of travelers over the age of 25. In Paris, six hostels are affiliated with the the Fédération Unie des Auberges de Jeunesse (FUAJ), the French member of HI (see chapter 13 for the federation's address).

Traveling Without Reservations

There are times when, even if you ordinarily travel with reservations, the chance to get away on the spur of the moment presents itself with no lead time to make plans. Although in Paris, this makes it more difficult to find the kind of room you want at a rate you're willing to pay, it's not impossible. Getting rooms without reservations is easiest, of course, during bad weather or when internal or external problems such as strikes or terrorist threats have caused cautious travelers to cancel their plans.

If you can avoid it, don't rely on (or advance any cash to) people at the airport or railway station hotel reservations desk. Instead, have them find out if anything's available at three or four hotels that sound promising. Then go to the one at the top of the list. Above all, never have a booking agency make arrangements before you know what its charges will be. Some demand outrageous fees.

FIVE TIPS FOR KEEPING HOTEL BILLS DOWN

As if room charges aren't high enough, the little extras itemized on your hotel bill can be a fiscal nightmare. To avoid unpleasant surprises:

1. Never call home through the hotel switchboard. The call may cost at least twice as much as it would have if you'd placed it through a pay phone.

2. Don't eat breakfast at the hotel unless it's included in the price and there's not a separate room-only rate.

3. Stop at a market to buy snacks and beverages rather than using those in your hotel room mini bar.

4. Find out if in-room movies are free *before* you even turn on their channel. In upscale hotels, they are often included in the room rate and are great for film fans. However, if they're not, the charges can be steep.

5. Avoid using room service until after you've studied the prices. Continental breakfasts can cost more than $20 in some hotels.

When you arrive at the first hotel, approach the front desk and ask if any discounts are available—for schoolteachers, North Americans, whoever. A business card helps you qualify for a business rate even if you're self-employed or don't work for a company the hotel does business with on a regular basis. If the person in charge at the front desk anticipates vacancies that night, you're likely to get a discount. How much depends, in part, on your technique as a negotiator: After you've been quoted the first discounted rate, ask if that's the best rate available. If the hotel takes credit cards, ask if there is a discount for paying cash. Pour on the personality. Don't be in the least confrontational, and you've a good chance to get a price break. If you don't and are traveling light, go on to the next hotel on your list. Unless the city is packed, if you persist, you'll get value for your money.

Before you make your final commitment and register, ask to see your room. If you're not satisfied, ask to see another. Also, upon registration, inquire as to whether there will be additional charges for laundry, television, or local phone calls, and how much those charges will be. If breakfast is included in the room rate, ask if there's a rate reduction if you choose not to breakfast at the hotel. If it isn't included in the rate, make sure to specify whether you will or will not be eating at the hotel. This can save potential check-out hassles.

So what if, despite your best efforts, the room you've chosen turns out to be a flop? If you haven't paid for the entire stay, check out other hotels. If you're leaving Paris the next day but plan to come back, invest a couple of hours investigating hotels that appeal to you. Ask to see a room or two. Write down the addresses of those you like best. That way, you'll be all set to write letters asking about deals *before* you take your next trip.

CHAPTER
3

Bon Appétit

I've heard it said that you can't get a bad meal in Paris. That's not quite true—almost, though. At least your chances of getting good (and sometimes great) food are far better than anywhere else in the world. You see, Paris has a gourmet history that goes back centuries. Part is myth, perhaps, but even the myths tend to bolster the pride French chefs take in creating the perfect soufflé, bakers in producing their baguettes and *pain du jour*. One reason people get excited about Paris dining is the number of different kinds of places where food is served; another is the wide variety of things to eat.

When discussion turns to prices, however, enthusiasm wanes, since the Paris restaurants with the big reputations—not to mention Michelin stars—often charge as much for one person's dinner as you would spend back home feeding a family of four for a week. Some of these restaurants specialize in elegant, classic dishes. Others have made their mark with creative dishes in keeping with whatever's the trend of the moment *(cuisine actuelle)*. Still others produce a combination of the two—traditional dishes with a contemporary twist.

According to food writers, restaurant dinners that cost less than $40 are considered inexpensive; under $60, moderate. Luxury meals, with costlier wines, will range from about $160 to $200 per person. At these restaurants, prices are usually the same for lunch as for dinner.

Fortunately, restaurants with "name" chefs, fancy appointments, and reputations for excellence aren't the only places where you can get memorable meals. There are also bistros, brasseries, cafés, *salons du thé*, and wine bars, hundreds of which serve either à la carte or prix fixe meals for about $20 to $30, or even half that amount.

Traditionally, bistros are small family-run restaurants, with Mom overseeing the dining room and Dad, the kitchen. Decor isn't fancy. Lace curtains at the windows, tile floors, wood chairs (not always matching), and serviceable tableware are standard. Handwritten or photocopied menus list a limited selection of home-cooked dishes. The dishes bistros serve most likely depend on which region of France the chef comes from.

In recent years, more contemporary bistros—with updated furnishings and modern cuisine—have arrived on the gastronomic scene. For the most part, however, the traditional whitewashed walls with framed prints, white linen tablecloths, and plates of *boeuf Bourguignonne* or *poule au pot* predominate.

Brasseries, as you've no doubt surmised, are the French equivalent of the British pub (*brasserie* is the French word for "brewery"). They're generally rather noisy, brightly lit, and cheerfully decorated, with the accent on Alsatian foods, wines, and—of course—beer. You'll almost always find the hearty combination of sauerkraut and sausages called *choucroute* among the no-nonsense dishes on the menu. Snacks, as well as meals, are available just about anytime a brasserie is open—usually from breakfast until the wee hours of the next morning, seven days a week.

The decor of the most elegant ones dates back to the early 1900s and the Belle Epoque, with its richly carved wood, etched glass, sculpture and stonework, fancy plaster cornice moldings and ceiling medallions, art glass, and ornate mirrors. Most establishments are large; some of them serve as many as 1,000 customers a day.

Cafés are perhaps the most casual of French eateries. The majority of them have sidewalk seating areas and often also have outside counters, dispensing everything from beverages and ice cream cones to sandwiches and pizza slices to passersby. If you wish to occupy a table, however, you must be served by a waiter, and prices are almost always substantially higher than if you buy it to eat off the premises. At sidewalk cafés in locations frequented by tourists, a cup of coffee or soft drink costs about $5. Prices for meals, however, are usually more realistic. These outdoor eateries are one answer for people who dislike cigarette smoke, since there's generally enough of a breeze to keep the air circulating.

You also might consider dinner at a sidewalk café at Sunday noon. It seems that everyone in Paris chooses that day to go out for lunch. The cafés are crowded, but the French, dressed in their Sunday best, make for marvelous people-watching.

Salons du thé (tea shops) have been popular Paris institutions—off and on—for more than 100 years. Their latest renaissance began in the 1980s and they've been growing in popularity ever since, though purists decry the fact that pâtisseries and cafés "that aren't really *salons du thé* at all" advertise that they are. True *salons du thé*, it is maintained, don't have a lot in common with cafés and brasseries. Whereas the latter tend to be noisy and very public—especially those opening to the sidewalk—the tea shops are subdued, cloistered, and genteel. No raucous laughter or honking horns intrude on conversation.

When a Paris tea shop incorporates a terrace, it's usually one that looks out on a garden, narrow passage, or quiet street. Interior decor may be English countryside, Louis XIV gilded swirls, or contemporary chic. But each of the shops prides itself upon properly made tea, be it darjeeling or a blend of raspberry and mango. As far as food is concerned, the typical tearoom offers light meals—quiches, soups, sandwiches—in addition to cakes, tarts, cookies, and other sweet treats.

Wine bars also serve light meals that go well with wine, which they sell by the glass. The kinds of food available vary widely, from ethnic specialties to make-your-own-salads to gourmet dishes. Like the other eating places, they often have tables on the sidewalk during mild weather.

Alimentary Alternatives

In addition to dining in traditional eateries, you can cut food costs in lots of other ways—all of them delicious and nutritionally as healthful as you want them to be. The following will give you some ideas that work in France's capital city—perhaps better than they do anywhere else in the world.

As I mentioned in chapter 2, the inclusion of a continental or full breakfast in your room rate can add $20 or more—money that can be more economically spent eating on your own. In addition, though there are exceptions, most hotel breakfasts included in the room rate aren't very imaginative—the continental breakfast of the four same kinds of rolls, the same two juice choices, and coffee or tea each morning. Even if everything is delicious, this can become boring by the third day, especially when so many interesting options are available elsewhere.

Sidewalk café breakfasts, although not cheap, still generally cost about 50 percent less than those served in hotel restaurants. Another inexpensive alternative is to keep a supply of breakfast foods on hand in your room (juice and/or yogurts on ice in the ice bucket, fresh fruit from a street market).

As far as I'm concerned, the breakfast that makes me feel most Parisian is a roll from the neighborhood boulangerie-pâtisserie with a cup of coffee or tea, all of which costs about $3. There are often small tables inside where you can eat as you watch the locals come in for their daily bread. Or if the weather's fine, choose a bench in the park or one that overlooks the Seine.

If a roll or two isn't enough to keep you comfortable for the whole morning, more's the pleasure, for all of Paris is a movable feast, with boulangeries, pâtisseries, charcuteries, traiteurs, and fromageries only a short walk from anywhere in the city. The following will give you an idea of what's available. Of course, there are hundreds of these shops, so my standards for choice have been quality, location in places convenient to tourists, and an extra something—taste, aroma, decor, ambience—that has made each special to me.

Boulangeries

If you have time to visit just one boulangerie, it ought to be that of Lionel Poilane, who is known as Le Roi du Pain (the King of Bread); he's perhaps the most famous baker in France. His shop, *Boulangerie Poilane,* is at 8, rue du Cherche-Midi (6e; 45-48-42-59; Sevres-Babylone or St-Sulpice Métro station). It's open 7:15 A.M. to 8:15 P.M., Monday through Saturday. The bread is quite acidic, very dense, and country loaves decorated with designs made of the dough *(pain décoré)* are a specialty.

Although the Poilane loaf has set the standard against which every other loaf in France is measured, it isn't my favorite. Poilane's shop, however, is. Whereas most other boulangeries dispense their wares from modern brass and glass cases, this tiny shop features wooden shelves with baskets on them, each containing different kinds of breads, rolls, cookies, and tarts. An old-fashioned scale is used to weigh bread when it is sold by the slice. The floors are tile, and painted scenes of rural France decorate the wall space not taken up by shelving.

As you might imagine, several of the best boulangeries are in the upscale areas of the city. Two I especially like in the 16th arrondissement are J. Darracq (2, rue de Chaillot; 47-20-

64-51) and Bonneau (75, rue d'Auteuil; 46-51-12-25). Try the big sugar cookies called *sables* if you need a little something to tide you over until dinnertime.

Another great boulangerie-pâtisserie is Moulin on rue St-Antoine just opposite the St-Paul Métro entrance (4e). Windows filled with tarts topped with glazed fruit, curls of chocolate, or slivered almonds, French pastries, and gorgeous *gateaux* lure you inside, where there's an equally extensive array of breads, croissants, brioche, and breakfast rolls.

I bought one of the best sandwiches I have ever eaten (smoked salmon, tomato and cucumber slices on a baguette-sized brioche) at Moulin for about $4. Another all-time great baguette came from a vendor's glass case on blvd Haussmann.

One of the most popular boulangeries in the eighth arrondissement is Julien (73, av Franklin D. Roosevelt; 43-59-78-76; St-Philippe-du-Roule Métro station), where the *pain au chocolat* and lemon tarts are favorites. In the ninth arrondissement, Caron (26, rue du Faubourg Montmartre; 47-70-33-70; Rue Montmartre Métro station) has a wood-burning oven right in the shop so you can watch the baker as you wait your turn at the counter.

Three other boulangeries sure to please are: Max Poilane (1er), 42, place du Marché St-Honoré; 42-61-10-53; Tuileries Métro station (Max is Lionel's brother); Boulangerie Artisande (5e), 6, rue Linne; 47-07-10-94; Jussieu Métro station (owner Gerard Beaufort is always creating new bakery items); and Gerard Mulot (6e), 76, rue de Seine; 43-26-85-77; Odeon Métro station (with the reputation of producing the best brioche in Paris).

You won't be in Paris long before you realize that while there are dozens of boulangeries that limit themselves to making bread, rolls, and the occasional apple turnover, there are even more boulangerie-pâtisserie combinations. These are especially useful when you're shopping for picnic fare or just grazing, because you can buy your sandwich and dessert in the same place.

At the boulangerie-pâtisserie on the square des Corolles in the suburb of La Defense, for example, you can buy baguette sandwiches filled with ham and cheese, sausage, or pork for about $2.40, French pastries for about $1.20, and—if you've been provident enough to bring along a beverage—your total cost for a filling lunch is about $4. A small bottle of Evian or a 12-ounce Coke costs a whopping $1.40 to $2 at most boulangerie-pâtisseries, but later in this chapter I'll tell you where to get beverages for much less.

Many of the boulangerie-pâtisseries are plain Janes, with little attempt made at decor or display. At the other end of the spectrum are places like Lenotre (16e; 48, av Victor Hugo; 45-02-21-21; Victor Hugo Métro station), where precisely arranged pastries, tarts, and petits fours dazzle under table-sized glass domes. *Gateaux* are glazed, beribboned, and sprinkled with sparkles. Chocolates repose in exquisitely decorated boxes trimmed with picture-perfect roses and bows.

You'll find these pâtisseries in all parts of the city. The rule of thumb is that the more lavish the displays, the higher the prices. However, this doesn't apply to taste. The least pretentious-looking items for sale in the plainest of pâtisseries are often delicious.

Fromageries

Like bakers in their quest for producing the perfect loaf, France's cheese sellers are fervent about properly aging each kind of cheese they sell—so fervent, in fact, that many of them take on the aging process themselves in caves under their stores. These usually small shops, while not so ubiquitous as boulangeries, pâtisseries, or charcuteries, are nonetheless a French institution and a must for travelers who appreciate the nuances of various cheeses. The best of the fromageries supply the Stiltons, Reblochons, and Camemberts served in Paris's top restaurants. Rather than paying the horrendous restaurant markup, by patronizing their suppliers you can buy wedges of your favorites at more appropriate prices for picnics in the park.

The aroma of these shops can be almost overwhelming, so I prefer those that are partially open to the street, such as Fromagerie Cler (7e; 31, rue Cler; 47-05-48-95; Ecole-Militaire Métro station). It's a part of the upscale food market that runs along two blocks of rue Cler. Another fromagerie that's just off the market is Marie-Anne Cantin (12, rue du Champ-de-Mars; 45-50-43-94). It's a charming shop with two aging cellars under it (one very humid for cheeses made of cow's milk, and the other very dry for goat cheese).

Cheese fanciers who read French won't want to miss Chez Tachon (1er; 38, rue de Richelieu; 42-96-08-66; Palais-Royal Métro station). Small, handwritten signs give the history of many of the cheeses on display, telling how they originated and have evolved.

One of the largest selections of cheeses is found in the tiny shop called La Maison du Bon Fromage (1er; 35, rue du Marché St-Honoré; 42-61-02-77; Pyramides or Tuileries Métro station. Whether you're looking for a Reblochon from the Savoie, a Swiss Fribourg, a strong, spicy Livarot from Normandy, a Langres from Champagne, or a St-Marcellin from Lyons, you've a good chance of finding it at La Maison: It carries some 200 different kinds of cheese (France alone produces about 180).

Lillo (16e; 35, rue des Belles-Feuilles; 47-27-69-08; Victor Hugo Métro station) is an elegant shop on one of Paris's posh market streets. La Ferme Saint-Hubert (8e; 21, rue Vignon; 47-42-79-20; Madeleine Métro station) is another fromagerie in an upscale area popular with tourists.

Whichever cheese shops you choose, be sure to ask which cheeses are best at that particular time, and don't hesitate to ask questions about the different varieties. Most cheese sellers will offer samples to customers who seem genuinely interested.

Charcuteries and Traiteurs

Charcuteries combine, on a limited scale, the products of the boulangerie, pâtisserie, and fromagerie with a whole host of deli items—sliced meats, jars of condiments, crocks of olives, and hundreds of other good things to eat. Traiteurs are shops that sell ready-prepared foods, either to be eaten cold or reheated. You'll frequently come upon shops that combine the features of both charcuteries and traiteurs, such as the pricey Fauchon, with its navy-and-white tile walls and case upon case of pâtés in puff pastry, herring, caviar, tagliatelle with tuna and basil sauce, and other *plats du jour*.

Like the fromageries, Paris's top charcuteries tend to supply its better restaurants with their pâtés, foie gras, and sausages. No matter which charcuterie you patronize, chances are you'll see many items you're not familiar with, or at least haven't tasted before. This is your chance, since the white-coated shopkeepers aren't at all displeased if you ask for single slices or small portions.

At Chedeville (1er; 12, place du Marché St-Honoré; 42-61-04-62; Tuileries Métro station), you can watch several butchers at work in what is one of the city's major charcuteries. Most shops, like Charcuterie Coesnon (6e; 30, rue Dauphine; 43-54-35-80; Odeon Métro station), are smaller, mom-and-pop affairs.

Of course, you won't be able to sample some of the charcuteries' bounty unless you're renting an apartment, since many of the sausages and such require cooking, but there are enough other choices that you won't be too disappointed.

As far as the traiteurs are concerned, although I love to look at the upscale establishments like Fauchon and Hediard (8e; 21, place de la Madeleine; 43-12-88-88; Madeleine Métro station), I prefer those with an ethnic orientation such as Noura (16e; 27–29, av Marceau; 47-23-02-20; Alma Marceau or Charles-de-Gaulle-Etoile Métro station), where Lebanese foods are featured. It's an attractively designed place, with dozens of main courses, salads, and desserts in its basket and glass cases. Although prices aren't as modest as those of most traiteurs specializing in Lebanese, North African, or Jewish cuisine, you can still get the makings for a gratifying meal for $10 to $15.

Among my nonethnic favorites is Au Royal Palais (16e; 29, rue du Docteur Blanche; 45-25-67-67; Jasmin Métro station). Even if you're not hungry when you're in the Auteuil area, you'll enjoy looking at the appetite-appealing window displays. A huge selection of salads, berry tarts frosted with confectioner's sugar, and main courses, attractively arranged, may make you change your mind about eating.

While most of us could spend hours looking at the spectacular displays in the traiteurs that are picture-pretty, the no-frills traiteurs—the equivalent of North American take-out shops—are far more practical when you're keeping an eye on cost. An economical way to find a meal, some have tables or chest-high counters on the premises. When they don't, or even if they do, you won't have to go far to find a wall or bench to sit on.

Add to all these epicurean opportunities the street markets, with their bountiful fruits and vegetables (don't touch them or you're liable to get a tongue-lashing by the vendor), and you'll find that it's possible to dine like a king without paying a king's ransom.

Sit-Down Dinners

No matter how tantalizing the food from Paris's specialty food stores and even its supermarkets may be, there are times when you want to sit down in a restaurant—or bistro, café, or brasserie—for a meal. After all, Paris *is* the Gastronomic Capital of the World.

Prix fixe (set price) meals—they're known as *formule* or *formula* in France—are usually a better value than you get by

SUPERMARKET SPECIALS

I don't care how much money you have to spend on food, you'll be missing the gastronomic boat if you don't—at least once—visit a supermarket. The biggest ones are all located in the suburbs, but many of them aren't far from Métro stations.

The best supermarket I've found in France—maybe anywhere—is Auchan, at La Defense. Now, I'm not talking about the neon-tubing and waterfalls-over-the-veggies kind of store, but rather the kind that carries great-quality food in abundance. The cheese department is enormous and regularly offers specials on several varieties at a time. You can get Camembert in approximately a 12-ounce size for about a dollar; herbed Boursin or a good Chèvres (goat cheese) for about $1.50; about eight ounces of Brie for around $1. Specialty cheeses, though more expensive, cost less than anywhere else I've seen.

In the produce departments, tomatoes actually have stems on them and avocados cost less than they do in North America. Fruit, much of it imported from Turkey and southern Europe, may cost a bit more than it does at home, but it goes for less than you have to pay at Paris's street markets. And in supermarkets, you are permitted to touch the merchandise—you even weigh it yourself, and a price label comes out of the scale.

Herbs and spices are generally less expensive than in North America, as are jams and jellies—a small jar of cherry jam costs about $1. There's a large selection of glacéed fruit, along with mixes for *crème pâtisserie* and *crème brûlée*, things like *eau de fleurs* and *eau d'orange* to put in home-baked cakes, and intriguing sprinkles and other decorations to put on them—all at reasonable prices.

It's in the cookie and candy departments, however, where you'll really save. Good-sized packages of sugar wafers sell for as little as 60 cents; chocolate candy bars manufactured in France cost as little as $1 for five when they're on special (the Let's Go bars, which taste a lot like Milky Ways, are delicious).

Auchan is a big French supermarket chain, and the La Defense store is located inside the shopping mall directly to the left of the Grande Arche as you're approaching it from the La

Defense Métro station (about a quarter of a mile away). Another recommended supermarket is one of the Leclerc chain, which is catercorner from the Hoche Métro station entrance in the suburb of Pantin. It's also part of a big shopping mall.

In the city itself, smaller stores of the Monoprix, Prisunic, and Franprix chains offer some savings, but aren't nearly as pleasant or economical as the suburban stores.

And now, as promised, a word about bottled water. If it's the only kind you drink when traveling abroad—and that's what most prudent travelers do—you will be appalled at the restaurant and street vendor prices of Evian, Perrier, and other name, or even nonname, brands. Not too long ago, following a late-evening arrival from the States, I was dying of thirst but due to a number of circumstances had neglected to buy the usual bottle of water for my hotel room. Desperate, I pulled a bottle from the mini bar, drank it down in two small glassfuls, then looked at the rate sheet. Seven dollars. Next morning, I lost no time asking directions to the nearest suburban supermarket where one-and-a-half-liter bottles of water cost about 60 cents. Supermarket soft drinks are around $2.20 a six-pack.

---

ordering à la carte. However, if you're not really that hungry or haven't a big appetite, you'll save by ordering only an item or two. If you order only one or two courses in some of the more pretentious restaurants, be prepared to withstand the withering looks and contemptuous attitude of your waiter.

But before you venture out to dine, a short course in courses is appropriate. The French refer to what we call appetizers as entrées and to what we call entrées as main courses. Dessert is the same in both vocabularies. Cheese is eaten either as a separate course before dessert or as a substitute for it. Coffee is served after dessert, and you'll always be asked if you want it *au lait* (with milk).

Whether credit cards are accepted, and which ones, varies with each eating place, as do hours and days they're open.

Many restaurants also close in July or August for vacation. Therefore, it's a good idea to phone ahead and make reservations so you're sure you'll be able to eat where you want. As for tipping, although service is included in the price of all meals, a tip—anything from a few francs to 5 percent of the bill—is appropriate for exceptional service.

The following suggestions, which include a variety of dining experiences, should provide quality meals while keeping your wallet in shape. Of course, chefs quit, their significant others dump them, or they have an occasional bad food day, so we can't guarantee you'll get the same quality of food as the people who recommended these eateries. Nonetheless, in this uncertain world, they're pretty sure bets.

Bistro Bizet (16e; 6, rue de Chaillot; 47-20-26-92; Iéna Métro station) is a quintessentially French charmer with white linen, peach walls, and framed posters of Bizet's operas as decoration. Two prix fixe meals are available, one served at midday only. The lunch special costs about $13 and offers a choice of two entrées, two main courses, plus a cheese or dessert course. The other, at about $17, expands the number of entrées to four (herring fillets with potatoes is a good choice); offers four main courses, including *boudin noir*, the traditional blood sausage; and includes dessert or cheese, plus a beverage (beer, wine, or mineral water).

Bistrot du 7eme (7e; 56, blvd de Latour Maubourg; 45-51-93-08; Latour Maubourg Métro station) features a $15 prix fixe lunch that could easily double as dinner. Appetizers include chicken liver salad and Norwegian smoked salmon, while sirloin steak with béarnaise sauce and veal scallops with mushroom and cream sauce are among the main courses. For dessert, try the chocolate charlotte—unless you prefer cheese. The ambience is traditional bistro, with white napery and framed posters as well as black-and-white sketches on the walls. If you order à la carte, expect to pay about $25, excluding wine.

Bofinger (4e; 3, rue de la Bastille; 42-72-87-82; Bastille Métro station) is the oldest Alsatian brasserie in town and has been designated a historic landmark. Opened in 1854, its interior dazzles with brass, glass, and all the trappings of opulence associated with the Belle Epoche. Though à la carte prices generally are horrendous, you can get a huge helping of *choucroute* and a fresh berry tart for not much more than $20. The prix fixe meals cost about $30.

Chartier (9e; 7, rue du Faubourg Montmartre; 47-70-86-29; Montmartre Métro station) is another Paris landmark. The bistro, established in 1892, features fin-de-siècle brass rails, wooden booths, huge chandeliers, and traditional fare, such as sole meunière, smoked tripe sausages and, of course, *pommes frites*. Whether you order a prix fixe meal or à la carte, you can count on spending no more than $20.

Jo Goldenberg (4e; 7, rue des Rosiers; 48-87-20-16; St-Paul Métro station), with its yellow-and-black tile facade, is located in the heart of the old Jewish quarter. Food is hearty and plentiful, with such main courses as stuffed carp and beef goulash as well as some very good soups. Meals are served on two levels, one of which is nonsmoking. Prices start at about $20 for a fixed price meal.

La Cigale (7e; 11 bis, rue Chomel; 45-48-87-87; Sevres-Babylone Métro station) features traditional bistro fare such as lamb chops with white beans, entrecôte and french fries, and a very nice salmon. For starters, there's a memorable pâté. The homemade tart or pastry of the day—despite the prix fixe bill of about $31—makes a fine ending. Wine isn't included, but a half pitcher of Beaujolais—your best bet—won't hike up the tab too much.

Le Durer (8e; 19, rue Yvonne le Tac; 46-06-00-08; Abbesses Métro station) offers a *formula* meal for about $20 that starts with six escargots, avocado and shrimp cocktail, and salad or onion soup gratinée. Main courses include salmon, grilled entrecôte, and leg of lamb. An aperitif, glass of wine, and dessert or cheese are also included in the price. Durer's decor tends to the formal, with dark reds and golds predominating.

Le Petite Chaumiere (4e; 41, rue des Blancs Monteaux; 42-72-13-90; Rambuteau Métro station), with its bentwood chairs and round tables with starched white linen, art-glass lamps, and framed prints on the walls, makes a great midday stop. For about $12, you get a choice of such starters as lentil salad, duck mousse, and soup du jour. Main courses run to substantial fare like ground steak and codfish fillet. Included in the price is your choice of dessert or coffee.

Restaurant à la Petite Chaise (7e; 36, rue de Grenelle; 42-22-13-35; Bac or Sevres Métro station, founded in 1680) is one of the eating places that claim to be Paris's oldest. Whether or not that's true, there's no disputing the value received for money spent at this quiet neighborhood restaurant. Though the interior is a bit shabby, the service is polite and the food very good. The three fixed price meals, all of which include red, white, or rosé wine, cost about $25, $30, and $36. Among the appetizers are snails, vegetable soup, pâté, and salad. The lamb, beef, and pork dishes are all good main course choices, and you have the option of either dessert or cheese for the third course.

Le Bistrot de Breteuil (7e; 3, place de Breteuil; 45-67-07-27; Duroc Métro station) is considered to have one of the best restaurant terraces in town, in large part because its umbrella tables are on a street where there's not as much traffic as in most parts of central Paris. Inside, greenery, flowerpots, and large windows create a light and airy atmosphere. The set price meals include the house aperitif (a white wine kir) and entrées such as foie gras, a fish terrine with lobster sauce, or warm goat cheese salad. Main dishes range from a *salé* of duck with lentils to the more usual rack of lamb and roasted chicken. The hot apple tart with crème fraîche is a popular dessert.

Les Zygomates (12e; 7, rue de Capri; 40-19-93-04; Daumesnil or Michel-Bizot Métro station) is one of the new bistros that serve a mix of traditional and contemporary fare. Entrées include a fresh tomato and basil mousse as well as an unusual artichoke and lamb's tongue combination. Main dishes include fresh fish, chicken with cream and chives, rabbit compote, and other country-style specialties.

Les Zygomates—like many French restaurants—goes all out during wild-game season (August through October), with venison, baby boar, and wild fowl on the menu. But food is only part of the reason to visit this off-the-tourist-path establishment. Housed in what was a turn-of-the-20th-century butcher shop, the bistro is a real charmer, with etched-glass panels of hunting scenes, painted tiles, marble counters, and lots of mirrors to reflect it all. The prix fixe meals cost about $13 for lunch and $24 for dinner.

Though reservations are recommended (and sometimes required) at many of Paris's eating spots, it is possible to use the stroll-and-search method of selecting a place to eat, especially if you set out for an early meal.

For this approach, one of the very best streets is rue St-Louis-en-l'Île, a quarter-mile stretch of small shops, boutique hotels, and eateries that bisects Île St-Louis. Among those I discovered on a recent Paris trip was L'Îlot Vache (corner of rue des Deux Ponts; 46-33-55-16; Sully-Morland Métro station), where the windowsills are crammed with miniature cows—mostly ceramic Holsteins. It's a pretty place with stone walls, pink linen, and candles. The $14 *formule* features some great options like fish soup, Roquefort salad, and herring for starters; grilled lamb or salmon with two sauces as a main course; and sorbet, chocolate mousse, or crème caramel for dessert.

Meal prices—like hotel rooms—are usually lower at eating places on the city's outskirts. For instance, on av Jean Jaures across from the Cités des Sciences et des Industries, lace-curtained bistros, cafés, and small brasseries charge 25 to 30 percent less than their central-city counterparts.

Most of the restaurants on the street serve $10 *formule* dinners that include wine, main course, and cheese or dessert. Somewhat fancier, Au Boeuf Couronne (19e; 188, av Jean Jaures; 45-08-11-15) features a seafood platter for about $24 from September through May, and the $30 *formule*, served year-round, includes the likes of spinach salad with Roquefort, *boeuf Bourguignonne*, and crème caramel in a setting of dark wood with wall sconces, ornate chandeliers, etched glass, and greenery.

When you're looking for a bit of refinement, the following trio of *salons du thé* should provide it.

At Tea and Tattered Pages (6e; 24, rue Mayet; 40-65-94-35; Falguière Métro station), items like clam chowder and crab cakes are on the menu. While you eat, it's perfectly all right to read one of the 15,000 used books for sale.

The decor at Angelina (1er; 226, rue de Rivoli; 42-60-82-00; Tuileries Métro station), with mirror- and mural-covered walls, is spectacular. Devotees say, however, that it can't compete with the house specialty, a decadently rich hot chocolate called Africain, that's made with melted candy bars.

Mariage Frères (4e; 30-32, rue du Bourg-Tibourg; 42-72-28-11; St-Paul Métro station) combines tea shop with tea merchant. About 300 varieties of tea from almost two dozen countries are for sale. The tea shop is at its best when strawberry tarts are in season, but it's great to browse around anytime.

Though you may not always save money, a great way to save time and rest your feet when you're visiting museums is to have lunch or dinner on the premises. At the Musée d'Orsay, for example, the former depot diner has become an opulent dining room where interesting salads and gourmet main dishes, like duck breast with five-pepper sauce, provide sustenance with a gourmet flair. There's also a snacks-and-pastry café on the museum's top floor.

Over at the Louvre, meanwhile, museumgoers can slow down for fast food at the Carousel du Louvre underground shopping mall's food court. Twelve self-service counters offer everything from Breton-style crêpes to Tex-Mex. You'll be wise to stick with the French specialties, however (the croque monsieur is an especially good choice), and stay away from the Chinese raviolis. Expect to pay about $10 for a meal including a beverage.

A Bistro Meal, a Glass of Wine, and . . .

Wine bistros are fast becoming an important part of the Paris dining scene. Generally smallish, with an intimate ambience, they're often hidden away on side streets. Whereas the city's wine bars emphasize wine, with light meals somewhat of the afterthought variety, wine bistros put equal emphasis on food. The wines are mostly from small wineries—perhaps produced by the owner's brother or a friend. Menu choices tend toward hearty bistro fare, though some of the wine bistros serve lighter, more sophisticated dishes.

L'Enoteca (4e; 25, rue Charles V; 42-78-91-44; Sully-Morland Métro station) is an Italian-flavored wine bistro that's housed in a stone building dating to the 16th century. With the best selection of Italian wines in the city, the bistro meals typically start with antipasto—eggplant, braised artichokes, and the like. Main courses, which change regularly, include the classic osso buco and a variety of pasta dishes with homemade pesto.

Le Passage (11e; 18, passage de la Bonne-Graine; 47-00-73-30; Ledru-Rollin Métro station) is known for wine, jazz, and some of the best bistro food around, from *cervelle de canut* (a mélange of creamy white cheese, chervil, chives, mint, chopped garlic, and tarragon) to homemade *andouillettes* (tripe sausages) and steak tartare. Portions are generous. Save room for *pots de crème*, which come in at least three delicious flavors.

Juveniles (1e; 47, rue de Richelieu; 42-97-46-49; Palais-Royal Métro station) is unusual in that it features wines from around the world at reasonable prices. The menu changes daily, featuring the likes of roasted cod with eggplant marmalade and terrine of guinea hen with onion compote. If you're in the mood for something lighter, fill up on Juveniles' excellent tapas with one of its Spanish sherries.

Speaking of wine, in many Parisian restaurants you can now keep the cost of your meals down substantially by ordering wine by the glass rather than by the bottle. At L'Oeillade (7e; 10 rue St-Simon; 42-22-01-60; Rue du Bac or Solferino Métro station), for example, an à la carte meal for two can cost more than $75 (prix fixe meals cost about half that amount), but prices for a glass of wine start at about $5.

At Brasserie Flo (10e; 7, cours des Petites-Ecuries; 42-46-15-80; Château-d'Eau Métro station), house wines—including an Alsation Riesling and Pinot Blanc, a red *vin de pays* from the Languedoc, Beaujolais, and Côtes du Rhône—cost just $4 a glass.

The cost reduction is even greater at the restaurants with Michelin stars, where the price of a whole bottle of wine can more than double the tab. At two-star Guy Savoy (7e; 18, rue Troyon; 43-80-40-61; Charles-de-Gaulle-Etoile Métro station), all but the most expensive wines on the list can be bought by the glass for about 16 percent of the bottle's price. At three-star L'Arpege (7e; 84, rue Varenne; 45-51-47-33; Varenne Métro station), two regional wines—a red and a white—are available at $8 a glass.

Although chocolates aren't considered food in the same sense as meat and potatoes, some of us don't think our gastronomic life is complete without them. When you decide to skip dessert and have a couple of chocolates instead, you won't have to go far to find a place to buy them, since Parisians think they're wonderful, too. Be prepared to pay a lot for your pleasure, however, if you buy any but the supermarket variety. The following shops will give you a visual treat as well as a gustatory one:

Michel Chaudun (7e); 149, rue du l'Université; 47-53-74-40; Invalides Métro station.

Jean-Paul Hevin (6e); 3, rue Vavin; 43-54-09-85; Vavin Métro station; and (7e); 16, av de la Motte Picquet; 45-51-77-48; La Tour–Maubourg Métro station.

La Bonbonnière Saint Honoré (8e); 28, rue de Miromesnil; 42-65-02-39; Miromesnil Métro station.

A La Mère de Famille (9e); 35, rue du Faubourg Montmartre; 47-70-83-69; Montmartre or Cadet Métro station.

Boissier (16e); 184, av Victor Hugo; 45-03-50-77; Victor Hugo Métro station.

If chocolate won't do it but an ice cream cone will, the place to go is Berthillon (4e; 31, rue St-Louis-en-l'Île; 43-54-31-61; Pont Marie Métro station). This is the most popular ice cream parlor in Paris, with more than 60 flavors—from *nougat au miel* (nuts and honey) to blackberry sorbet.

Saving the Best Tips for Last

As I mentioned earlier, although meals in most full-fledged restaurants cost the same whether they're served at lunch or dinnertime, bistros and brasseries often have lunch specials. Frequently they're the same items that will be served at dinner, but if you eat them early enough—usually before 3 P.M.—you'll save a lot of money. For example, at Leon of Bruxelles, a Belgian brasserie chain that specializes in mussels, you'll pay a dollar more for exactly the same sized portions of mussels and *pommes frites* at 3:30 P.M. that you would have an hour earlier. (I lost track of the number of mussels in one serving at six dozen.) There are other eateries, however, where the fixed price lunch menu is available until 8:30 or 9 in the evening.

Eating your main meal at lunchtime may have another advantage besides saving you money. The atmosphere is relatively smoke-free during the middle of the day. Late in the evening, when Paris eats dinner, restaurant air gets hazy, since the ordinance calling for nonsmoking areas is seldom enforced.

Coffee and wine in Paris eateries generally add a sizable amount to the bill. Although you can get a $1 cup of coffee at the Galeries Lafayette cafeteria and a few other places in the city, this is the exception rather than the rule. And while some house wines are adequate, others leave much to be desired. The least expensive wines on the menu are usually a better choice, and some establishments now sell wine by the glass.

Don't forget to keep on the lookout for bargains. You're most likely to find brochures advertising two-course meals and those containing discounts for meals—especially for newly opened eateries—in the racks at travel centers and in hotels. You'll find more dining specials in winter than the busy summer season, especially during the holidays. And sometimes, you'll find discounts in unexpected places. When you go to the fashion show at Printemps department store, for example, you're handed a coupon good for a 10 percent discount on lunch.

If you plan to be in Paris for several days or weeks, you might consider investing in the *Paris Directory* (see chapter 13) put out by Entertainment Publications. The directory will entitle you to 25 percent discounts at more than 300 dining spots, including a handful of one- and two-star restaurants. According to *Consumer Reports Travel Letter*, which tested the plan, personnel at some of the places appeared to be unfamiliar with the program but gave the discount after they were shown the name of their establishment in the directory.

Wherever you go, don't worry about getting in over your head financially. According to law, restaurants must post their menus so that they can be read from outside the building.

The great French chef Auguste Escoffier is attributed with the saying, "Good cooking is the source of true happiness." Savvy travelers say that it's even a truer source when you can find it while keeping your travel budget intact.

SO SPLURGE A LITTLE

If your Paris dream is eating in a restaurant that's been awarded a Michelin star or two, indulge yourself. You may find that it doesn't cost as much as you thought it would—especially if you keep a couple of guidelines in mind.

Experts in the culinary field maintain that the difference in the number of stars a restaurant receives doesn't depend on the food—especially the difference between two- and three-star establishments. True, a high standard of food preparation is necessary in order to get any stars at all, but the number depends on other criteria, such as opulence of decor, quality of menu, linens and tableware, distance between tables, rest room amenities, and the like. As a result, you're almost as sure to get an outstanding meal in a one-star as a three-star restaurant. Your surroundings may not be so sumptuous or the china so fine, but if your objective is to experience a gourmet meal created by one of the country's top chefs, you won't miss the trappings of luxury.

Since a restaurant's prices seem to escalate with each mention received in newspapers, articles, and books, you'll do well to rely on recommendations of people whose culinary judgment you trust and steer clear of "name" restaurants. In general, meals at establishments that rely on repeat customers, such as businesspeople who frequently entertain clients, provide better value than those at spots that cater to tourists and people determined to be seen at the "right" places.

A case in point is the one-star Les Muses restaurant in Hotel Scribe (9e; 1, rue Scribe; 44-71-24-24; Opéra Métro station). It doesn't have a reputation as an "in" spot. The dining room furnishings are very fine but won't knock your socks off. The food, on the other hand, is outstanding.

The prix fixe lunch/dinner for about $55 (excluding wine) is superior to those of many two- and three-star restaurants. After an entrée such as smoked salmon, you might have a sautéed bay prawns with satay sauce and spinach in a puff pastry, or wild mushrooms and marinated scallops on a bed of lettuce.

Main course choices include filet of beef with chestnut sauce, and chicken breast stuffed with snails and pecans. Unless you're an expert, when more than a dozen cheeses are wheeled to your table on a trolley for the next course, have one of the knowledgeable waiters select five or six varieties for you.

Dessert choices include those on the pastry cart as well as six more listed on the menu, including a wonderful apple shortbread combination with orange butter. The finale—just when you're certain you can't eat another bite—is a two-tiered plate of what must be the most delicious petits fours ever created, along with coffee or tea. The crusty rolls served with the meal are remarkable, too. It's also possible to eat at Les Muses for less: There are prix fixe meals for about $42.

To sample top chefs' creations without paying full-fledged restaurant prices, you might eat at their lower-priced bistros. Michel Rostang and Guy Savoy are among the chefs who have augmented their status restaurants with less expensive satellites. Rostang has one at 10, rue Gustave-Flaubert in the sixth arrondissement called Bistro d'a Côte Flaubert (42-67-05-81; Courcelles Métro station).

Savoy is connected with several satellites, including one Bistrot de l'Etoile at 19, rue Lauriston (16e; 40-67-11-16; Charles-de-Gaulle-Etoile Métro station); another with the same name at 75, av Niel (17e; 42-27-88-44; Charles-de-Gaulle-Etoile Métro station); Cap Vernet (8e; 82, av Marceau; 47-20-20-40; Charles-de-Gaulle-Etoile Métro station); and Les Bookinistes (6e; 53, quai Grands Augustins; 43-25-45-94; St-Michel Métro station).

Other spin-offs include Tour d'Argent's Rotisserie du Beaujolais (5e; 19, quai Tourville; 43-54-17-47; St-François-Xavier Métro station) and Goumard-Prunier's Gaya Rive Gauche (7e; 44, rue du Bac; 45-44-73-73; Rue du Bac Métro station).

If you won't be happy until you've dined in a Michelin-starred restaurant, but don't want to pay the astronomical prices, you may want to check out a new option. François Reverse, who founded the French travel agency Degriftour, has come up with a Web site offering discounted prix fixe meals at France's top restaurants. After you have connected to the site (http://www.degriftour.fr), search for "Les Grandes Tables," then click on "Ile de France." Select restaurants and dates to review their set menus. You can also make your reservations by following the instructions given on the Web page. Cost per person will probably run from about $80 to $100, but will include wine, after-dinner coffee, and service charges—and will be only half to two-thirds of the regular price.

Getting From Here to There

When you look at maps of some cities, they make sense right from the start. Paris doesn't. Rues, avenues, and boulevards run horizontally, vertically, diagonally—sometimes changing names in the process. Every so often, they're interrupted by squares or triangles or circles of land, usually called *places*, but sometimes *étoiles* or *squares*, from which still more streets radiate at a variety of angles. Then there's the River Seine, which flows every which way through the city, with some 32 bridges spanning it. Actually, the Seine follows a roughly east-to-west course through the central city, so what is referred to as the Rive Gauche (Left Bank) is south of the river and the Rive Droite (Right Bank) is more or less north.

Despite all this, after you've studied the map and spent some time in on-site exploration, Paris is one of the easiest cities in the world to navigate.

Paris is divided into 20 geographical districts, called arrondissements, which are encircled by the multilane blvd Peripherique that separates the city from its suburbs. The arrondissement numbering system begins with the area around the Louvre as the first arrondissement (abbreviated 1er). North of it is the second arrondissement (abbreviated

2e, like all the arrondissements that follow it, with only the letter *e* after the number).

As you're facing the map, to the right of the second arrondissement is the third, and below that is the fourth. Below the fourth and across the river is the fifth. Then, proceeding clockwise in spiral fashion, are the succeeding arrondissements. Only six of them (5e, 6e, 7e, 13e, 14e, and 15e) are on the Left Bank.

You'll need some study time with a map to get the scheme memorized, but you'll find it's a very effective means of locating the places you wish to visit. The arrondissements most popular with tourists are the first, where many major points of interest are located (the Louvre, the Jardin des Tuileries, Palais Royal, and the Forum des Halles shopping mall are some), and the eighth, where you'll find the most elegant hotels, shops, and restaurants, as well as several palaces and the Arc de Triomphe. (Actually, the latter is at the junction of the 8e, 16e, and 17e.) Montmartre is in the 18th arrondissement. The fifth and sixth are known as the Latin Quarter because courses used to be conducted in Latin at the Sorbonne and other universities located there. The Hôtel de Ville, Notre Dame, the Centre Pompidou, and Île St-Louis are all in the fourth arrondissement.

Within the arrondissements are the traditional neighborhoods, former villages, and *communes* (communities), which go back hundreds of years and are still known by their original names. Take Belleville, for example. It has traditionally been the area of Paris where immigrants settle. Parts of the neighborhood are in the 11th, 19th, and 20th arrondissements. Another neighborhood, the Marais, goes back to the days when the marshes *(marais)* were drained and grand homes were built on the reclaimed land. It's primarily in the fourth arrondissement.

Then there's Menilmontant, where singer Edith Piaf spent her childhood. Its commercial district now is a mix of African health food and exotic grocery stores, fabric shops, and Arab butcher shops, where roasted goat heads are among the wares for sale. The former wine village of La Goutte-d'Or has become another of Paris's ethnic areas, with people of more than four dozen nationalities living there.

There are the also the upscale neighborhoods of Auteuil and Passy; neighborhoods Montmartre, Montsouris, and Plaisance, where affordable housing in the early 20th century attracted artists and writers, and whose artistic history now attracts tourists; and Charonne, Butte-Aux-Cailles, and Rhine-et-Danube, which each has a distinct personality that sets it apart from other areas of the city.

The Money Angle

Not only is Paris easy to understand once you have the lay of the land, but it's also a place where you can save big bucks on transportation. Believe it or not, you can start saving when you begin making preparations for your trip.

If you plan to take a variety of day trips from Paris and/or excursions within France, you'll want to buy a France Rail-pass, which you must buy before you leave home. I'll talk more about rail passes in chapter 10, but when you arrive in Paris the important thing to know is that two extra vouchers come with your pass at no extra charge. One is good for a ride on the RER (Réseau Express Régional or Regional Express Network) from the airport to any Métro station in the city on the day of your arrival, and the other is for transport to the airport when you depart. Since the one-way Charles-de-Gaulle trip costs about $6.30, and the Orlyval RER trip about $7, you've already saved $12.60 to $14.

As I mentioned in chapter 1, two airports serve Paris—Charles-de-Gaulle and Orly. Once you've touched down at either one, cleared customs, and retrieved your baggage, you'll have several options in addition to the RER to get to Paris, some of which are far less expensive than others.

From the Charles-de-Gaulle Airport (CDG), even if you aren't flying Air France you can catch its buses, which leave every 12 minutes for city terminals near the Arc de Triomphe and Porte Maillott, and every 30 to 60 minutes (depending on the time of day) for Gare Montparnasse, the railroad station that most of Paris's high-speed trains use.

The Arc de Triomphe/Porte Maillot buses leave Charles-de-Gaulle (the transatlantic flight terminal for all lines but Air France and Continental) at Door 34, and Door 26 for Montparnasse. At Aérogare 2 (the domestic terminal), they leave from Doors 5 and 6. Individual tickets cost about $9.10 to Arc de Triomphe and Porte Maillot ($18.20 round-trip) and $10.50 ($17 round-trip) to the train station, but there are discounts for groups of four or more. Buses run from 6 A.M. to 11 P.M.

RER trains run every 15 minutes from 5 A.M. to 11:59 P.M. To get to the trains, you must catch the shuttle at Door 28 of Aérogare 1 or Door 5 at Aérogare 2. The ride to the Gare du Nord takes about 25 minutes (but figure 2 minutes more for each additional stop). As I mentioned, RER tickets cost about $6.30 from the airport to any Métro station in Paris. This is a real money saver if your hotel is close to a station and your baggage is so light that you can avoid taking a cab.

Speaking of luggage, don't attempt riding the RER or subways—especially during rush hour—if you have more luggage than you can hold on your lap or shove under a seat at the end of the car. If you do put your luggage under a seat, be sure you can see it at all times.

The Roissybus, which goes to place de l'Opéra on rue Scribe in Paris, leaves every 15 minutes from doors 10 and 12 at CDG2, Door 30 of CDG1, and Door A of Hall T9, and costs about $6.75.

Taxis can cost anywhere from around $40 with light traffic to $100 when it's bumper to bumper, depending upon the time it takes to get to your hotel. (Fares are higher after 7 P.M., and there are extra charges for luggage.) Under ordinary conditions, taxis take little more than half an hour to get to most destinations in Paris. Taxi lines at Charles-de-Gaulle are outside doors 7 and 16.

Although taxis are expensive for one or two people traveling alone, when traffic is relatively light and you don't have any heavy suitcases, for four people sharing they can be the most economical transportation in terms of time, energy, and money. (Some cabs, however, have a three-passenger limit.)

Air France buses also serve Orly. The Paris terminal is at Invalides, but the driver will drop passengers off at Porte d'Orléans or Duroc Métro station if requested to do so. The buses leave every 12 minutes. Tickets cost about $7 ($11.90 round-trip). The buses depart from Orly Sud (the international terminal) at Door 5 and from Orly Ouest (the domestic terminal) from Door E. The trip between Orly and Invalides takes about half an hour under normal traffic conditions.

Linked with Paris through the RER railway system, Orlyrail trains leave every 15 minutes, from 5:35 A.M. to 11:17 P.M., and take about 45 minutes to reach Gare d'Austerlitz. Other stops are St-Michel/Notre Dame, Musée d'Orsay, Invalides, and Champ de Mars/Tour Eiffel. Shuttle buses from Orly Sud (Door H) and Orly Ouest (Door F) take passengers to the RER station. A one-way ticket costs about $4.90.

A newer system, called Orlyval, connects by shuttle with RER line B, which goes to stations including Denfert-Rochereau, and continues all the way to Charles-de-Gaulle Airport. It costs about $8. Trains leave every four to eight minutes, and the trip between Chatelet Métro station and Orly takes 30 minutes.

The RATP bus number 215, called Orlybus, goes from the airport to the Denfert-Rochereau Métro station in south Paris every 13 minutes. There you can connect with Métro lines to various parts of the city. The bus costs about $4.90. Public transportation service at both Charles-de-Gaulle and Orly begins at between 5:30 and 6 A.M. and operates until 11:30 or

11:45 at night. The buses leave Orly Sud from Door H and Orly Ouest from Door J. Under normal traffic conditions the trip takes about 25 minutes.

Taxis from Orly usually cost less than from Charles-de-Gaulle: Whereas the latter is about 19 miles north of Paris, Orly is only 9 miles south. Still, if yours is a Right Bank hotel (north of the river) and you're traveling during heavy traffic after 7 P.M.—and traffic *can* be heavy at that time—expect to pay a bundle.

A recently inaugurated service, the Paris Airports Service, provides direct van transport between either of the two major airports and anywhere you want to go in Paris. Rates from Charles-de-Gaulle Airport are about $22 for one person and $27 for two, with additional price breaks for groups traveling together. From Orly, the cost is about $18 for one person and $21 for two, and the vans can take up to eight passengers. The company doesn't take charge cards, however.

Once you're in the city and have settled into your hotel, getting around becomes far less expensive. It's estimated that about 10 million people live in Paris and its immediate environs. You'll find that despite the large population and relatively few skyscrapers, it's a very compact city. It's also very flat. (The one major hill tourists have to contend with—leading up to Sacré Coeur in Montmartre—is served by a funicular.)

Although the claim that you can walk from one end of the city to the other in two and a half hours seems an exaggeration, the average walker *can* cover a great deal of territory in a day. In addition, unless the workers are on strike, you can also rely on the excellent Métro and bus systems to get anywhere you want to go.

The underground transport system is vast, with 13 lines (plus four RER railway lines) and more than 275 stations. Like every underground system, it is advertised as easy to use. Like all the others, however, it isn't always that uncomplicated, particularly at a station where several lines connect. Travel life becomes much easier—not to mention more efficient—when you have a map of the Métro system. Maps of the city are available from the tourism offices.

You'll also find that you're far more likely to get on the wrong train or go in the opposite direction if you're in a hurry. The best plan is to plot your course while you're still in your hotel room, writing down the station where you want to stop, the numbers of the lines you have to connect with, and the name of the last station on each of those lines. That way, after your ticket has been gobbled up and spit out again by the turnstile and you're through the gate, you'll have a foolproof plan to follow. Connecting lines (referred to as *correspondance*) are clearly marked on the station walls, with arrows pointing the way to trains going in each direction.

The big drawback with taking the Métro—other than not seeing the territory you're passing through—is that some stations (Montparnasse, Chatelet, Bastille, and Charles-de-Gaulle-Etoile, among others) require ascending and descending hundreds of steps and walking what seems like several blocks to make connections.

Once you're on the trains, however, it doesn't take long to get from place to place. At the end of each car are four fold-down seats, which I find preferable to the facing bench seats in the middle of the car for two reasons. First of all, there's usually more legroom, and second, you can get on and off quickly—and this is a real plus, since stations on lines you're not familiar with can come up more quickly than you anticipate.

The Métro operates from 5:30 A.M. to 1:15 A.M. Although it is relatively safe, it's best to avoid traveling through the tough parts of the city after the evening rush—especially on the last run of the night. Check with your hotel's concierge or front desk if you're uncertain of the area. Beware, too, of pickpockets during times when the cars are crowded.

Single Métro tickets cost about $1.10. A one-day pass, which provides unlimited travel on Métro and RER lines within the city as well as buses, costs $7.70. A two-day pass costs $12.60; three-day, about $16.80; five-day, $29.50.

Anything other than the one-day pass is no deal at all, since for about $13, you can buy a weekly Carte Orange (Orange Card), which begins on Monday and is good for seven days. The only catch is that you must have a passport-type photo. I have brought black-and-white proof sheet photos from home and head shots of the appropriate size cut out of color prints, which have filled the requirement.

Since you have to take at least six Métro or bus trips to justify buying a one-day pass, it saves money only for people who plan to spend just one day taking several public conveyances. Even then, the *carnet*—10 tickets for about $8.12—is usually a better deal, since the tickets can be used anytime.

Unless I'm impatient to get someplace, the bus is my favorite way—other than walking—to explore the city. Like the Métro, the buses provide extensive transportation that takes you to within two or three blocks of almost anywhere in Paris. Even in heavy traffic, if you have a window seat, the slow ride and frequent traffic delays aren't wasted time; they allow you more time to watch the passing parade. Most bus rides require only one ticket, but on very long trips, two may be necessary.

Tickets for the Métro and buses are interchangeable. You can either buy your bus tickets in advance at any Métro station and most *tabacs*, or get them on board the buses. Free maps of the Métro, bus, and RER routes are available at the stations and many hotels. After you board a bus, insert your ticket into a small box at shoulder level (located behind the driver) until you hear a click that means the ticket has been validated.

The symbol marking most Métro stations is a circle with a large yellow M inside it, while other stations still can be identified by the original green Art Nouveau canopies and rail-ings, with the word MÉTROPOLITAIN spelled out in full. Red-and-yellow signs indicate bus stops. Many of them have shelters with benches inside, which makes waiting much more pleasant during inclement weather.

Taxis, which more often than not take only three passengers at a time, have a basic charge of about $1.80 to $2.10 that's on the meter when you begin your ride. The charge for the number of kilometers traveled is added to this amount. The daytime rate within the 20 arrondissements, known as Tariff A, is about 55 cents per kilometer from 7 A.M. to 7 P.M. Tariff B, effective in the same area between 7 P.M. and 7 A.M., is about 90 cents a kilometer. In the suburbs, Tariff B is charged during the day and Tariff C ($1.20 per kilometer) is charged at night.

There's usually a supplement of about $1.40 for a fourth passenger, and each bag that must be put in the trunk (theoretically of 11 pounds or more) costs an additional $1. If you call for a taxi, you have to pay for the distance the driver has to travel to get to you. Furthermore, if the taxi driver takes you to the special taxi bays at railroad stations or some bus terminals, there's a charge of about 60 cents. A charge of about 50 cents is levied for each animal you have with you—not something that concerns most travelers, but Parisians grumble about it.

Alternative Energy

Whether you decide to wander aimlessly, follow your own itinerary or one from a walking guide, or take a commercial tour, strolling Paris on fine days could well be your trip's highlight. For anyone in reasonable condition, the hike from the Arc de Triomphe to the Louvre is an easy one. And for people who like to stop and smell the roses, there are plenty of those—as well as benches—in gardens along the way.

The Left Bank, Île de la Cité, and Île St-Louis are other favorite strolling areas. Other less well-known spots (I'll explore them in chapter 6) are equally appealing and easy to explore on foot. And whereas at home you may jog primarily for exercise, finding scenic paths in Paris can add a memorable dimension to your visit. Bois de Vincennes on the east side of Paris has both a one-mile and a nine-mile route. Bois de Boulogne, on the western edge of the city, has even more miles of pathways through its woods and meadows.

You can jog along loops at places like Luxembourg Gardens and the Tuileries, too—best in marginal weather, when the joggers aren't out in force. What you'll probably enjoy most is creating your own routes in the city's finest residential neighborhoods—past the embassies in the 8th and 16th arrondissements, perhaps.

Though I wouldn't recommend riding a bicycle through Paris traffic, quiet streets and the two big parks—Bois de Boulogne and Bois de Vincennes—are perfect for bicycling (see chapter 6).

Whatever mode of transportation you choose, be sure to take time to really savor the sights along the way. They'll provide you with memories mere money can't buy.

5

Everything That Money Can Buy

Just once, I'd like to get on a plane bound for Paris with nothing but a suitcase full of money, for nowhere in the world can you find a more stylish selection of things to buy—from table linens and haircuts to mountain climbing gear and lingerie. Unfortunately for those of us with American dollars, most of the items for sale these days are—as the French would say—*très cher*. Nonetheless, there *are* bargains if you know how to go about shopping for them.

Haute and Not-so-Haute Couture

While Paris is no longer as dominant in world fashion as it was a quarter century ago, the city is still synonymous with high-style clothing. Spring and fall showings of the major couturiers continue to attract the lion's share of attention from the fashion press, and all of us still covet clothes with Paris designer labels. So let's talk about the highest of high fashion first. Even though most people cannot or do not wish to spend the money required to buy designer clothes, it doesn't cost a cent to look at them. And knowing what's commanding top dollar fashionwise will guide you when looking for bargains later.

First of all, it's important to understand that there's a difference between haute couture and other fashion houses. Original haute couture garments are one of a kind, designed by a couture house listed with the Fédération Française de la Couture, whose rules for classification are very strict. There are less than two dozen of these houses, and many of the most talented designers are not on the list.

Prices for these haute couture creations are beyond the reach of almost everyone. However, they are a major inspiration for mass-market clothing. Ready-to-wear clothes produced by top Paris designers at the nondesignated fashion houses are also expensive, but prices don't approach those of haute couture.

Not so long ago, couture houses and big-name designer shops were primarily concentrated on rue du Faubourg-St-Honoré, but today you'll find them on several additional Right Bank streets and, increasingly, on the Left as well.

Avenue Montaigne currently is one of the most prestigious addresses, but there are many others, as you'll see from the following list of some of the top designers' salons and boutiques. Although the majority of these designers specialize in women's apparel, a number of them design clothes for men as well.

Pierre Balmain (8e); 44, rue François; 47-20-35-34; Franklin D. Roosevelt Métro station.

Jean Cacharel (9e); 34, rue Tronchet; 47-42-12-61; Madeleine Métro station.

Pierre Cardin (8e); 27, av Marigny; 42-66-68-98; and Pierre Cardin Prestige (8e); 82, rue du Faubourg-St-Honoré; 42-65-26-88; both Champs-Elysées-Clemenceau Métro station.

Jean-Charles de Castelbajac (1er); 31, place du Marché St-Honoré; 42-60-41-55; Tuileries Métro station.

Celine (8e, women's clothing); 36, av Montaigne; 49-52-12-01; Alma Marceau Métro Station; and (16e, men's clothing); 3, av Victor Hugo; 45-01-80-01; Victor Hugo Métro station.

Chanel (1er); 31, rue Cambon; 42-61-58-15; Tuileries Métro station.

Christian Dior (8e); 30, ave Montaigne; 40-86-28-00; Alma Marceau Métro station.

Courreges (8e); 40, rue François; 53-67-30-00; Franklin D. Roosevelt Métro station.

Jacques Fath (8e); 36, rue du Faubourg-St-Honoré; 42-68-03-46; Concorde Métro station.

Louis Feraud (8e); 88, rue du Faubourg-St-Honoré; 55-27-88-88; Champs-Elysées-Clemenceau Métro station; and (6e); 95, rue de Seine; 46-34-26-97; St-Germain-des-Pres Métro station.

Jean-Paul Gaultier (11e); 30, rue du Faubourg-St-Antoine; 44-68-84-80; Bastille Métro station.

Hubert de Givenchy (8e); 3, av George V; 44-31-50-23; George V Métro station.

Hermes (8e); 24, rue du Faubourg-St-Honoré; 40-17-47-17; Concorde Métro station.

Lacoste (8e); 95, av des Champs-Elysées; 47-23-76-00; Franklin D. Roosevelt Métro station.

Christian Lacroix (8e); 73, rue du Faubourg-St-Honore; 42-68-79-00; Concorde Métro station.

Lanvin (8e); 15, rue du Faubourg-St-Honoré; 44-71-33-33; Concorde Métro station.

Guy Laroche (8e); 28, rue du Faubourg St-Honoré; 40-06-01-70; Concorde Métro station.

Lolita Lempicka (4e); 2, rue des Rosiers; 48-87-09-67; St-Paul Métro station; and (8e); 78, av Marceau; 40-70-19-22; Alma Marceau Métro station.

Thierry Mugler (8e); 49, av Montaigne; 47-23-37-62; Alma Marceau Métro station.

Nina Ricci (8e, samples are for sale downstairs); 39, av Montaigne; 49-52-56-00; Alma Marceau Métro station.

Rodier (6e); 38, rue de Sevres; 45-48-33-39; Sevres-Babylone Métro station.

Sonia Rykiel (6e); 175, blvd St-Germain; 49-54-60-60; St-Germain-des-Pres Métro station.

Yves Saint Laurent (16e); 5, av Marceau; 44-31-64-00; Alma
   Marceau Métro station.
Jean-Louis Scherrer (8e); 53, av Montaigne; 56-57-00-00;
   Franklin D. Roosevelt Métro station.
Louis Vuitton (16e); 78 bis, av Marceau; 47-20-47-00; Alma
   Marceau or Franklin D. Roosevelt Métro station.

Top designers more closely identified with other countries
have Paris shops, too. Among them are:

Kenzo (Takada) (8e); 27, blvd Madeleine; 42-61-04-14; Made-
   leine Métro station.
Hanae Mori (8e); 19, av Montaigne; 47-23-52-03; Franklin
   D. Roosevelt Métro station; and (8e); 5, place de l'Alma;
   40-70-05-73; Alma Marceau Métro station.
Emanuel Ungaro (8e); 2, av Montaigne; 53-57-00-00; Alma
   Marceau Métro station.
Valentino (8e); 17, av Montaigne; 47-23-64-61; Alma Mar-
   ceau Métro station.
Gianni Versace (8e); 62, rue du Faubourg-St-Honoré; 47-42-
   88-02; Concorde Métro station; and (8e); 41, rue François;
   47-23-88-30; Franklin D. Roosevelt Métro station.

Unless you're determined to buy the absolute latest in
designer clothes, you can save from 20 to 70 percent by visiting the stores that sell them at a discount. Most of these
stores have the word *stock* in their names. This means they
have relationships with designers that allow them to sell last
season's clothes a minimum of three months after they've first
come out. Needless to say, the amount of discount is propor-
tionate to the time that has elapsed since an item's debut on
the fashion runways.

Because Paris fashions are usually of classic design and since
they don't become totally accepted in North America until two
or three years after they appear on the Continent, garments
from previous years' collections can be very smart buys. Some
of the "stock" stores handle clothes of only one designer; others,

of several. Most are located on rue d'Alesia in the 14th arrondissement, but there are also about a dozen stock stores on rue
St-Placide (St-Placide Métro station) and still others scattered
about the city. The following is only a sampling:

Pierre d'Alby Stock; 92, rue d'Alesia (men's, women's, and
children's clothing).
SNC (Yves Saint Laurent); 64, rue d'Alesia.
Jean-Louis Scherrer (12e); 29, av Ledru-Rollin; Ledru-
Rollin Métro station.

Even at "stock" establishments, these Paris creations don't
come cheap. Expect prices for suits from last year's collections to start at about $250 to $350. And whether you're
buying from a salon or a "stock," in order to get a good deal,
you should know how much couturier clothes cost at home.
Also be aware that although prices are often about the same
all over the world, designers sell the rights to use their names
and designs to garment makers in other countries, so both
quality and styles may vary.

The Lowdown on High-Fashion Showings

Showings of the haute couture collections, the highlights of
each fashion year, are traditionally held in January and July,
although there's a trend toward earlier dates, such as October and April. While the openings are free to members of
the fashion press and customers who receive invitations,
they're otherwise virtually impossible to get into if you haven't
a connection with someone involved in a show—one of the
models, the person in charge of accessories, the producer.
Since most of us don't, we have to be content with the alternatives—the weekly fashion shows offered by Printemps and
Galeries Lafayette department stores. These shows are first-
rate and perhaps the best free entertainments you'll find in
the city.

Admission to the Friday fashion shows at Printemps (also on Tuesday during summer) is by ticket. These are found virtually all over town—in giveaway entertainment guides, in tourist office brochures, at hotel concierge desks. The shows start at 10 A.M. on the seventh floor under the spectacular artglass dome, where guests are seated at tables in the store's restaurant, Café Flo. They're fast-paced shows, lasting about an hour and a half, with models wearing outfits created by a wide variety of designers. A handout lists prices of the items modeled. And while you're on the seventh floor, don't miss the uplifting stained-glass memorial dedicated to former employees who gave their lives in the service of France.

You can attend the 11 A.M. fashion shows on Wednesday at Galeries Lafayette by phoning 48-74-02-30 for reservations. Shows are also presented every Friday at 2:30 P.M., April through October.

Speaking of department stores, the three leaders—Printemps, Galeries Lafayette (both on blvd Haussmann) and Samaritaine (on the Right Bank at Pont Neuf)—are great places to find good buys, especially if you're lucky enough to visit them on sale days. Department store sales are traditionally held in January or February and July or August. However, there's a growing trend to have them at other times as well.

For example, at Samaritaine's big sale at the end of October, sale booths line the walkway and street between the store's two buildings. I found compact discs starting at about $6 for jazz and $4 for classical, along with silk ties for about $15. Inside the store, most items were selling for 20 percent off.

Samaritaine is also the place to go if you want to bring home a jacket (about $39), checked pants (about $36), or a toque (about $19) to your favorite chef. Even if you don't find anything to buy in this working-class department store, the Art Nouveau architecture is worth a visit. Also, the store's restaurant on the 10th floor features great vistas, as does its free rooftop viewing area.

I've found bargains at Galeries Lafayette and Printemps, too, such as wool berets for about $10 and charming gift wrap for about $2. Also, be sure to check out the linen and homeware departments for kitchen towels, pot holders, and utensils with a French flair. Coupons for a 10 percent discount at the three stores (Samaritaine also offers 20 percent off on perfume and cosmetics) are in display racks at tourist offices and hotels. You must present your passport to take advantage of this offer.

The discount department stores, such as Monoprix and Franprix, are worth a spin through, too. Alhough quality isn't always the highest, some specials, such as novelty underwear, socks, and tights, are worth buying.

There are also two kinds of complexes—shopping arcades and malls—that born-to-shop types won't want to miss. Oldest of the city's shopping arcades, passage des Panoramas (2e; 11, blvd Montmartre) dates back to 1803. Though it is rather down at the heels, many of the other 19th-century arcades have been restored so that their glass roofs sparkle, their marble gleams, and their brass shines. As a result, your interest may turn out to be more architectural than commercial, because prices are generally high.

Most of the best shopping malls are located in such suburbs as La Defense and are much like those we have in North America. Though many of the items for sale are made in Taiwan or Sri Lanka, the design is usually European. Some of the best buys I've found in the malls are housewares, such as soufflé dishes (at about $8) and madeleine tins (at about $6), but I've also bought clothes, including good-quality lamb's-wool sweaters from a closeout rack for about $10 each.

Although closing hours vary, most stores open at 9:30 or 10 A.M. Some of the smaller stores close all day Monday, while some open at 3 P.M. Most stores close on Sunday, but an increasing number of the larger stores are open then and on holidays as well. Remember, too, that not all stores are open during the vacation month of August.

Buying Beauty at a Bargain

Local experts in the art of makeup—and who among Parisians is not?—swear that the Prisunic store at 109, rue la Boetie (8e; 42-25-27-46; St-Philippe-du-Roule Métro station; the front door of the store opens onto the Champs-Elysées) has the best-stocked makeup counters of any of the chain's 21 stores. Monoprix, with more than 30 locations, is the other Paris chain where you'll find glamour at cut-rate prices.

Herboristerie du Palais Royal (1er; 11, rue des Petits-Champs; 42-97-54-68; Bourse Métro station) isn't inexpensive, but its stock is extensive and includes products such as carrot face oil that you might not be able to find at home.

At any drugstore, be on the lookout for Vichy's facial cleanser (it contains angelica, cornflowers, mallow, and veronica) and Clarin's Morning Face Wash (coconut oil, jojoba, and licorice). For professional facials with prices that won't make you frown, try one of the 17 Gisele Delorne salons located in the city.

Checking Out the Markets

Paris is almost as famous for its markets as as it is for its fashions. Due to the high price of real estate, almost all of the flea markets are now located in the suburbs, but street markets where food and flowers are sold add enchantment to all parts of the city.

Largest of the flea markets and the one most tourists know about is Marché aux Puces. With more than 3,000 stalls in addition to street vendors and indoor shops, it's located just outside the Peripherique, which encircles the city, between Porte de Clignancourt and Porte de St-Ouen (Porte de Clignancourt Métro station).

Marché aux Puces actually is made up of a series of markets that cover an area of more than 75 acres. Several are named for the streets they are on, and each has its own character. Among the best are Marché Biron on rue des Rosiers, a high-quality antiques market where you can get a *Guide des Puces* (flea market guide); Marché Cambon, with beautifully displayed antique furniture; Marché Paul Bert, specializing in art, silver, jewelry, and furniture; Marché Vernaison (textiles, notions, and such are among its best buys); and Marché Jules Valles, where the standouts are its turn-of-the-20th-century objets d'art.

Though Marché aux Puces is intriguing and great for browsing, it's not a buyer's market. One Parisian who's an expert on the subject says, "No one who lives in Paris shops there. That's where all the tourists go, so the prices have gone up, up, up." Instead, she says, Paris residents go on Saturday and Sunday to Puces de Vanves, a mile-long stretch of both licensed and illegal, unlicensed vendors on the southern edge of the city (the main part of the market is on av Georges-Lefenstre). This market isn't as organized or professional as Marché aux Puces, but you've a better chance of finding bargains.

There's a wide array of merchandise—everything from bins and bags of treasures and junk to cheap plastic place mats and brass andirons—but the best buys, locals say, are secondhand furniture and bric-a-brac. The nearest Métro stop is Porte de Vanves. You can also reach the market by taking the bus that runs along the Peripherique.

Meandering Through the Markets

Of the street markets, rue de Buci (6e)—behind the church of St-Germain-des-Pres—is marvelous. With food and flower stalls lining both sides of rue de Seine and rue de Buci, sidewalk cafés, and a backdrop of typically Parisian buildings, it makes you happy just to be there. Never mind that it has the reputation of being the most expensive in Paris. You can capture hours' worth of memories without spending a centime. The market is close to the St-Germain-des-Pres Métro station.

FLEA MARKET MANNERS AND MOVES

1. Dress down. If you look prosperous, the prices quoted will be higher.
2. Check to see if the market is located in a safe neighborhood and whether its advisable to go there alone, after dark, or not at all.
3. Keep any significant amount of money in a money belt or a pouch out of sight. Pickpockets love crowded markets and the jammed Métro cars traveling to them.
4. Remember that brand-name merchandise sold on the street may be stolen goods or counterfeit.
5. Not everything sold at Paris markets can be brought back to the United States legally. Certain animal skins, tortoiseshell, and other goods are illegal.
6. Carry a lot of change and small bills. You'll get a better deal if you pull out the amount you want to pay and say, "This is all the money I have with me."
7. Never pay the asking price.
8. Be prepared to carry away what you buy. Porters are often scarce or nonexistent, except in the more upscale markets.

Other colorful Left Bank markets include those on rue Cler (7e; definitely upscale, with some great fromageries; Ecole-Militaire Métro station), rue Mouffetard (5e; try the fresh bread at 115; Censier-Daubenton Métro station); and blvd Raspail (6e; especially popular on Sunday, when it becomes a market for organically grown produce; Rennes Métro station).

Marché Place d'Aligre (12e), with its covered indoor butchers' market and outdoor food and flower stalls, is more like a North African bazaar, with an exotic selection of olives, peppers, and the like in addition to the traditional French market staples. It's noisiest on weekends, when militants of various political persuasions harangue the crowd. Though it's somewhat hard to find, you can reach the market from Ledru-

Rollin Métro station by following rue du Faubourg-St-Antoine to rue Crozatier. Rue d'Aligre goes off Crozatier to the right, a few yards from the intersection. Not open on Monday, the market closes at about 1 P.M.

Another intriguing market, Marché Château-d'Eau (10e; corner of rue du Château d'Eau and rue Bouchardon; Château d'Eau Métro station), gives you glimpses of Paris in days gone by. Butchers wash slabs of meat at the market's fountain and there's not a tourist in sight, as neighborhood residents go about their daily shopping.

Marché aux Vieux Papiers (av de Paris; St-Mande Tourelle Métro station), in the suburb of St-Mande, is a market specializing in old postcards, stamps, letters, and other paper collectibles held on Wednesday from 10 A.M. to 6 P.M. To avoid investing serious money in a counterfeit item, don't make any important purchases here unless you're an expert or have one with you. There's also a stamp market, Marché aux Timbres, off the Champs-Elysées on av de Marigny (8e; Champs-Elysées Métro station) on Thursday, Saturday, and Sunday. It opens at about 10 A.M.

The larger flower markets are between Notre Dame and the Palais de Justice on Île de la Cité (it becomes a bird market on Sunday; 4e; Cité Métro station), at place de la Madeleine (8e; Madeleine Métro station), and at place de Ternes between Parc de Monceau and Arc de Triomphe (17e; Ternes Métro station). Anemones, chrysanthemums, poppies, carnations, Dutch irises, orchids, roses, and dozens of other flowers brighten even the grayest of Paris days. And since flowers are one of France's best bargains—prices start at about $4 a bunch—why not take some back to your hotel room?

Scoping Out the Secondhand Shops

Even if you wouldn't be caught dead in a thrift shop back home, you may have a lot of fun poking through those in

Paris. First of all, they're less frantic than flea markets. Second, there's often a Gallic charm to even the tacky trinkets. Finally, you might get a real bargain—say a pretty dish or a paperweight—especially if it's a slow day. Scattered in most parts of the city, the best thrift shops are sponsored by organizations with affluent members, just as they are in the United States. None of the shops listed below is important enough to base an entire day's excursion around, but they're all worth poking through if you're going to be in the area anyway.

Boutiques Emmaus (11e; 54, rue de Charonne; Ledru-Rollin Métro station) offers a big selection of clothes and household goods. Open Monday through Wednesday and Friday 2 to 5:30 P.M., Thursday and Saturday 9:30 A.M. to 5:30 P.M.

L'Armée de Salut Thrift Store (13e; 12, rue Cantagrel; 45-83-54-50; Boulevard Massena Métro station). Professional dealers dig around at this Salvation Army thrift shop, and new merchandise arrives daily, so experts say it's one of the best of its kind in the city. Open Tuesday through Saturday 9 A.M. to noon and 2 to 6 P.M. By the way, the shop is in a building designed by Le Corbusier and constructed—complete with sealed windows and air-conditioning—in 1932.

Les Orphelins Apprentis d'Auteuil Thrift Store (16e; 40, rue la Fontaine; Michel-Ange-Auteuil Métro station). Furs, jewelry, and Chanel suits are said to be specialties of this shop, sponsored by a religious institution established to teach trades to orphans. On the day I visited, the jewelry was definitely ordinary and the Chanel suits several years old. However, as in most thrift shops, new merchandise arrives frequently.

Reciproque (95, 101, and 123 rue de la Pompe; Pompe Métro station). This is considered the best source of used couture clothing, though most items cost from about $200 to $2,000. I also found that the various shops smelled like old clothes, and some garments had not been cleaned since they had been worn. A Parisian customer, though, said that she visits often, examines the clothes carefully, and finds great buys, even if they do cost $300 and more.

If you happen to be on Paris on the first or third Saturday of the month, you might want to drop by the American Church (7e; quai d'Orsay at R. J. Nicot; Alma Marceau Métro station), which holds rummage sales from 2 to 5 P.M. on those days. Nothing costs much, with most prices from about $1 to $10.

Window-Shopping Par Excellence

When writing guidebooks, I'm always tempted to include antiques in the entertainment chapter rather than the one on shopping. This is especially so when writing about Paris, for most of the quality antiques are terribly expensive and therefore of the "just-looking" variety. But while you may be only looking, you don't want to waste time looking at anything but the best. The following will give you a sampling of the crème de la crème.

Louvre des Antiquaires (1er; 2, place du Palais Royal; Palais-Royale–Musée du Louvre Métro station) houses some 250 dealers all under one roof. Several of the dealers carry only one type of merchandise, such as naval antiques, time-pieces, light fixures, or decorative garden items.

Another good place to wander is along rue St-Paul (4e; St-Paul Métro station), where you'll come upon shops like Fuc-shia Dentelle (2, rue de l'Ave Maria; 48-04-75-61), focusing on antique christening and wedding gowns, beaded bags, embroidered shawls, and garments of all kinds decorated with lace inserts. At Les Saggittaires (17, rue St-Paul; 40-29-06-08), windows are decorated with hurricane lamps in all shapes, sizes, and designs.

The Left Bank street where you'll perhaps see the most elegant antiques the city has to offer is quai Voltaire (7e). Although each shop has only a few items in its windows, the pieces on display are virtually all treasures.

If you're planning to buy antiques that cost a bundle, be sure to get some proof of their authenticity. While dealers are generally reliable, producing fake antiques has been big business in France for years, with whole factories devoted to fabricating period furniture—complete with nicks and subtle scratches—that looks as though it were made centuries ago. By the way, the most important antiques event in the world is the Biennale International des Antiquaires, held at the Grand Palais every other year.

Travelers with an ongoing interest in antiques might consider timing their Paris visits to coincide with the annual celebration of Carre Rive Gauche, the association of about 100 antiques dealers whose shops lie within the area bounded by quai Voltaire, rue du Bac, rue de l'Université, and rue des St-Pères.

In late May, for about 25 years, the galleries and boutiques have held open house from 11 A.M. to 10 P.M. (8 P.M. on Sunday) from Tuesday evening through Sunday. The streets are decked with greenery and banners; the shops, with gorgeous bouquets of flowers. Dealers go out of their way to find really unusual objects to display, and the event is considered a prestigious one.

As a result, on opening night you'll not only see priceless antiques but also international celebrities and socialites dressed to the nines. If you want to avoid the crowds, follow the advice of top interior decorators who go on Tuesday afternoon, before the affair is officially open.

Like antiques, the products in Paris's gourmet food palaces and candy stores are pricey but fascinating to look at. For example, take Fauchon (8e; 26, place de la Madeleine at rue de Seze; 47-42-60-11; Madeleine Métro station). With more than 20,000 different products, its tantalizing aromas and artful displays make it a contender for the title of World's Ultimate Gourmet Food Store.

Among the most prestigious candy sellers is Debauve & Gallais (2e; 33, rue Vivienne; 40-39-05-50; Bourse Métro station; and 7e; 30, rue des St-Pères; 45-48-54-67; St-Germain-des-Pres Métro station). The chocolates and their wrappings are as fancy as you'll find anywhere. Prices are, too—at about $40 for a pound.

Unlike antiques and furniture stores, the gourmet shops and confectioneries aren't concentrated on various streets in the city. On the contrary, they're scattered about. Even less affluent neighborhood shopping districts will have at least one confectioner and specialty food store with merchandise that looks as good—or even better—than it tastes.

Flo Prestige, for example, has boutiques in five arrondisse-ments, some of which are less fashionable than others. While it's primarily a catering company, the shops contain dozens of comestibles suitable for gourmet giving. Petrossian is another company whose gastronomic temples decorate the city. Among its specialties are caviar, truffles, foie gras, and various confits—all attractively packaged.

Less expensive, but nonetheless delightful, are the products for sale at l'Epicerie (4e; 51, rue St-Louis-en-l'Île; 43-25-20-14; Sully-Morland Métro station). In this tiny shop, floor-to-ceiling shelves contain spices and condiments, vinegars and jams, each category identified by different-colored check tops tied with raffia. You'll find everything from confiture of prunes, ginger, and port wine to pistachio vinegar; currant jelly to mint marmalade.

For bargain-priced but high-quality food gifts to bring home to gourmet friends, try one of the large supermarkets. Cans of escargots cost about $6, jars of marmalade about $2. There are cheeses at less than a third of what you would pay in North America (I counted 20 kinds of goat cheese in one market), mixes for crème caramel and other French desserts, several varieties of specialty mustards, and other condiments (see chapter 4 for supermarket locations).

While you're at the market, you'll find other bargains—bistro plates for about $4 each, Teflon brioche and tart pans (about $4), and Emile Henri serving dishes ranging from $8 to $12; two ramekins go for about $4—far less than they sell for in the United States.

Rue du faubourg-St-Antoine (11e; Bastille or Ledru-Rollin Métro station) is populated by craftspeople, many of whom make furniture. Their workshops also are located in courtyards and narrow passages that connect area streets to each other. St-Antoine is the street to follow if you want to see the finest in French furniture design. The shops aren't large—most have only a few pieces in their display windows—and each seems to specialize in furniture from a different period. Sophisticated wrought-iron furniture in a lovely shade of green is in the window of Scene d'Interieur (79, rue du Faubourg-St-Antoine); elegantly upholstered traditional pieces are at Merisier de Qualité (number 31). Louis XIV, Louis XVI, Art Nouveau, art deco—you'll see them all as you pass by.

Rue du Paradis (10e; Château d'Eau Métro station) is the street to prowl for porcelain, since it's lined with shops specializing in tableware. Quality ranges from cheap pottery to the most exquisite china.

Finding Fabric and Findings

Paris fashions look great because of their design, true, but also because of the variety of fabrics and findings available to their designers. Though not all of these materials can be procured by people who aren't in the garment business, many of them are available.

Although it's highly publicized as the place in Paris to go for fabrics and notions, the area at the base of Sacré Coeur in Montmartre on rue Charles Nodier and adjacent streets (18e; Anvers Métro station) is bargain territory only for people who really know their goods and have a great deal of time to spare. Most of the fabrics for sale are of questionable quality and not especially good design, so diligent searching is necessary.

Even though their prices are higher, in the long run you'll be happier by shopping at regular fabric stores, such as the following:

Entrée des Fournisseurs (3e); 8, rue des Francs-Bourgeois; 48-87-58-98; St-Paul Métro station (notions only).

Fabric Bouchara (9e); 54, blvd Haussmann; 42-80-52-19; Havre-Caumartin Métro station.

Henri Maupiou (2e); 2, rue de la Paix; 42-61-08-27; Opéra Métro station (very expensive, but definitely worth the price if you plan to put together your own Paris creation).

Toiles de Mayenne (16e); 83, av Paul Doumer; 44-88-32-33; La Muette Métro station; (6e); 3, rue Lobineau; 44-07-33-81; Mabillon Métro station; and (6e); 78, rue Seine; 43-54-62-25; Odeon Métro station.

Tissroy (8e); 97, av Victor Hugo; 47-27-61-01; Victor Hugo Métro station.

Underneath the Arches—and Arcades

The handsome arches of an abandoned railroad viaduct at 9–129, av Daumesnil (12e) have been glassed in and converted into one of Paris's newest showplaces, Le Viaduc des Arts.

The workshops, exhibit spaces, and galleries underneath the arches showcase a wide range of arts and crafts, from cabinetmaking and ironwork to lace making and photography. Not only can you watch the artists, artisans, and designers at work, but you can also buy the items they produce.

The upper level of the viaduct has become part of Promenade Plantée (Bel-Air or Dugomonier Métro station), a walkway (with bicycle path) that stretches about 2.7 miles (4.5 km) from the Opéra Bastille to Bois de Vincennes. The promenade follows the old railroad bed through embankments and short tunnels, offering spectacular views of the city at their exits.

The covered arcades of Paris make shopping a memorable experience even if you don't spend a franc. With vaulted roofs and patterned mosaic tile floors, the passages were constructed from 1800 to 1847 and are usually lined on both sides by shops.

The most delightful of the arcades are those with glass ceilings, buttressed with intricate wrought-iron or other decorative supports. The detail on the storefronts and pillars, designs on the floors, and ornate light fixtures illuminating them ensure that no two of the shopping arcades are alike.

During the mid-1800s, there were more than 100 of these shopping galleries in the city. Now, there are fewer than 20. Predecessors of present-day department stores, the arcades provided shoppers with an alternative to the dirty roadside businesses of the day. The reputations of the arcades varied; many catered to the less desirable elements of society.

With the advent of the department store in the mid-1880s, the arcades became unnecessary, and many were abandoned or fell into disrepair. Classified as historical monuments in 1970, several of the 20 or so remaining galleries have been renovated to their former glory and house upscale shops and restaurants, while a few cater to specific kinds of businesses such as antiques dealers, ethnic shops, or discount stores.

Four of the arcades are in the second arrondissement, three of them within about two blocks of each other (passage Choiseul at 44, rue des Petits-Champs, 4-Septembre Métro station, built in 1827; Galerie Colbert at 6, rue des Petits-Champs, Bourse Métro station, built in 1826; and Galerie Vivienne at 4, place des Petits-Champs, Bourse Métro station).

Built in 1823, Galerie Vivienne, with its trendy clothes, gourmet food store, brasserie, and wine shop, is one of my favorites. It's also the place where you can gaze at the sumptuous Wolff et Descoutes fabrics or sip a cup of tea at A Priori Thé (tables are both inside and outside in the passage). The most elegant arcade of its day, the Galerie Vivienne is neoclassical in style, with stucco bas-reliefs, walls painted in a cheerful yellow, and mosaic floors. It's especially popular on weekends.

Another charmer, which is also easily accessible to most tourists, is Galerie Vero-Dodot (1er; 19, rue Jean-Jacques Rousseau; Palais-Royal Métro station). Wainscoted storefronts with Corinthian columns, a diamond-patterned floor, and shops where you can buy everything from leather goods to antique dolls and architectural salvage make it especially interesting.

Three arcades are located across the boulevard from one another in Montmartre. Passage des Panoramas (2e; 11, blvd Montmartre and 10, rue St-Marc) is the oldest of the passages and was built in 1799–1800. It was named for the panoramas (grand-scale, circular illuminated paintings of Jerusalem, London, Rome, and other world capitals) that were exhibited there when the passage opened in 1800. The panoramas were removed in the early 1830s.

Passage Jouffroy (9e; 10, blvd Montmartre), with its great glass and wrought-iron roof, built in 1845, is one of the newest. It's the place to go if you're looking for old prints and illustrations, or antique books and toys. Among its more interesting shops is CINEdoc (45–53, passage Jouffroy; 48-24-71-36), with an enormous collection of film-related photos, posters, books, and old movies. Across the street, passage Verdeau (9e; 31 bis, rue du Faubourg Montmartre; Le Pelletier Métro station), built in 1847, is occupied by shops selling items such as old comics and secondhand books.

Among the other arcades are:

Passage des Pavillons (1 er); 6, rue du Beaujolais; Pyramides Métro station.

Passage du Caire (2e); 2, place du Caire; Sentier Métro station.

Passage du Grand Cerf (4e); 145, rue St-Denis; Etienne Marcel Métro station. Built in 1825.

Galerie de la Madeleine (8e); 9, place de la Madeleine; St-Lazare Métro station. Built in 1845.

Passage Royale (8e); rue Royale; Concorde Métro Station.

Passage Brady (10e); between 46, rue du Faubourg-St-Denis and 43, rue du Faubourg-St-Martin; Château d'Eau Métro station). Businesses in this arcade are primarily East Indian cafés, grocery stores, and barbers.

Passage de l'Industrie (10e); 42, rue du Faubourg-St-Denis; Strasbourg-St-Denis Métro station. Built in 1827.

Shouldn't-Miss Specialty Shopping

"So many shops, so little time" is the plaint of Paris visitors who enjoy looking for the out-of-the-ordinary, in both quality and design. The following is only a sampling of what France's capital has to offer.

Demons et Merveilles (6e; 45, rue Jacob; 42-96-26-11; St-Germain-des-Pres Métro station) is one of the most colorful shops in the city, with merchandise from Afghanistan, Pakistan, India, Morocco, and Tunisia. The embroidered jackets from Kashmir, elaborate fezzes from Afghanistan, and wooden boxes from Pakistan are especially attractive.

Pylone (4e; 57, rue St-Louis-en-l'Île; 46-34-05-02; Sully-Morland Métro station) is filled with clever novelties—many of them made of latex—neckties, bibs, and ice cube trays, suspenders with jazz musicians on the straps, umbrellas in clear primary colors with matching tulip handles, vases, and pitchers shaped like fish.

The table linens, bedspreads, pillows, and lamp shades at Patrick Frey (6e; 7, rue Jacob; 43-26-53-13; St-Germain-des-Pres Métro station) are stunning and, though expensive, a good home investment.

It's said that no one who is serious about cooking leaves E. Dehillerin (1er; 18 and 20, rue Coquilliere; 42-36-53-13; Les Halles Métro station) without making a purchase. Perhaps the

most complete kitchenware store anywhere, it offers a choice
of copper molds in two dozen different designs, wire whisks
in every conceivable size, copper kettles, carbon and stainless-steel knives, teakettles, colanders, and everything else you
need to fully equip a kitchen.

Quality souvenirs of Paris in the form of ceramic miniatures of its buildings—storefronts, bistros, boulangeries—are
a specialty at Saint Louis Posters and Gifts (4e; 23, rue St-
Louis-en-l'Île; 40-46-91-65; Sully-Morland Métro station).
Originals cost from about $56 to $600, but replicas sell for
about $22 to $37.

At the Musée d'Orsay boutique (7e; 1, rue de Bellechasse;
40-49-48-14; Solferino Métro station), items for sale are based
on works by artists featured in the museum. Among the more
outstanding objects is tableware featuring motifs from Cézanne
paintings. A ceramic pear and apple centerpiece costs about
$56; a large pitcher costs about $100.

At Kim (1er; 91, rue de Rivoli; 42-60-23-41; Louvre-Rivoli
Métro station), the accent is on cashmere, with men's and
women's sweaters in a variety of styles and prices starting at
about $100.

Although there are booksellers' stalls on both sides of the
Seine, most of their wares are written in French. The most
convenient source of English-language books and magazines
is W. A. Smith (1er; 248, rue de Rivoli; 44-77-88-99; Concorde
Métro station). Be sure to check out the free magazines and
brochures at the entrance.

Brentanos (2e; 37, av de l'Opéra; 42-61-52-50; Pyramides
Métro station) is another bookstore that's easy to find, and
it's one of the oldest—and best—English-language bookstores
in the city.

When you're looking for bring-home gifts for bridge-playing
friends, stop by Le Boutique du Bridgeur (1er; 28, rue de
Richelieu; 42-96-25-50; Palais-Royal Métro station) where
score pads, playing cards, and other accoutrements of the

game are for sale. Another shop carrying merchandise that is extremely specialized is A l'Olivier (4e; 23, rue de Rivoli; 48-04-86-59; Hôtel de Ville Métro station), which features all manner of oils, whether for cooking, massage, or shampoo. Madeleine Gely (7e; 218, blvd St-Germain; 42-22-63-35; Rue du Bac Métro station) specializes in umbrellas and canes, whereas Le Rideau de Paris (7e; 32, rue du Bac; 42-61-18-56; Rue du Bac Métro station) handles lace bistro curtains and traditional French dish towels.

Hôtel des Ventes Drouot Montaigne (9e; 9, rue Drouot; 48-00-20-80; Richelieu-Drouot Métro station) holds estate sales and auctions of everything from rare objets d'art and period furniture to everyday household items and trinkets from abroad. If you have any intention of buying, be sure to arrive in advance of the afternoon auctions so that you can look over the merchandise. Another interesting browsing spot is Credit Municipal de Paris (3e; 55, rue des Francs-Bourgeois; 44-61-64-00; Rambuteau Métro station), the municipal pawnshop.

I can't imagine spending a day in Paris listening to tapes and CDs, even if you can do it for free. But it's possible at FNAC Music Shop (12e; 1, rue de Charenton; 43-42-04-04; Bastille Métro station) if no one is waiting in line behind you. Just find an empty slot, put on the headphones, and choose your tunes by touching a computer screen.

Aux Vieux Campeur (5e; 48, rue des Ecoles; 53-10-48-48; Cluny–La Sorbonne or Maubert Mutualité Métro station) is the largest camping and mountain climbing gear company in France. From sleeping bags and dehydrated foods to belay devices and rope bags, the selection is huge in this store that covers an entire city block.

At Au Chene-Liege (15e; 74, blvd du Montparnasse; 43-22-02-15; Falguiere Métro station), all items—and there are hundreds of them—are made from cork. Place mats, coasters, paper, clock mountings, book coverings, serving dishes, and furniture are only a few of the articles for sale.

GLOSSARY OF SHOPPING TERMS

bijouterie—jewelry store
boulangerie—bakery
brocante—used items
charcuterie—delicatessen
dégriffe(s)—signifies discount store
épicerie—grocery store
fabrique à la main—handmade
fèves—charms baked into Epiphany cakes, usually made
    of porcelain, available at kitchen supply stores and flea
    markets
fripes—antique clothes
grand magasin—department store
kiosque à journaux—newstand
librairie—bookstore
magasin de chaussures—shoestore
magasin de photographie—camera store
marché—market
mercerie—notions shop
parfumerie—perfume store
passage (rhymes with *massage*)—a shopping arcade
pâtisserie—pastry shop
pharmacie—drugstore
santons—carvings of French country characters
solde or *promotion*—additional markdowns
soldes—seeing this word following a designer's name means
    that sale merchandise is sold there
stock—discount stores usually have this word in their names
supermarché—supermarket
village—group of antiques stores or stalls under one roof

A final word on shopping. Always ask shopkeepers when
their next sale will be. Who knows? It may start the following
day. Hermes's sales, for example, take place both in March

and October, while in June and December top designers donate items to the big sale at Porte de Versailles called Braderie de Paris. Rodier regularly features specials—often as much as 30 percent on specific items such as sweaters, which puts them into the affordable class.

A bargain or not, the ultimate criterion in evaluating the worth of an item is its value to *you*. Years later, will you regret your failure to buy that enchanting, but outrageously expensive, silk flower arrangement? The fabric that would have looked so grand on the breakfast room chairs? The sport coat that was so impeccably cut? If the answer would seem to be yes, I have a suggestion. Try to get it for at least a bit less than the merchant is asking, and convince yourself that it's enough of a bargain to buy.

I have a friend who maintains that *everything* is negotiable. He recommends asking whether a store that accepts credit cards gives a discount for cash. Since stores have to pay a certain percentage of each credit-card transaction to the institution that issues the cards—Visa, American Express, or whatever—managers are usually happy to have cash for the sale without having to wait for it. While this strategy is most effective in the smaller shops, it works surprisingly often in department stores. Even if you're not successful, remember that purchasing the item—whatever its cost—will most likely be less expensive than making a return trip to Paris to buy it.

CHAPTER

6

Seeing the Sights

When you ask people who adore Paris why the city is so special, they'll give you many reasons. Chances are one of them will be "because there's so much to look at." Thanks to the excesses of the Louis and other rulers, Paris has an unprecedented abundance of extravagant buildings and impressive monuments. Presidents of the past few decades haven't held back, either, when it has come to renovation, construction, and other sightly improvements.

The Belle Epoche and Empire periods, the efforts of Baron Haussmann to make the city more elegant, and the fondness Parisians have for well-kept parks have contributed a great many pleasant scenes as well. As a result, it's possible to spend your entire Paris stay admiring its embarrassment of architectural riches and immaculate public gardens, never spending a cent except for transportation from one place to another.

Even if you've not been to Paris, you have undoubtedly heard about and seen pictures of many of the standard sights. Most spectacular is the Tour Eiffel (Eiffel Tower; 7e; Champ de Mars; 44-11-23-65; Bir-Hakeim Métro or Champ de Mars RER station), built by Gustave Eiffel and star of the 1889 Universal Exhibition. Said to be the most famous monument in the world (by Parisians, at least), it rises to a height of 317 meters (about 1,040 feet) and makes a great point of reference if you've lost your way.

Another landmark that's recognizable around the world is the Arc de Triomphe (Arch of Triumph, 8e, place Charles de Gaulle; 55-37-73-77; Charles-de-Gaulle-Etoile Métro station). The monument, inaugurated in 1836, was built to the glory of the French army. It contains a museum chronicling its history, and you can experience the panoramic view from its top by paying about $6. The arch looks impressive anytime, but it's especially splendid when illuminated at night or when a military band, resplendent in dress uniform, is playing in front of it. The band concerts usually take place on national holidays or during periods "when the government feels the people's spirits need a patriotic boost," according to one Parisian.

The Cathedral of Notre Dame de Paris (4e; place de Parvis de Notre-Dame; 42-34-56-10; Cité Métro or Chatelet–Les Halles or St-Michel–Notre Dame RER stations) is another of the sights every Paris visitor feels compelled to see. Rightly so, for this Gothic masterpiece, constructed between the 12th and 14th centuries, is one of the most important ecclesiastical buildings in the world. Though entrance to the cathedral is free, you must pay about $6.20 to climb the 387 steps to the viewing area and about $5 to tour the crypt. The museum entrance fee is about $2.25. The cathedral is open Sunday through Friday 8 A.M. to 7 P.M.; it's closed on Saturday between 12:30 and 2 P.M. Hours for viewing from the tower, entrance to the crypt, and museum vary. Free lectures are presented in French and foreign languages (phone for information).

The 14th-century Conciergerie (1er; 1, quai de l'Horloge; 53-73-78-50; Cité Métro or St-Michel–Notre Dame and Chatelet–Les Halles RER stations) is typical of 14th-century civil architecture. In the 15th century, the lower floor of the palace was converted into a prison, and the cells—including Marie Antoinette's—may be visited. Open summer, 9:30 A.M. to 6:30 P.M.; winter, 10 A.M. to 5 P.M. Admission is about $5.

The Pantheon (5e; place du Pantheon; Cardinal-Lemoine Métro or Luxembourg RER station) was formerly a church, but since the French Revolution it has been the necropolis of great Frenchmen, serving as the final resting place for 61 of them—including Voltaire, Rousseau, Hugo, and Zola. Open 9:30 A.M. to 6:30 P.M. in summer, 10 A.M. to 5:30 P.M. in winter. Admission costs about $5.

The Basilique du Sacré Coeur (18e; parvis du Sacré Coeur; 42-51-17-02; Anvers Métro station) was built as a result of the public's wishes following their defeat in the Franco-Prussian war of 1870 and the Paris Commune uprising of the next year. Although access to the basilica is free, there's a charge of about $3 to visit the dome and the crypt.

Ste-Chapelle (1er; 4, blvd du Palais;53-73-78-51; Cité Métro or St-Michel–Notre Dame RER station), a 13th-century jewel, was built by the order of St-Louis to contain the crown of thorns. The stained-glass windows are outstanding. Entrance to the church, open 10 A.M. to 5 P.M., is about $5.

Opéra National de Paris (9e) is a triumph of 19th-century theatrical architecture, built by Charles Garnier and opened in 1875. It costs about $5 to go inside the hall, which is open Monday through Saturday 10 A.M. to 5 P.M.

The Bastille Opéra National de Paris (12e; place de la Bastille; 40-01-19-70; Bastille Métro or Gare de Lyon RER station) was inaugurated in 1989 and is one of the controversial new buildings that most visitors like but many Parisians think are dreadful. The building is characterized by the transparency of its facades and the use of the same materials on the interior as the exterior.

Tour Montparnasse (15e; rue de l'Arivée; 45-38-52-56; Montparnasse-Bienvenue Métro station) is another 20th-century addition that many Parisians aren't sure they like. The tower's 56th and 59th floors are open to the public for a fee of about $8.40. Open 9:30 A.M.to 11:30 P.M. in summer (closes an hour earlier in winter).

The Eglise de la Madeleine (8e; 14, rue de Surene; 44-51-69-00; Madeleine Métro or Auber RER station) looks more like a Grecian temple than a church with its impressive Corinthian columns. Inside are a magnificent organ and mosaics. The church is open Monday through Saturday 7 A.M to 7 P.M., Sunday 7 A.M. to 1:30 P.M. and 3:30 to 7 P.M.

Chapelle Expiatoire (8e; 29, rue Pasquier, square Louis XVI; 42-65-35-80; St-Augustin Métro and Auber RER stations) was built on orders of Louis XVIII as a memorial to Louis XVI and Marie Antoinette. It is located on the site of a cemetery where 3,000 victims of the Revolution of 1789–1799 are buried. It's open Wednesday, November through January, 10 A.M. to 1 P.M. and 2 to 4 P.M.; it opens earlier and closes later during other months of the year.

There are other interesting sights as well—the Hôtel des Invalides, Bastille Square, Hôtel de Ville (City Hall), the Louvre, the Petit and Grand Palaces, for example, plus dozens more. But how do you go about looking at even a fraction of the sight-seeing possibilities without spending a fortune? You might take a commercial sight-seeing tour, but for the most part, as tours go, they are extremely expensive. For example, a three-and-a-half-hour guided tour of Notre Dame and the Louvre costs around $30 and up; a three-hour trip that includes the second floor of the Eiffel Tower and a one-hour Seine cruise costs $40 or more.

The full-day Paris tour with a lunch cruise costs about $125 or more. Companies like Espace Limousines (14e; 48, rue Sarrette; 47-91-41-63; Alesia Métro station) advertise sight-seeing for up to seven passengers at about $50 to $100 an hour with a three-hour minimum—not a bad deal if you have seven people in your party.

Although it's also possible to hire a guide plus a four-person sedan for four hours at $525, which works out to about $32 an hour per person, most of us don't travel to Paris with six other people or want to spend $131 for a half day's touring when we travel with three. If we're looking after our wallets, then, we need to be self-reliant in finding the way from one point of interest to the next.

If you are willing to pay about $21, the commercial survey tours such as Cityrama give you a good idea of the lay of the land. They're drive-bys, with no stops along the way, but they do go down that grand boulevard of Paris, the Champs-Elysées, as well as past 10 other points of interest on both the Right and Left Banks. Another tour, also costing about $21, takes participants past the city's illuminated sights and flood-lit monuments.

People who don't mind (or prefer) seeing the sights without commentary can look at just about all of them by riding the city buses. A combination Métro and bus pass will cost you a fraction of the money charged for commercial tours, and if you want more than a drive-by you'll be able to get on and off at will. Some of the best routes to take—and a sampling of the points of interest they pass—follow:

Number 21—Opéra, Palais Royal, Musée du Louvre on the Right Bank; follows the Left Bank to blvd St-Michel and Jardin du Luxembourg.

Number 22—The Arc de Triomphe, Gare St-Lazare, and Opéra are only a few of the points buses on this route pass as they wend their way through the ritzy 8th and 16th arrondissements. This is a great route for seeing how affluent Parisians live.

Number 24—One of the longest bus routes, it takes you past sights like place de la Concorde, Gare d'Austerlitz, Gare de Lyon, the Omnisports complex, and Centre Culturel Americain.

Number 42—Tour Eiffel and Parc André Citroen as well as a short stretch of the Champs-Elysées.

Number 47—Forum des Halles and Notre Dame.

Number 49—Grand Palais, Invalides, and Ecole Militaire.

Number 52—La Madeleine, rue Faubourg-St-Honoré, Arc de Triomphe, as well as Bois de Boulogne.

Number 58—Jardin and Palais du Luxembourg, Les Deux Magots café, Île de la Cité, rue de Rivoli, and Hôtel de Ville.

Number 73—Musée d'Orsay, place de la Concorde, Champs-Elysées, Arc de Triomphe, and La Defense.

Number 82—One of the best routes for passing by loads of important sights, this one goes by Palais des Congres, Arc de Triomphe, Tour Eiffel, Invalides, Gare Montparnasse, and Jardin du Luxembourg.

Number 84—Another of the best sight-seeing routes, this one goes past the Pantheon, Jardin du Luxembourg, Eglise St-Sulpice, Musée d'Orsay, place de la Concorde, Eglise de la Madeleine, Parc Monceau, as well as through the St-Germain-des-Pres district.

Number 96—This route follows along the boulevards St-Germain and St-Michel, through Île de la Cité, the heart of the Marais, and the 20th arrondissement. Sights it passes by include Palais de Justice, Conciergerie, place du Chatelet, and Hôtel de Ville.

The most interesting bus rides for my money (and they don't take a lot of it) are those that follow a route around the periphery of Paris. If you look at a map, you'll see that the city is encircled by a wide roadway called the Peripherique, which separates Paris from its suburbs. Paralleling the Peripherique inside the city limits is a series of interconnecting boulevards that also form an irregular circle (actually, it's more of an oval). Buses travel this route frequently, stopping at the *portes* (main arteries with Métro service nearby) to the various suburbs. What makes this trip so interesting is that you get an overview of Paris that no organized tour will give you. You'll see neighborhood playing fields, sports stadiums, and shopping districts patronized only by the people who live nearby. There are huge blocks of faceless housing projects and vast acres of beautifully tended parks. There are street stalls with secondhand clothing and the French sky-rise headquarters of companies like Sony and Mercedes-Benz.

Alhough stops are frequent, they give you more time to absorb the surroundings. Buses are identified by the letters PC rather than the usual numbers. I like to make this trip, which takes a minimum of two and a half hours on Sunday morning, when traffic is relatively light. If you've bought a *carnet* of Métro and bus tickets, the whole trip costs you about $1.80.

Maps that include all the bus routes are available at the Office de Tourisme and at major Métro and railway stations.

Viewpoints—Theirs and Mine

In my view, looking at Paris from great heights is best left to the birds. Much of the city is on level ground, and a vast majority of its buildings are of similar height. Because of this, and the often hazy skies over Paris, viewing the city from a rise in elevation or a building that's only a few stories higher than most of its surroundings is far more interesting than panoramic views. If you must—and it's a very clear day—go to the highest level of the Tour Eiffel or Montparnasse. But I'm with the legions who say it's just not worth the money or the horrendous lines.

Instead, use the money for lunch at the 10th-floor terrace restaurant of Samaritaine department store or the 9th-floor tearoom of Musée d'Institut du Monde Arabe, where the views aren't so all-encompassing but have a lot more character. At Institut du Monde Arabe, you'll be looking at Île St-Louis and the Bastille as well as the Seine—an intensely interesting slice of the Parisian landscape. At Samaritaine, there's also an observation deck where the 360-degree view of the city is absolutely free.

For other viewpoints that won't cost you a cent, go to the overlook in front of Sacré Coeur in Montmartre and the square outside the Grande Arche at La Defense. The outdoor escalator at Centre Georges Pompidou provides vistas from yet another aspect.

The nightly rates at the prestigious—and recently renovated—Raphael Hôtel (8e;17, av Kleber; 45-02-16-00; Kleber Métro station) are breathtaking. And so are the 360-degree views from its roof garden. You can have the views without staying at the hotel by buying a cocktail at the bar on the rooftop terrace.

The three dozen or so bridges crossing the Seine in Paris provide still more opportunities for picture-perfect views. On one of the most famous, Pont des Arts, you'll get marvelous perspectives of Île de la Cité on your left as you're crossing to the Left Bank and of the Louvre on your right. Pont Philippe offers spectacular views of the church of St-Gervais and Hôtel de Ville. From Pont de la Concorde, you'll be in sight of both place de la Concorde and Palais-Bourbon.

For an album full of photos if you're carrying your camera—and a lifetime full of pictorial memories if you aren't—take a walk along the river, crossing to the other side each time you come to a bridge. On the return trip, cross the bridges in the opposite directions. The riverside stretch from Pont de la Tournelle and Pont Marie (they connect Île St-Louis with the Left and Right Banks) to Pont D'lena is about two miles long, and one of the most picturesque strips of real estate in the world.

When you've taken a sidewalk stroll or two, you might try ambling along the quays underneath the arches of the bridges. It's a great way to get a closer look at their elegant ironwork and sculpted stone, and to watch the fishermen as they wait for the fish to bite.

Or you might choose to walk along one of the city's canals. Though St-Martin canal goes underground at blvd Richard-Lenoir just north of place de la Bastille, its original canal bed has been transformed into an area of gardens, markets, and playgrounds (Bastille Métro station). Also, outside the Bastille Métro station in the opposite direction, you'll be just steps away from Port de Plaisance de Paris, at what used to be the entrance of the St-Martin canal from the Seine and is now a marina.

French Walk-Abouts

Even better than seeing Paris from the window of a vehicle is experiencing it at ground level in the fresh air (provided you stay away from the exhaust-filled boulevards). While you'll be able to discover places to explore on your own, the following will give you some ideas of where to begin.

Perhaps you'll want to take a number 52 bus to the Porte d'Auteuil stop, then spend a few hours meandering around one of the city's most pleasant—and prestigious—residential areas. After admiring the bunches of fresia, dahlias, and Dutch irises at the flower shop across from the bus stop, walk along rue d'Auteuil, a shopping street with upscale charcuteries, fromageries, and the like.

Step inside one of the pâtisseries for a *sable glacé* (glazed sugar cookie) or madeleine (a lemon-vanilla cookie, similar to pound cake) to munch, then proceed on your journey. You may choose to stroll along rue la Fontaine, past houses built by Guimard. At number 14, his masterpiece, Castel Beranger, as well as buildings at numbers 17 through 21, illustrate the renowned architect's Art Nouveau style.

When you reach the headquarters building of Radio France, turn left on rue L'Assomption to av Mozart, the district's commercial artery with upscale boutiques and other businesses. Or follow any street that looks interesting—and they all do.

Even more intriguing are the alleys. One of them, at 55, rue du Docteur Blanche, leads to the first two Parisian houses, Villa LaRoche and Villa Jeanneret, built by 20th-century architect Charles-Edouard Jeanneret, better known as Le Corbusier. Today, the houses (8–10, square du Docteur Blanche; 42-88-41-53) illustrate various components of the architect's revolutionary style. A stone's throw away, the buildings on rue Mallet-Stevens were almost all designed by the art deco architect Mallet-Stevens, who lived at number 12.

Another wonderful area for strolling is the Marais, where many magnificent mansions of the 17th and 18th centuries have been, or are being, restored. After the 1789 revolution, the neighborhood went into a decline. Artisans and poorer members of the working class moved in, followed by Jews from Russia and central Europe fleeing persecution. In 1965, the government rescued the neighborhood, which had by that time become a slum. It was protected as a historic neighborhood, and plans were drawn up for its restoration. Now, the remnants of past poverty are disappearing, being replaced by boutiques and art galleries, restaurants, and private residences. Showplace of the district is the charming place des Vosges, whose stone and brick houses have been completely restored to their former glory.

Not all of the Marais has been gentrified yet, however, so you'll be able to find vestiges of its nonglory years along streets like rue François Miron, rue des Archives, and the busy rue St-Antoine.

For centuries Paris, for a number of reasons, has been known as the City of Light, not the least of which has been its tradition of leadership in the arts and the Enlightenment. You'll discover a second reason as you walk along the Seine just before sunset. That's when the buildings on the river's banks are bathed with the softness of light that drew painters to Paris, and the Eiffel Tower looks as if it were made of spun gold filigree. The third reason will also be illustrated on your walk as the city's famous streetlights, first instituted during the reign of Louis XI (with torches), are turned on. Walk from east to west on either side of the river to get the sunset's total effect.

Another route I like starts at Notre Dame (Cité Métro station). From the cathedral's front entrance, go clockwise around the periphery of Île de la Cité to Pont St-Louis. Along the way, you'll pass by the statue of Henry Vert Galant, the Conciergerie, and the flower market. If you're tired when you come to the bridge, walk across the street to the lovely park behind Notre Dame to rest on one of the benches. If not, cross the bridge to Île St-Louis and make a circle of the island. When you're back at your starting point, stroll down rue St-Louis-en-l'Île, with its shops, restaurants, and small hotels (cross Pont Sully to the Sully-Morland Métro station).

When you temporarily tire of row upon row of Belle Epoche and Empire buildings, take a breather at La Defense, the area created for corporate headquarters of French and international companies. La Grande Arche—a giant and unadorned arch so big that it could contain Notre Dame Cathedral—is the centerpiece of this sky-rise development of dramatic contemporary buildings. Though the Parisians may look askance at the break from tradition, most Americans see La Defense as proof that the French are as capable of great architectural design today as they have been in the past.

On Saturday evening, blvd du Montparnasse is a favorite, too. Never mind that it's more crowded than at any other time of the week. In fact, that's part of the reason for going. It's so alive. Queues at the movie theaters extend out into the street. All the tables at the pavement cafés are filled. Crêpe makers and pizza vendors at sidewalk stands do a brisk business. There's a holiday feeling in the air that you find only at special times in cities around the world.

Montmartre evokes two different scenes in most people's minds—the Moulin Rouge world of Henri Toulouse-Lautrec and the narrow streets captured on canvas by Maurice Utrillo. Although the area has changed since the 19th century, you can get glimpses of those days by walking along streets like rue Constance and rue Lepic (check out the turn-of-the-20th-century tiles at the Lux Bar, number 12).

Don't miss the pink neo-Gothic manor at the end of Impasse Marie-Blanche, either. Or the view of Paris rooftops as you descend rue Tholoze. And be sure to walk to Regyn's Montmartre hotel on rue des Abbesses for great views of the Guimard-designed Métro station entrance through the trees. It's one of the two Paris Métro stations with their original green wrought iron intact.

Wandering around the Left Bank is gratifying almost anywhere you choose to go—but be sure to take a map, because it's easy to get twisted around. I prefer to steer clear of the main boulevards and walk along the narrower streets, where you'll find pleasures with a quintessentially French accent: pocket parks with nursemaids chatting while they gently push navy blue prams back and forth; streets like rue de la Huchette where sword swallowers, jugglers, and other street performers entertain; walks along the various quays, where artists' stalls, boats on the river, and views of buildings such as Notre Dame vie for your attention.

Sunday morning is the best time for this Left Bank walk, especially when your last destination is Luxembourg Gardens, which is definitely a Sunday kind of place. Bring along a book and spend some time reading, if you like, or watch the children sailing boats on the pond (see chapter 11).

Wherever you walk, take time to enjoy the sights along the way at Métro entrances, near monuments, and in other unlikely locations: men in business suits playing a lunch-hour game of *boules* (sort of a cross between horseshoes and shuffleboard, and played with balls); children's carousels (modern versions with their iridescent racing cars and rocket ships as well as those with the traditional gilded curlicues and pastel ponies).

If you most want to take time to smell the roses while you're walking, Paris parks are the place to go. The largest of them all, Bois de Boulogne, is situated on the western edge of the city. Created from a much larger forest, the park is so vast, with so many paths to follow, that you can hike uninterrupted by throngs of people. The park is also a favorite with bicyclists and horseback riders.

Within the Bois, which Napoleon III had patterned after London's Hyde Park in the mid–19th century, are several gardens—the Shakespeare (planted with vegetation mentioned in the Bard's plays), the Bagatelle (famous for its *folie*, or folly, and its rose garden), and Jardin d'Acclimation, an amusement area for children (see chapter 11). There are lakes for boating and two racecourses, as well—Longchamp, where the fashionable Grand Prix is run each June, and the Auteuil. The park is open 24 hours daily, but don't go there at night. After dark, it becomes the domain of hookers and muggers.

Bois de Vincennes, on the eastern edge of Paris, was once, like Bois de Boulogne, a royal hunting ground. And like Bois de Boulogne, under orders of Napoleon III it was transformed into an English-style park.

With a variety of paths to follow, around ornamental lakes and through the gardens of the Parc Floral, up the steps to the recently restored Château de Vincennes or through the zoo (see chapter 11), the park is an effective antidote to Parisian traffic. The château, by the way, served as everything from a prison to a porcelain factory before its restoration.

Just about every tourist has walked through, or at least by, Jardin des Tuileries (Tuileries Garden), but the people who really enjoy these areas of green grass surrounded by manicured hedges are the Parisians themselves. You'll see them out in force each Sunday, strolling along the paths, sitting in the green metal chairs surrounding the ponds and savoring ice cream cones bought from vendors. The park is a convenient lunch and rest-ing station when you're spending the day at the Louvre.

Parc Monceau (Monceau Métro station), from the toll house at the blvd de Courcelles entrance to the Corinthian colonnade around the edge of its miniature lake, is an out-door museum of architectural antiques and statues, sur-rounded by some of the lovliest flowers and greenery in Paris. It's a park that seems to be made for sitting on a bench and reveling in the beauty around you.

One of Paris's most interesting open spaces, Parc André Cit-roen (15e; Balard Métro station) is a futuristic combination of greenery, sculptures, and water: waterfalls, fountains, orna-mental lakes, and a canal. Ten distinctive gardens offer a vari-ety of botanical experiences. Each of the Theme Gardens represents one of the five senses. The Changing Garden goes through a metamorphosis each season. And while the White Garden was created for play, the Black Garden is centered on serenity. *Spontaneity* is the byword at the Garden of Move-ment; and Central Park, dominated by two large greenhouses, is for people who favor hothouse plants.

The modern Parc Georges Brassens (Convention Métro station), also in the 15th arrondissement, occupies the site of the old Vaugirard abattoirs. One of its most interesting features is a rock climbing practice zone. There's also a scented garden, created especially for people who are blind. The park is the site of festivities during the October grape harvest.

Parc de Bercy (12e; Bercy Métro station), on the Seine, was formerly a warehouse district. With a romantic garden, a vegetable garden, an orchard, and a scented-flower garden in addition to vast lawns, it's a park most visitors from abroad don't know about.

From May through September, the city of Paris sponsors free concerts in about 20 of the city's parks and gardens. Concert schedules are available in the town halls of every Paris district, at the reception desk of the Paris Town Hall (Hôtel de Ville), and at the Paris Tourist Office on the Champs-Elysées. You can also get information by telephoning 40-71-76-25.

Paris by Boat

To admire the beauty of Paris from another angle, consider taking a *bateaux mouche* ride on the river. Although dinner cruises are outrageously expensive ($100 and more per person), a one-hour ride in a *bateau mouche* costs about $7. The *bateaux mouche* are operated by several different companies whose flat-bottomed passenger boats are very much the same: rows of seats, some outside, some enclosed by glass. The routes are nearly identical as well—from near the Eiffel Tower to Île St-Louis, going around both it and Île de la Cité, and back to the dock. If you want to get away from the tape-recorded commentary, sit at the back of the boat, where it isn't so intrusive.

During summer months, the BatOBus also operates a passenger service along the Seine. With five stops between the Eiffel Tower and Île de la Cité, single trips cost about $1.80. The better deal is an all-day pass for about $9, which enables you to get on and off the boat at will. With the pass you'll be able to sightsee by water all day long and take a complete circuit at sunset, when the river is at its very best.

It's possible to cruise Paris's canals, too. The trips take three hours and go between the city's center and Parc de la Villette (see chapter 11).

Pedal Pushing

If you like to go on bike rides at home, you'll love Paris. I'm not suggesting that you pedal down the Champs-Elysées, but rather wander the nooks and crannies of Paris that you otherwise might not get to explore. Bike rentals aren't cheap (about $18 a day, $28 for 24 hours, $99 a week), but you'll be able to cover a great deal of territory.

There are bike tours, too. Paris à Velo, C'est Sympa! (4e; 37, blvd Bourbon; 48-87-60-01; Pont-Marie Métro station), offers tours that cover from 10 to 15 miles in two and a half to four and a half hours. There are several itineraries, including one that winds through the 19th and 20th arrondissements.

Mountain Bike Trip (15e; 6, place Etienne Pernet; 48-42-77-77; Felix-Faure Métro station) offers a tour that includes most of the major Parisian sights (including those along the Champs-Elysées). A seven-hour tour is offered by Three Ducks Youth Hostel (15e; 6, place Etienne-Pernet; 48-42-57-87; Felix-Faure Métro station). Bicycle tour charges include the use of helmets.

You'll frequently find flyers with discount coupons for both boat and bike tours. Look for them at tourist offices, hotel brochure racks, hostels, and other places where non-Parisians tend to go, such as the American Church information area.

7

Museums and Galleries

To properly describe all the treasures in Paris museums would take a rather large book—and many have been written. If you're an artist, collector, or museum enthusiast, you probably already have several of them. However, if museums aren't the major reason you want to visit Paris, the following mini guide should send you in the right directions.

My museum credo is that *really looking* at the pictures, archaeological treasures, or toys in one part of a single museum beats racing around in a museum marathon and remembering nothing about any of them six months later. Therefore, this chapter focuses on a handful of the must-see museums—those the critics consider the most important in Paris—and several others that even people who don't usually like museums will love.

The Master Museums

Few people would argue that Paris has the greatest number of important museums of any city in the world, including the megastar, Musée du Louvre (1er; rue de Rivoli; 40-20-53-17; Palais-Royal/Musée du Louvre Métro station). Now that its billion-dollar expansion has been completed, the Louvre can claim the distinction of being the largest museum anywhere. To see it all would be a humongous project, which could take years to accomplish thoroughly. As a result, many Louvre visitors come away frustrated after trying to do the whole place in an afternoon.

I'll admit that on my first visit, I did the "six-minute Louvre," madly dashing from the *Mona Lisa* (so disappointingly small) to the *Winged Victory of Samothrace* (impressive) to the *Venus de Milo*, just to be able to say that I had seen them. Then I came to my senses and spent the rest of the time admiring the dramatic oils by Delacroix. On each subsequent visit, I've concentrated on just a few artists whose work interests me most.

You may find it easier than I to retain visual material, but if you don't, pick up a floor plan of the museum at the entrance. Take a few minutes to look it over, then decide which collections you want to see most: works by Rubens, Rembrandt, Brueghel, or other northern Europeans; Islamic, Roman or Etruscan, Oriental, or Greek antiquities; objets d'art such as tapestries and jewelry. It will be a tough but necessary choice: After all, there are about 30,000 items on display.

Before its reincarnation, the Louvre was drab, musty, and suffered from insufficient lighting. Then in the early 1980s, American architect and museum specialist par excellence I. M. Pei began making changes on his drawing board. Today, with the addition of a central glass pyramid and three smaller ones, a "city of light" has been created under the museum's two large courtyards. Art treasures are displayed in renovated salons and galleries whose decor now rivals the works on exhibit. The biggest triumph of all, perhaps, was the wresting of the Richelieu Wing from the Ministry of Finance, which had occupied it since 1871. Seven floors of offices, stripped of their paneling and false ceilings, have been transformed into three floors of magnificent exhibition space.

The 17-year-long restoration effort, completed in 1998, has doubled the area of gallery space and increased the number of exhibits by 25 percent. The Richelieu Wing, inaugurated in

1993, contains the Louvre's incomparable collection of 17th-to 19th-century French paintings. The Denon Wing, reopened in 1997, is dedicated to the museum's Italian paintings and drawings—that's where you'll find the *Mona Lisa*. The most recently reopened of the wings, the Sully, holds a treasure trove of Egyptian and Middle Eastern art and artifacts.

Typically Parisian, the Louvre's Musée des Arts de la Mode et du Textile chronicles two centuries of French haute couture and lesser fashions. There are 18th-century gowns of satin, damask, and silk as well as creations by top contemporary designers such as Karl Lagerfeld and Christian Lacroix.

The Louvre is open Wednesday 9 A.M. to 9:15 P.M., Thursday through Monday 9 A.M. to 5:15 P.M. Admission is about $6.40 for adults, except after 3 P.M. and on Sunday, when it's $4.20. Seniors pay half price at any time (as they do in most Paris museums), and there's no entry fee for people under the age of 18. Guided tours in English—for which there is a charge—are conducted daily at 10 A.M., 11:30 A.M. and 2 P.M. (except on Tuesday, when the museum is closed, and on Sunday).

The Musée d'Orsay (7e; 1, rue de Bellechasse; 40-49-48-84; Solferino Métro station) is a must-see museum in my book—not only for the works of art it contains, but also for the fabulous job its architects did in converting an old railway station, the Gare d'Orsay, into a remarkably attractive space for displaying that art. The d'Orsay is the place to go to see major works by impressionists—Monet, Manet, Renoir—and postimpressionists such as Cézanne, van Gogh, Gauguin, and Toulouse-Lautrec. Also on exhibit are paintings by the fauves (wild beasts) of the early 20th century: Matisse, Derain, and de Vlaminck among them. Other works range from a Charles Rennie Mackintosh chair to the *Gates of Hell* sculpture by Auguste Rodin. Since exhibits at the d'Orsay encompass the period from 1848 to 1914, it's a museum that satisfies a wide variety of artistic tastes. The d'Orsay's bookstore is huge, with most of the books in French. The museum is open Tuesday through Sunday 10 A.M to 5:30 P.M. (Thursday until 9:15 P.M.); admission is about $5.60 for adults and about half that amount on Sunday, and $4.20 for seniors and students at all times. Maps are available at the entrance.

The third of the major museums that has made big news in the art world during the last quarter century is the Centre Georges Pompidou—also known as the Beaubourg (4e; place Beaubourg; 44-78-12-33; Rambuteau Métro and Chatelet–Les Halles RER stations). Built "inside-out" in 1977, the Pompidou's exterior is a fantasy of air and water ducts, pipes, steel struts, and all the other structural necessities customarily covered up by brick or some other building material. Inside, corridors from the huge and undistinguished-looking central core lead to various galleries and activity venues. Due to unanticipated crowds, the Beaubourg's interior was badly in need of an overhaul in the late 1990s, when Renzo Piano and Jean-François Bodin were commissioned to do a complete renovation. With work now finished, the museum was recently reopened.

Although the building's exterior is not to everyone's taste, the quality of the works of art inside it is undeniable. The fifth level is dedicated to works created from 1905 to 1960. Included among them are Henri Matisse's *Sorrow of the King*, and *Man With a Guitar* by Georges Braque.

The fourth level is devoted to contemporary art, such as the whimsical *Ben's Store* by Vautier Benjamin, along with works by Andy Warhol and Jasper Johns. The first and sixth levels are reserved for major exhibitions of contemporary artists and movements, and include furniture and furnishings as well as fine art. Library areas occupy the second and third levels. The Pompidou is open noon to 10 P.M. weekdays except Tuesday, 10 A.M. to 10 P.M. Saturday and Sunday. General admission costs about $4.90, and there are additional charges for the special exhibits. Incidentally, the plaza outside the Pompidou is a show in itself, with street performers and self-proclaimed artists providing the entertainment.

Lesser—but Nonetheless Brilliant—Museums

Even though they aren't as well known as the Big Three, a number of other art museums in Paris would be considered stars in other cities. One of the finest collections of 18th-century art is that of the Musée Cognac-Jay (3e; 8, rue Elzevir; 40-27-07-21; St-Paul or Chemin Vert Métro station). Bequeathed to the city by the founders of the Samaritaine department store, it includes works by Boucher, Chardin, and Watteau as well as furniture, porcelain, jewelry, and other objets d'art. The collection is housed in the elegant Hôtel de Donon in the Marais. The building dates to 1575, but has an 18th-century extension and facade. It's open 10 A.M. to 5:40 P.M. Tuesday through Sunday; the admission charge is about $4.20.

The Grand Palais (8e; 3, av General-Eisenhower; 44-13-17-17; Champs-Elysées-Clemenceau Métro station) is an imposing building used only for temporary exhibitions such as the 1995 spectacular featuring the works of Paul Cézanne. Reservations for these artistic blockbusters are necessary. Otherwise, you'll spend precious hours in line. Hotel concierge desks can make the reservations for you. Admission prices vary with the exhibits.

Musée d'Art Naïf—Max Fourny (18e; 2, rue Ronsard; 42-58-72-89; Anvers Métro station) features naive paintings (those created by artists who have little formal training) from around the world. If you're fond of folk art, this is the place to go. However, be sure to call in advance, because the museum can be closed when special exhibitions are being put in place—a real disappointment if you've made a special trip. Open Tuesday through Sunday 10 A.M. to 6 P.M. Admission is about $5.60.

Musée Picasso (3e; 5, rue de Thorigny; 42-71-25-21; Chemin Vert, St-Sebastien Froissart, or St-Paul Métro station) claims the largest collection of Pablo Picasso's art to be displayed in one museum. Turned over to the French government in lieu of death duty payments, the works include not only those done by Picasso, but also paintings by Degas, Cézanne, Matisse, Renoir, and others that belonged to the artist. Open Wednesday through Monday 9:15 A.M. to 5:15 P.M. (Wednesday closing at 10 P.M.). Admission is about $5.30.

Musée Jacquemart-André (8e; 158, blvd Haussmann; 42-89-04-91; St-Philippe-du-Roule Métro station) has an outstanding Renaissance and 18th-century art collection, showcased in an equally grand 19th-century town house. Since this museum is not as well known as it ought to be, there are fewer people around than at most—a big plus in a city where the general complaint about museums is that they're too crowded. Open Wednesday through Sunday 1 to 6 P.M. Admission is about $6.70.

Musée de la Musique (19e; Cité de la Musique; 221, av Jean Jaures; 44-84-44-84; Porte de Pantin Métro station) presents about 900 musical instruments, artfully displayed, which range from those of the 16th century to top-quality trombones, keyboards, and synthesizers like those in use today. Also among the exhibits are music-related paintings, sculptures, and sketches. Instrumental demonstrations, interactive areas, and recorded tours with headphones enhance the experience. Admission for adults is $6.30; children 6 to 18 $4.20; and under 6 $2.10. The museum is open Tuesday through Saturday from noon to 6 P.M. (7:30 P.M. on Friday), Sunday 10 A.M. to 6 P.M.

Musée National du Moyen-Age-Thermes de Cluny (5e; 6, place Paul Painleve; 53-73-78-00; Cluny–La Sorbonne Métro or St-Michel–Notre Dame RER station) contains one of the world's finest collections of medieval art. Appropriately housed in a medieval mansion erected by the abbot of Cluny and completed in 1500, the museum's treasures include two Books of Hours from the 15th century, ruins of Gallo-Roman baths built on the site in A.D. 200, the Lady With the Unicorn tapestry series, and 21 of the 28 stone heads of the kings of Judah (circa 1220). Open Wednesday through Sunday 9:15 A.M. to 5:45 P.M., with adult admission about $4.20.

Musée Carnavalet (3e; 23, rue de Sevigne; 44-59-58-58; St-Paul Métro or Chatelet–Les Halles RER station). Two historic mansions, the Hôtel Carnavalet and the Hôtel le Peletier de St-Fargeau, provide the setting for exhibits that trace the history of Paris from its origins to contemporary times. Entire rooms, decorated in the style of various eras (among them the re-creation of a jewelry store in 1900 and the reconstruction of an early-20th-century hotel ballroom), are impressive. Open Tuesday through Sunday 10 A.M. to 5:40 P.M. Admission is about $4.60 for adults, with special expositions costing more.

Galerie National du Jeu de Paume (1er; Jardin des Tuileries, place de la Concorde; 47-03-12-50; Concorde Métro station). This impressionist art museum was built on the site of what was originally a tennis court built by Napoleon III in 1851. In 1986, the museum's collection was moved to Musée d'Orsay. Now the building is used for contemporary art exhibits, usually retrospectives of established artists. Annually, the museum is the setting for Festival d'Automne, an invitational show that features contemporary art, including the avant garde. Open at various times throughout the year. Admission varies with the event.

Musée de l'Orangerie (1er; Jardin des Tuileries, place de la Concorde; Concorde Métro station). This museum, which focuses on works of the impressionists, is closed for extensive renovation. Planned changes include the conversion of exterior walls to glass in response to Claude Monet's request that as much natural light as possible would reach his Water Lilies series. Upon the renovation's completion, the Orangerie's marvelous collection of works by Monet, Cézanne, Matisse, Modigliani, Picasso, Renoir, Rousseau, Utrillo, and other great artists will be rehung and rearranged. The museum is scheduled to reopen in autumn 2001.

Bibliothèque Nationale Richelieu; Musée du Cabinet des Medailles et des Antiques; Musée Vitrines de Arts du Spectacle (2e; 58, rue de Richelieu; Bourse Métro station). Manuscripts that had become the property of medieval kings form the nucleus of the library's collection. To these manuscripts, a copy of every book produced in France since 1537 has been added by law. Two Gutenberg Bibles and original manuscripts by famous French authors, as well as the world's most valuable collection of photographs and engravings, are among the library's treasures. The huge collection of books, periodicals, and recordings has been transferred to the Bibliothèque National Tolbiac near the Gare d'Austerlitz in the 13th arrondissement.

First-century silverware and other valuable items including coins, jewels, and medals are showcased in Musée du Cabinet des Medailles et des Antiques, part of the National Library (47-03-83-40). Open Monday through Saturday 8 A.M. to 6 P.M.; admission is about $3.

Arts du Spectacle (passage Colbert, between 6, rue des Petits-Champs and 4, rue Vivienne; 47-03-81-26; Bourse Métro station), under the entertainment department of the National Library, is the venue for temporary exhibits with subjects ranging from costumes and puppets to musical comedy posters and mime. Open Monday through Saturday 1 to 5 P.M., Sunday, noon to 6 P.M. Closed holidays. Admission is about $3.

Bibliothèque National de France François Mitterand (Tolbiac; 12e; quai François-Mauriac; 53-79-53-79; Quai-de-la-Gare Métro station). Built to augment the existing Bibliothèque Nationale Richelieu, Tolbiac was designed by Dominique Perrault and is definitely avant garde. Centerpiece of a plan to turn around a decaying riverfront area, the building's distinguishing features are four huge L-shaped towers. In addition to being the repository for specific categories of the library's vast collection of materials, the facility also serves as a public library. Open Tuesday through Saturday 10 A.M. to 7 P.M., Sunday noon to 6 P.M. A day pass costs about $2.10.

Musée de l'Histoire de France (3e; Hôtel Soubise; 60, rue des Francs-Bourgeois; 40-27-60-96; Rambuteau Métro station; also Hôtel Rohan; 87, rue Vieille du Temple; Hôtel de Ville

Métro station). Hôtel Soubise contains documents from the National Archives dating from the Merovingian period to the present day. Even if you're not interested in the documents, you may want to visit the museum: This mansion is considered one of the most magnificent in the Marais. The interior decoration, created between 1735 and 1740 by the most gifted artists of the day, is exquisite, and the courtyard is equally pleasing. Open Wednesday through Monday 1:45 to 5:45 P.M. Admission is about $2.10. Hôtel Rohan is part of the museum, but is used only for temporary exhibits of documents.

Musée Kwok-On (4e; 41, rue des Francs-Bourgeois; 42-72-99-42; St-Paul Métro station). On display is the marvelous collection of items relating to Asian theater and its traditions gathered by the museum's patron, Kwok-On. Costumes, musical instruments, masks, and shadow puppets as well as props used in street festivals in China, India, Japan, and Southeast Asia are among the pieces on display. Open Monday through Friday 10 A.M. to 5:30 P.M. Closed holidays. Admission is about $3.75.

Musée National d'Histoire Naturelle (5e; Jardin des Plantes, 57, rue Curvier; 40-79-30-00; Jussieu Métro or Gare d'Austerlitz RER station). The Grande Galerie de l'Evolution opened in 1994. Its multimedia production tells the story of evolution with lifelike stuffed animals, music, reader boards, touch-the-screen databases, and videos. You'll find sea creatures on the lower level. Four of the older museums—entomology, minerology, paleobiology, and paleontology—are also part of the museum, but aren't as impressive as the Grande Galerie. The Grande Galerie is open Monday and Wednesday through Sunday 10 A.M. to 6 P.M. (Thursday to 10 P.M.). Admission is about $5.60. The older museums are open Monday and Wednesday through Sunday, 10 A.M. to 5 P.M. Admission ranges from about $2.10 to $4.20.

Musée National des Arts Asiatiques Guimet (16e; 6, place d'Iéna; 47-23-61-65; Iéna Métro station). Undeniably one of the world's leading Asian art museums, the Guimet exhibits the finest Khmer (Cambodian) art in the Western Hemisphere. Originally on display in Emile Guimet's home in Lyons, the collection was moved to Paris in 1884. Among the most important items are a number of large Khmer temple sculptures; Buddhas from India, Indonesia, Japan, and Vietnam; and religious objects from Tibet. Open Wednesday through Monday 9:45 A.M. to 6 P.M.; admission is about $3.75.

Espace Montmartre Salvador Dali (18e; 11, rue Poulbot; 42-64-40-10; Abbesses Métro station). Moving lights focus first on one, then on another of Dali's paintings hung in this dark underground museum. The artist's voice adds a surrealistic touch, in keeping with both the persona of the painter and his individualistic artistic style. Many of the paintings are Dali's less familiar works. Also on display are his illustrations for such books as *Alice in Wonderland* and the *Decameron* by Boccaccio. The museum is open from 10 A.M. to 6 P.M. Admission is about $5.60.

Musée de la Mode et du Costume (16e; 10, av Pierre 1er de Serbie; 47-20-85-23; Iéna or Alma Marceau Métro station) focuses on fashions, uniforms, and other clothing from the 18th century to the present. Several of the garments in this collection of more than 100,000 outfits have been donated by celebrities such as the late Princess Grace of Monaco and top French fashion designers. Open Tuesday through Sunday 10 A.M. to 5:40 P.M. Admission is about $4.90 for adults.

Manufacture Royale des Gobelins (13e; 42, av des Gobelins; 44-61-21-69; Les Gobelins Métro station), where more than 5,000 tapestries and carpets have been created since the national company was formed in 1662, offers guided factory tours Tuesday through Thursday at 2 P.M. They cost about $7.40. The entrance fee, including the tour, is about $4.90 for adults.

Among the numerous other Parisian museums dedicated to art and the antiquities is Institut du Monde Arabe (5e; 23, quai St-Bernard; 40-51-3-38; Cardinal-Lemoine Métro station). This establishment centers on the art and civilization of the Arab/Islamic world from its beginnings to the present

(Tuesday through Sunday 1 to 8 P.M.; about $5.60 for adults). Another excellent art repository, Musée Marmottan—Claude Monet (16e; 2, rue Louis-Boilly; 42-24-07-02; La Muette Métro station), focuses on a fabulous collection of paintings by the impressionists (Tuesday through Sunday 10 A.M. to 5:30 P.M.; admission for adults is about $5.60; for children, about $3.50.

While several museums don't charge admission on Sunday, more and more of them are discontinuing this practice. You may want to buy a museums and monuments card, which offers admission and priority access to permanent collections of 65 museums and monuments in Paris and the greater Paris area. These cards, which can be purchased at the museums and monuments, tourism offices, and major underground stations, cost about $11.20 for one day, $22.40 for two days, and $33.60 for five. The passes don't permit access to temporary exhibitions or guided tours, but one of their major advantages is that you don't have to wait in ticket lines. However, the one-day pass isn't a bargain unless you visit at least three museums with an average entrance fee of $5 (or the Beaubourg all-day pass plus one of the more expensive museums). You need only go to an average of two museums a day to make the five-day pass pay dividends.

National museums are closed on Tuesday, except Musée d'Orsay, which closes on Monday. Closing day for municipally funded museums is Monday. And remember, if you're visiting Paris in August, be sure to check whether the museums you wish to visit are open at all; several of them close during that month.

THE OUT-OF-THE-ORDINARY

Although most of Paris's museums are traditional, some of the others' reasons for existence are based on items you didn't know were so numerous or varied or—weird. This sampling goes from the sublime to the sewers. Musée Baccarat (10e; 30 bis, rue de Paradis; 47-70-64-30; Gare de l'Est Métro station) chronicles the evolution of crystal objects from 1828 to the present, with more than 1,200 items in this dazzling collection. Open Monday through Friday 9 A.M. to 6 P.M., Saturday 10 A.M. to 12 P.M. and 2 to 5 P.M.; admission is about $2.10 for adults.

Musée Pierre Fauchard (16e; 22, rue Emile Ménier; 45-53-40-05; Porte Dauphine Métro and Avenue Foch RER stations). Dentists and dental assistants will like this one, but you have to phone ahead to get in. It includes dentistry-related paintings from the 17th-century Dutch School, dentist's chairs, cabinets and instruments, antique books, and late-19th-century toothbrushes among its exhibits. Open Wednesday 2:30 to 5:30 P.M. by appointment only. Free admission.

Musée de la Contrefaçon (16e; 16, rue de la Faisanderie; 56-26-14-00; Porte Dauphine Métro station) focuses on the crimes of forgery and counterfeiting through the ages. Among its exhibits are imitation labels and money, along with rip-off products such as perfume and clothing. It's a small museum—only one room—but fascinating. Open Monday and Wednesday 2 to 4:30 P.M., Friday 9:30 A.M. to noon; admission is about $2.10 for adults.

Musée Pierre Marly—Lunettes et Lorgnettes (1er; 380, rue St-Honoré; 40-20-06-98; Concorde Métro or Invalides RER station) displays spectacles, opera glasses, and binoculars from the 13th century. From monocles and pince-nez to microscopes and telescopes, more than 3,000 items make up this most unusual collection. Open Tuesday through Saturday 10 A.M. to noon and 2 to 6 P.M.; the entrance fee is about $2.80 for adults.

Musée de la Serrure (also known as Musée Bricard; 3e; 1, rue de la Perle; 42-77-79-62; Chemin Vert Métro station) focuses on antique security devices, including a 17th century-device that shot any person at the door who tried to insert the wrong key. Open Tuesday through Saturday 10 A.M. to noon and 2 to 5 P.M. Closed August and the last week of December. Admission is about $4.20, and it's worth that amount just to see the elegant 1685 mansion in which the museum is housed.

Musée de la Franc-Maconnerie (9e; 16, rue Cadet; 45-23-20-92; Cadet Métro station) is located in the rear of a Masonic temple and documents the history of Freemasonry in Europe. Among the displays are insignia, paintings, and ceremonial robes. Open Monday through Saturday 2 to 6 P.M. Admission is free.

Musée de l'Eventail, Atelier Hoguet (10e; 2, blvd de Strasbourg; 42-08-19-89; Strasbourg-St-Denis Métro station) is a small museum that contains artistic fans dating from the 17th century. The technical room contains a workbench and fan frame, illustrating how fans are made. Open Tuesday 2 to 5 P.M.; admission is about $4.20 for adults.

Musée des Collections Historiques de la Prefecture de Police (5e; 1 bis, rue des Carmes; 43-29-21-57; Maubert Mutualité Métro station) follows the history of the Paris police force from the mid–16th century to the present. Exhibits include uniforms, weapons, and documents pertaining to famous cases. Open Monday through Thursday 9 A.M. to 5 P.M., Friday 9 A.M. to 4:30 P.M. Admission is free.

Musée de la Chasse et de la Nature (3e; 60, rue des Archives; 42-72-86-43; Rambuteau Métro station). Housed in an extravagant 17th-century mansion, this museum contains paintings by the likes of Monet, Rubens, and Brueghel, fine porcelain, furniture, and other items all decorated with hunting and nature themes. This museum is not for everyone, since some of the pieces on exhibit are chillingly graphic. Open Wednesday through Sunday 10 A.M. to 12:30 P.M. and 1:30 to 5:30 P.M. Admission is about $4.20 for adults.

Musée National des Monuments Français (16e; Palais de Chaillot, 1, place du Trocadero et du 11 Novembre; 44-05-39-10; Trocadero Métro station) presents major French monuments from the Middle Ages to the 19th century in full-scale reproductions. Open Tuesday through Sunday 10 A.M. to 6 P.M. Admission is about $2.95 for adults.

Musée des Arts Forains (12e; 53, av des Terroirs de France; Dugommier Métro station). This re-creation of a fairground from the Belle Epoque contains carnival rides, game booths, and other fair-related items. The museum is especially interesting on special days when music plays—all the mechanical carousels and other exhibits are set in motion. Open Saturday and Sunday 2 to 7 P.M. Admission for adults is about $5.90.

Musée de Radio-France (16e; 116, av du President Kennedy; 56-40-15-16; Ranelagh Métro or Kennedy–Radio France RER station) contains what is billed as "the finest collection of sound and picture devices in Europe." Features include a "sound tour" from the wireless to present-day technology. Guided tours, which cost about $3.50, are conducted at 10:30 and 11:30 A.M. and 3:30 and 4:30 P.M. While you're there, inquire about the free concerts that Radio France presents on Sunday throughout the year.

The French Ministry of Defense sponsors three Paris museums. Musée de la Marine (Maritime Museum) (16e; Palais de Chaillot, 17, place du Trocadero et du 11 Novembre; 53-65-69-69; Trocadero Métro station) contains models of warships since the end of the 17th century, sail and steam vessels, merchant ships, fishing boats, and exploration vessels as well as figureheads and other items related to the sea. It's one of the largest maritime museums in the world. Open Tuesday through Sunday 10 A.M. to 6 P.M.; admission isabout $5.30.

Musée de l'Armée (7er; Hôtel National des Invalides, 6, place Vauban; 44-42-37-72; Invalides Métro or RER station) is one of the leading military museums in the world. Arms, armor, and uniforms from the ancien régime and the Napoleonic era to World War II are displayed in one of Paris's grandiose buildings. Open Tuesday through Sunday, 10 A.M. to 6 P.M. (it closes one hour earlier in winter); adult admission is about $5.30. For information on Musée de l'Air et de l'Espace (Air and Space Musem), see chapter 11.

Musée des Egouts de Paris (7e; place de la Résistance at quai d'Orsay; 53-68-27-81; Alma Marceau or Pont de l'Alma Métro or RER station) explains the layout, workings, and history of Paris's sewers. Constructed under Napoleon III, the sewers were used as escape routes during the Nazi occupation. Open Saturday through Wednesday 11 A.M. to 5 P.M. (it closes one hour earlier in winter). Admission costs about $3.50.

Gallery Gazing

As you might imagine, there are art galleries galore in Paris—just check a Paris telephone directory, and you'll see that the number of them is overwhelming. Many are impeccably decorated salons where original works by important artists, past and present, are for sale. Others represent the not-so-well known. Add to these established galleries the crude backdrops set up by sidewalk artists on the Left Bank and you'll have a lot of free entertainment.

The following will give you an idea of the range of commercial galleries you'll encounter.

Galerie Denise Rene (7e; 196, blvd St-Germain; 42-22-11-02; Rue du Bac Métro station; and 3e; 22, rue Charlot; 48-87-73-94; Filles-du-Calvaire Métro station) handles classics of the first half of the 20th century, including works from the dada movement during World War I.

The Maeght Gallery (7e; 42, rue du Bac; 45-48-45-15; Rue du Bac Métro station) specializes in works by such greats as Chagall, Kandinsky, Braque, and Miró.

Galerie Agathe Gaillard (4e; 3, rue du Pont-Louis-Philippe; 42-77-38-24; Pont-Marie Métro station) is one of Paris's best photography galleries. In the past, it has featured exhibits of the works of Cartier-Bresson, Ansel Adams, and other legendary photographers.

The Yvon Lambert Gallery (3e; 108, rue Vieille du Temple; 42-71-09-33; Hôtel de Ville Métro station) showcases a sampling of French, German, Italian, Japanese, and American artists, including the whimsical Frenchman Philippe Favier.

Works at the Vidal Saint Phalle Gallery (4e; 10, rue Tresor; 42-76-06-05; St-Paul Métro station) include those of Spanish sculptor Jaume Plensa and the late Henri Michaux, a Belgian-born poet and painter.

The Galerie de France (4e; 54, rue de la Verrerie; 42-74-38-00; Hôtel de Ville Métro station) and Durand-Dessert (11e; 28, rue de Lappe; 48-06-92-23; Bastille Métro station) frequently present shows by individual artists.

One of the streets where you'll find a number of galleries is rue St-Louis-en-l'Île. Another that's great for gallery hopping is rue de Seine in the sixth arrondissement. If you would like to talk to the Parisian artists of today, and perhaps see them at their easels, here are a few places you might look for them.

Quai de la Gare Artists (13e; quai de la Gare; Boulevard Massena Métro station) isn't a gallery, exactly, but rather a series of old warehouses that have been or are in process of being renovated by artists as studios and living quarters. Off and on during the year, groups of these artists arrange shows and offer tours of their studios.

Another collection of artists' studios, La Cité Fleurie (13e; 65 blvd Arago; St-Jacques Métro station), is grouped behind old prison walls and a tumbledown garden. If you ask, some of the artists will let you see their studios and show you their work, just as Picasso, Gauguin, and Modigliani possibly did when they lived there years ago.

Though the paintings of many street artists look like they are a product of the paint-by-numbers school, others among those sketching the Seine are serious art students who may be the Renoirs and Corots of tomorrow. When you come upon an artist's work you like, whether it be in a commercial gallery or drying on an easel on Pont Marie, think twice before you dismiss the idea of buying it. After all, that painting or water-color or pen-and-ink sketch may turn out to be your all-time favorite souvenir of Paris and the centerpiece of your living room wall museum at home.

CHAPTER
8

Activities and Entertainment

Years ago, an Englishwoman who had logged countless thousands of travel miles told me, "In Paris, it seems silly somehow to spend time doing things that you can do *anywhere*. Especially when you can find such a lot of entertainment that's so utterly . . . French." If you think about it, her point is well taken. So I have decided to follow her lead and focus this chapter on activities and entertainments that are typically French.

Becoming a French Chef

Paris is acknowledged as the gastronomic center of the universe. And since master chefs are willing—for a price—to share their knowledge, people who want to learn more about preparing haute, regional, or nouvelle cuisine have their choice of an array of cooking classes and demonstrations.

Some of the finest are offered by the Ritz-Escoffier Cooking School. In 1898, Cesar Ritz opened his hotel, with Auguste Escoffier as his chef. Across from the kitchens where Escoffier cooked, the Ritz-Escoffier Ecole de Gastronomie Française on rue Cambon in the first arrondissement (43-16-30-50; Concorde or Madeleine Métro station) now teaches the art of French cooking to students from around the world. Throughout the year, cooking and pastry-making demonstrations featuring chefs from the school are presented Monday and Thursday. At some sessions a guest chef, such as Jean-Paul Duquesnoy, Jacques Cagna, or Gerard Besson, prepares an appetizer, main course, and dessert. You can attend a demonstration for about $67. The English translation at the session I attended was perfect, because the interpreter, a cooking school student who was born and raised in Paris, has an American mother. Half-day workshops are also presented throughout the year and cost about $98. (There's a 10 percent discount for students who take five of these sessions.)

During the year, courses of various lengths—from 1 to 30 weeks—are presented, essentially for people who already are chefs or plan to be. They range in price from about $812 to $24,780. A one-week course, "All About Wine," as well as those that cover such subjects as "Brasserie and Bistro Desserts" and "French Bread Baking," cost Americans about $200 less than they did three years ago. Since instruction is offered Monday through Friday, the courses are fairly easy to fit into visitors' itineraries.

Reservations are made by writing to the Hotel Ritz (15, place Vendome, 75001 Paris), though the entrance to the cooking school is actually at 38, rue Cambon, behind the hotel.

Parlez-Vous Français?

If you've always wanted to improve your foreign-language skills, this is your chance. A one-week course, with three-hour classes Monday through Friday, costs less than $200. The series costs about $300 if you choose courses that last five hours each day. Both morning and afternoon classes consist of small groups of about 8 to 10 students. Most groups are multinational and composed primarily of people who live in Paris and need to use the language at work.

The method at l'Institut Parisien de Civilisation Françaises (15e; 87, blvd Grenelle; 40-56-09-53; Bir-Hakeim Métro station) is one of total immersion, with no English spoken in class. Before students are put in classes, they're given a simple test to determine their level of competence in the language (see chapter 13 for more information).

Exploring the Underworld

The Catacombes (14e; 1, place Denfert-Rochereau; 43-22-47-63; Denfert-Rochereau Métro station) contain the bones of some six million dead collected from Paris's ancient cemeteries. The maze of tunnels, used in World War II as a hiding place by members of the French Resistance, are macabre to say the least. If you go, do take a flashlight and stick close to your guide so you won't get lost. Open Tuesday through Friday 2 to 4 P.M., Saturday and Sunday 9 to 11 A.M. and 2 to 4 P.M.; admission is about $4.20.

Not everyone wants to tour the Catacombes, but visiting the city's regular cemeteries is just about as much of a Paris tradition as the London pub crawl. The last resting places of the leading lights of the art, literary, political, and industrial worlds, the cemeteries are also interesting because of their statuary, monuments, and tombs—often in a state of disrepair that adds to the drama of their settings. Among the most fascinating are the following.

Cimetière du Père Lachaise (20e) is the largest in Paris and the final resting place of the rich, talented, and famous. Artists Corot, Daumier, Delacroix, Modigliani, Pissaro, and Seurat; writers Gertrude Stein, Balzac, La Fontaine, Molière, Proust, and Oscar Wilde; and actresses Sara Bernhardt and Simone Signoret are all entombed here. Enter by the way of the main entrance off blvd de Menilmontant (Père Lachaise, Philippe Auguste, or Gambetta Métro station). Although admission is free, you'll want to spend about $2 for a detailed map that shows the location of the celebrity tombs.

Cimetière de Montmartre (18e; av Rachel; Place de Clichy Métro station), on the west side of Butte Montmartre, contains the tombs of writer Emile Zola, composer Hector Berlioz, and painter Edouard Degas.

Cimetière Montparnasse (14e; main entrance off blvd Edgar Quinet; Edgar Quinet Métro station) is where existentialist Jean-Paul Sartre and his lover Simone de Beauvoir are entombed, as are composer Camille Saint-Saens, playwright Samuel Beckett, industrialist André Citroen, author Guy de Maupassant, and poet Charles Baudelaire. You can get a free "Index des Célébrités" at the main entrance.

The most visited tomb of them all is Napoleon Bonaparte's at Les Invalides (7e; Esplanade des Invalides; 45-55-37-67; Invalides Métro station). Like the Russian matrushka dolls, the emperor is entombed in a coffin within a coffin within a coffin—six layers of them.

Formerly a home for old, impoverished, or disabled soldiers, Les Invalides is an imposing structure that, despite the pompous facade, embodies the best of French classical architecture. Open April through September, daily from 10 A.M. to 6 P.M.; October through March, daily from 10 A.M. to 5 P.M. Admission is about $5.40.

Once you're in Paris, it won't take long to discover how the French feel about their poodles and Pekingese. So you won't be surprised to learn that Cimetière des Chiens, bordering the Seine in the suburb of Asnières-sur-Seine, contains thousands of graves where the beloved dogs are buried. Each grave marker bears an inscription in tribute to its departed canine (Gabriel-Peri Métro station).

Free guided tours of Hôtel de Ville (4e; place de l'Hôtel de Ville; Hôtel de Ville Métro station) are conducted Monday at 10:30 A.M. The tours, which begin at the north entrance on rue Lobau, show visitors the interior of this Renaissance-style reconstruction of the original city hall—a masterpiece of crystal chandeliers, marble, richly embroidered tapestries, and gold leaf. The original structure was burned down during the 1871 Paris Commune uprising.

Other very French tours, also free, are offered the first Saturday of every month at 2:30 P.M. at l'Observatoire de Paris (14e; 61, av de l'Observatoire; Port Royal RER station). Built under Louis XIV, the observatory is the seat of the International Time Bureau. Its four sides face the four points of the compass, and a copper wire set into the floor defines Paris's north–south axis. The tours are conducted by astronomers.

It will cost you an admission fee to tour the Conciergerie (1er; 1, quai de l'Horloge; 53-73-78-50; Chatelet Métro station), but most students of French history find it fascinating, although grisly. Located on the lower floor of the Palais de Justice, it was originally the residence of the Comte des Cierges, who was in charge of taxes and lodgings. Later the rooms were converted into a prison.

Prisoners numbering about 2,600, including Marie Antoinette, were held there during the Revolution of 1789–1799. Even revolutionary judges Danton and Robespierre were imprisoned in the Conciergerie before being beheaded. The Gothic-style building also contains an 11th-century torture chamber. Open in winter from 10 A.M. to 5 P.M., and in summer from 9:30 A.M. to 6:30 P.M.; admission is about $4.60.

Sitting in *Places*

One of Parisians' favorite activities is sitting outdoors—at sidewalk cafés, on benches or fountain steps, in parks and squares, on the banks of the Seine or its bridges. Although I've mentioned pavement cafés in the dining chapter, it was in the context of eating rather than as an activity. But the sidewalk cafés that serve good food aren't necessarily the best for sitting with a glass of wine, cup of coffee, or bottle of mineral water and watching the world go by. That beverage will be expensive—probably $4 to $5—but waiters won't hassle you to buy a second, so you can sit literally for hours.

When you're looking for a terrace café with a view, go to any of those on rue Jean du Bullay on the west side of Île St-Louis. For nostalgia, Deux Magots (6e; 170, blvd St-Germain; 45-48-55-25; St-Germain-des-Pres Métro station) was once the gathering place for Sartre, de Beauvoir, and their intellectual friends. Now it's at its best off season, after the masses of tourists have vacated the sidewalk tables.

The nearby Café de Flore (6e; 172, blvd St-Germain; 45-48-55-26) was another hangout of Sartre's. Albert Camus, Guillaume Apollinaire, and Pablo Picasso were also regulars. La Closeries de Lilas (14e; 171, blvd du Montparnasse; 40-51-34-50; Port Royal RER station) was the haunt of Henry James, Samuel Beckett, and Ernest Hemingway. Today, French film stars can be glimpsed beneath its green-and-white awnings.

As far as bench sitting goes, the best people-watching spots are along the Champs-Elysées. However, you'll have to go early on Bastille Day (July 14), when tanks, artillery, and various regiments parade up the avenue. Bench space disappears quickly, too, on the last day of the Tour de France, when cyclists ride up the Champs-Elysées to the Arc de Triomphe and back again for their final lap.

Other good places to park yourself are the parklike *places* (squares). Among the best, Montmartre's old village square, place du Tertre (18e; Abbesses Métro station), is a delight in the early morning before the "artists" and tourists arrive en masse. Also hectic by day, place de la Concorde (8e; Concorde Métro station), with its floodlit fountains and statues bathed in lamplight, is lovely at night after the traffic has thinned.

For the most serene sitting, choose the little pocket parks like place Rodin off av Leopold II in Auteuil (16e; Ranelagh Métro station) and the churchyard of St-Julien-le-Pauvre (5e; 1, rue St-Julien-le-Pauvre; St-Michel Métro station).

When basking in the sun by the Seine, you can choose to sprawl on the cement embankments close to the water or sit on a bench at street level. There are seating ledges, too, built into some of the bridges. Even if you're a closet artist at home, don't feel embarrassed about bringing out your sketch pad—or acrylics and easel, for that matter—when the spirit or the view moves you.

A Day at the Races

There are eight horse-racing tracks in Paris, several of which are within the Peripherique. If you're going for class, choose Longchamp in the Bois de Boulogne (16e; buses go to the track from Porte d'Auteuil Métro station). The French dress up when they go to the races, so you get a fashion show along with the racetrack excitement. *Paris Turf* is the name of the racing publication that will give you tips and turf times.

Speaking of sports, Parisians have a number of good swimming pools where you might want to get in a few laps. Among them are three that are easy to get to:

Henry-de-Montherland (16e); 32, blvd Lannes; 45-03-03-28; Rue de la Pompe Métro station.

Piscine Bertrand-Dauvin (18e); 12, rue René-Binet; 44-92-73-42; Métro station.

Piscine de la Porte de la Plaine (15e); 134, rue du General Guillaumat; 45-33-56-99; Porte de Versailles Métro station.

TV Watching

One of the reasons for staying at hotels in the moderate, first-class, or deluxe categories—and it's a compelling one for me—is that almost all of them have cable TV or some other system that provides a diversity of stations. This means that when you're too tired to walk another block but too wide awake to consider sleeping, you can watch your choice of French television programs as well as those on channels from Germany, Switzerland, the British Isles, Luxembourg, and other European countries on occasion. Whether you know the language usually isn't that important, though some of the game shows, sitcoms, and soap operas can be confusing if you don't.

The quality of programming is generally high, with concerts by major symphony orchestras, ballet, and folkloric performances. Musical competitions among choruses from various countries, instrumental groups, and operatic hopefuls are popular, too. Gardening and cooking demonstrations, travelogues, and weather reports are among the easiest noncultural programs to understand.

Getting a Haircut

One of the things you'll notice about Parisians in general is how well their hair is cut. Since it takes time and attention to be well trimmed, getting haircuts can be included in this chapter as a legitimate activity. Furthermore, having your hair attended to in a foreign country is always an interesting experience—and in this case should be a successful one.

While having your hair styled by a major-league hairdresser will cost more than most of us care to spend, in an ordinary unisex salon you'll pay about $26 for a haircut, $23 for a shampoo and blow dry. If you want to get out for a lot less and are willing to gamble, you can have a cut, shampoo, and blow dry at one of the city's many beauty schools for about $10.

An Afternoon (or Evening) at the Movies

Without question, for Parisians, the most popular place to go for entertainment is the cinema. After all, Paris is the self-proclaimed Cinema Capital of Europe, and filmmaking is considered so important that it is subsidized by the French government. If you have any doubt about the industry's importance, you need look no farther than the cinema pages in the weekly enterainment tabloid, *Figaroscope*. It devotes

16 or so pages to movie reviews and listings that include more than 300 titles showing currently.

The movies that are reviewed—and there are about 200 of them in each issue—are those from which you'll probably want to choose. Reviews include the year the film was made and the country in which it was made; whether it is in color or black and white; its duration in minutes; names of the principal actors; and a brief synopsis of the plot, along with subjective comments. They also tell whether foreign films have been dubbed in French (vf—*version française*) or are in their original language and have French subtitles (vo—*version originale*).

Most of the films shown in Paris movie theaters are made in France, followed by a sizable number from the United States. Over the course of a year, there are also films shown from just about every country in the world where movies are made. The reviews in a single issue of *Figaroscope* included films from New Zealand, Morocco, Germany, Great Britain, Iran, Spain, Japan, Italy, Portugal, Vietnam, Tunis, Hong Kong, Canada, Belgium, Cuba, Gabon, Australia, Russia, Greece, Holland, Venezuela, China, and Mali. In addition to the commercial theaters, the Musée d'Orsay and other cultural facilities show movies from time to time.

Several cinemas frequently present festivals centering on certain actors, directors, countries, or genres. These, too, are often listed in newspaper entertainment sections and the weekly and monthly tourist publications. To know which films to choose, read the foreign film reviews in major newspaper entertainment sections before you leave home, jotting down the names of those that have received the best notices. If you can read just a bit of French, skim reviews in *Figarascope* and other newspapers to figure out how the reviewer feels about a particular film. Phrases like *"un classique du genre"* and *"bonne humeur—communicative"* translate pretty easily.

Foreign film fans will be delighted to find that the cinema is one of Paris's most economical entertainments, with tickets costing about $5 to $6.60 for first-run films. At some theaters, seats are up to 40 percent cheaper on Wednesday. A number of theaters also sell passes that entitle the bearer to attend a certain number of movies at a reduced price—for instance, 5 for about $25 or 10 for $35. At others, "fidelity cards" give the holder a free ticket after a specified number of tickets— usually 5 or 10—have been purchased.

Be on the lookout, too, for those special days, advertised in newspapers and on TV, when one theater or a group of them presents its annual promotions. On one day in June, for instance, you can go to movies for the price of a single ticket plus one franc (about 14 cents) for each subsequent film you attend on that day. By planning your strategy carefully, a American expat told me, it's possible to see six full-length films, though it is a bit of a rush getting from one theater to another.

In the first week of February, all the cinemas in the city participate in "18 Heurs—18 Francs." Tickets for all films beginning at 6 P.M. that week sell for about $3.60. Most cinemas begin showing movies in the early afternoon, with others opening in either late morning or early evening. During the winter of 2000–2001, when several cinemas were advertising films at 20 francs (most of them in the late morning or afternoon), I saw David Lean's classic *Lawrence of Arabia* for about $2.80.

Most of the larger cinemas show several movies simultaneously, so be sure you join the right queue. When you enter a movie theater, you will be shown to your seat by an usher, who will expect a tip. Two or three francs will do. If you don't tip, you'll probably be reminded by the usher that he or she receives no wages from the cinema management. To avoid this, palm the tip after you've received the change from your tickets.

After-Dark Enticements

In addition to the cinema, Paris offers a host of other entertainments after the sun goes down. On the cultural scene, you have a variety of options on any given night. As in the rest of

Europe, admission to most cultural events costs less than to comparable entertainments in North America.

Legitimate theater is a treat for people who understand French. Even when you don't, if the story is one you're familiar with, you may enjoy attending a play, because the acting, stage sets, and costuming are generally superb. Comedie-Française is, of course, the best known of the Parisian theaters, specializing in works by such French literary giants as Molière (Jean-Baptiste Poquelin), Jean Racine, and Pierre Corneille as well as works by William Shakespeare and those of contemporary playwrights.

Comedie-Française (1er; 1, place Colette; 44-58-15-15; Musée du Louvre Métro station) puts 112 cheap seats on sale before its performances. They cost from about $4 to $7, depending on the production. Get there about an hour before curtain time to get a good place in line.

Other major theaters include the Odeon Theatre de l'Europe (6e; place Paul-Claudel; 44-41-36-00; Odeon Métro station), which presents plays from other countries in their original languages, and Theatre National de Chaillot (16e; place du Trocadero; 53-65-30-00; Trocadero Métro station), a huge underground auditorium where mainstream European productions and musical revues are staged. The building also contains a studio that features experimental theater.

The Theatre National de la Colline (20e; 15, rue Malte-Brun; 43-66-43-60; Gambette Métro station), with two performance spaces where contemporary dramas are staged, and the Huchette (5e; 23, rue de la Huchette; 43-26-38-99; St-Michel RER station), which specializes in Ionesco plays, are also in the dramatic forefront. Although café-theater is a Paris tradition, it's generally an expensive proposition—you'll save money by going to the theater and having a light supper either before or after.

Paris's only major ballet company—the French National Ballet—headquarters at the resplendent Opéra Paris-Garnier. Repertoire includes classics as well as more contemporary works, including choreography by George Balanchine, Agnes de Mille, and Twyla Tharp. The good news is that most ticket prices at the Opéra de Paris-Garnier range from about $8 to $61, depending upon the performance and seat location. The bad news is that very few seats are available to nonsubscribers. Thirteen days before each performance, 300 tickets go on sale to the general public. Be at the box office before it opens (Monday through Saturday at noon), because the cheapest tickets generally go first.

The back seats of the boxes go on sale at 1:30 P.M. the day before a performance. Any remaining seats are sold at reduced prices to students just before a performance is to begin.

Foreign companies such as the Martha Graham and Alvin Ailey appear at the Opéra as well as other venues. The Theatre de la Ville (1er; 2, place du Chatelet; 42-74-22-77; Chatelet Métro station), has become Paris's major venue for modern dance. Ticket prices run from about $28 to $32. Price reductions are offered if you buy tickets for a minimum of four different productions.

Traditional operas and symphony concerts are presented at the new Opéra de Paris Bastille (12e; 120, rue de Lyon; 36-69-78-68; Bastille Métro station), and other major venues as well. Although the Opéra Bastille is one of the most controversial opera houses in Europe, no one can deny that its technological capabilities are unsurpassed.

Productions of both classic and modern operas often are given avant-garde interpretations, making full use of video screens, neon lighting, and a sorcerer's bag full of state-of-the-art stage mechanisms.

At the Opéra Bastille on certain French holidays, concerts are often presented free of charge in their honor, but you must write in advance for tickets. When you ask the French National Tourist Office for information, find out if a free concert will be offered while you're in Paris.

The Opéra Comique, also known as Salle Favart (2e; 5, rue Favart; 42-44-45-40; Richelieu-Drouot Métro station), specializes in operettas but also mounts productions of full-scale operas.

Three major symphony orchestras are based in Paris, with the Salle Pleyel (8e; 252, rue du Faubourg-St-Honoré; 45-61-53-00; Ternes Métro station) the city's principal concert hall. The hall is headquarters for the Orchestre de Paris. The other two major symphony orchestras—the Orchestre National de France and the Orchestre Philharmonique—are a part of the state-operated Radio France. They often perform in the Maison de Radio-France hall or at Theatre des Champs-Elysées (8e; 15, av Montaigne; 49-51-50-00; Alma Marceau Métro station), which is owned in part by Radio France.

Other popular settings for operas, concerts, and ballet are Theatre National de Chaillot (16e; place du Trocadero; 47-27-81-15; Trocadero Métro station), the Grande Salle of the Centre Georges Pompidou, the Grand Amphitheatre de la Sorbonne, and the Auditorium du Musée d'Orsay.

While it was once possible to attend a free concert at one of Paris's churches every night of the week—and often have a choice of several—there's a growing trend toward charging admission.

Almost every night, there are concerts at the impressive Ste-Chapelle, a building constructed in 1241 to house holy relics and considered the finest example of Gothic architecture in Paris (4, blvd du Palais; 43-54-30-09; Cité Métro station). During one month's time, for example, performances included a celebration of medieval music, Vivaldi's *Four Seasons* and Mozart's *A Little Night Music*, an homage to Maria Callas, the original version of *Carmina Burana*, and programs of adagios and sacred arias. Tickets for most of the programs cost from $18 to $30, with reduced rates for students.

Eglise St-Louis-en-l'Île is another church that presents a number of concerts each month, with artists ranging from a soprano and string orchestra from Armenia to a vocal ensemble from London. St-Julien-le-Pauvre (5e; 23, quai de Montebello; 42-26-00-00), Maubert-Mutualité, and St-Gervais-St-Protais (4e; place de l'Hôtel de Ville; 42-72-64-99; Hôtel de Ville Métro station) are other churches with a reputation for presenting fine concerts.

Occasionally, the churches mentioned above present free concerts, especially in summer. Among the churches that offer free musical programs on a regular basis is St-Eustache (1er; 1, rue Montmartre; 42-33-28-29; Chatelet Métro or Les Halles RER station). Notre Dame (4e; place du Parvis–Notre Dame; 43-26-07-39; Notre Dame Métro or St-Michel RER station) presents organ concerts on Sunday at 5:30 P.M.

Eglise St-Merri (4e; 76, rue de la Verrerie; 42-71-93-93; Chatelet Métro station) offers concerts every Saturday at 7 P.M. and Sunday at 4 P.M. At St-Sulpice (6e; place Sulpice; 46-33-21-78; St-Sulpice or Odeon Métro station), organ concerts follow Sunday mass beginning at 11:30 A.M.

Prices at the opera houses and the main classical music venues range from about $10 to $110; from about $6 to $30 for performances in churches. In addition, free musical programs are presented in parks and gardens during summer, including Champs de Mars (40-71-76-47), Parc Floral of Bois de Vincennes (43-43-92-95), Parc Georges Brassens (40-43-04-78), and Parc des Buttes-Chaumont (49-52-53-55). Since concert times vary, phone the individual park for its concert schedule.

Concerts at Radio France (16e; Maison de la Radio, av du President Kennedy; 42-40-15-16; Ranelagh Métro station) often feature the New Philharmonic Orchestra (NOP), rated by some critics as the best in France. Though admission is charged for many Radio France concerts, others are free.

A series of summer concerts called "Paris Quartier d'Eté" presents classical and contemporary music. The most expensive tickets to those concerts that charge admission are $30. Other performances are free. Held at indoor and outdoor sites including the church of St-Eustache and the Grande Arche at La Defense, the festival runs from the middle of July to mid-August. To find out what's going on, you can consult any one of the weekly or monthly entertainment magazines or call the 24-hour events hot line at 47-20-88-98.

Three outlets of Kiosque Theatre—one opposite the west side of the Eglise de la Madelaine, one at Chatelet–Les Halles RER station, and the other in the courtyard of the Montparnasse train station next to the Montparnasse Tower—sell theater tickets at half price for performances on that day. The tickets are generally for the most expensive seats, and a commission of about $2.50 is charged. This can be a good deal when the seats are good ones and you pay only about what you would pay for an inferior seat. The kiosks are open Tuesday through Friday 12:30 to 7:30 P.M., Saturday 2 to 7:30 P.M., and have signs that say BILLETS (tickets).

It is possible to get discounts of 20 to 40 percent on festival, concert, and theater tickets at ticket agencies in the FNAC department stores at either 136, rue de Rennes (6e; 49-54-30-72; Montparnasse-Bienvenue Métro station) or 1–7, rue Pierre-Lescot (1er; 40-41-40-00; Chatelet–Les Halles RER station). To be eligible for the discounts, you must have a Carte Alpha, which you can also purchase at these locations for about $15. Cards are valid for one year. The agencies are open Tuesday through Saturday 10 A.M. to 7 P.M.

When you ask the personnel at hotel reception and concierge desks to make reservations for performances, you're apt to see them typing on a keyboard and pulling up information on small computer screens. Minitel, which is now a common convenience in French homes, businesses, and public buildings, provides access to theater information as well as everything from an electronic phone directory to United Press International (UPI) news.

You can use Minitel to reserve and pay for theater tickets with your Visa or Eurocard. First you must call up Spectamatic (36-15-MATIC) or Ticketel (36-15-TICK), then follow the prompts. When you give your credit-card number at the theater box office, you'll be handed your ticket. However, ordering by Minitel will cost you surcharges from 10 to 15 percent.

Billetel terminals operate on the same principle as Minitel. They're located throughout Paris in places such as the Etoile, Forum, and Montparnasse FNAC stores; Auber and Chatelet–Les Halles RER stations; the Cités des Sciences et des Industries; the Centre Georges Pompidou; and Galeries Lafayette. You reach Billetel by punching in 36-15-BILLETEL on a Minitel keyboard. You'll be given a password so you can pick up your ticket from a Billetel machine. This method also involves surcharges.

Booking agencies charge a commission of 22 percent. Therefore, if you want to save a hunk of change, buy your tickets directly from the box office. In most cases, you can phone in advance and the tickets will be waiting for you at the theater.

Come to the Cabaret . . . Maybe

Cabaret shows are expensive, and if you've seen the shows in Las Vegas you probably won't be impressed. Expensive though they may be, Paris's big-name reviews pack 'em in. At Bal du Moulin Rouge (9e; 82, blvd de Clicjy; 53-09-82-82; Blanche Métro station), made immortal by Henri Toulouse-Lautrec's posters and Hollywood's 1950s movie, the combination dinner-dance, champagne, and floor show costs from about $110 to $139 per person, depending on menu choice.

The Crazy Horse Saloon (8e; 12, av George V; 47-23-57-35; George V or Alma Marceau Métro station) charges about $40.60 for two drinks and a seat at the bar. Two tableside drinks run $63 to $78.40. What you pay depends on how close your seat is to the sophisticated strippers.

Folies Bergère (9e; 32, rue Richer; 42-46-77-11; Cadet or Rue Montmartre Métro station) offers dinner, a seat in the stalls for the 7:30 show, and a half bottle of champagne for about $114 a person.

At Le Lido (8e; 116 bis, av des Champs-Elysées; 45-63-11-61; George V Métro station), the dinner-dance, champagne, and show cost from about $114 to $142. You can watch the show from the bar for about $54.

When you choose to go to the cabarets via commercial tour, they will cost you even more. Two drinks plus the Crazy Horse show cost about $122 on a commercial tour. Tours that include drinks at a "typical cabaret in the heart of Montmartre," followed by either the Moulin Rouge or Lido 9:30 show with a half bottle of champagne, cost about $166 per person. The dinner-dance and show at the Moulin Rouge or the Lido will cost as much as $256 per person.

Commercial tour companies also offer X-rated tours with names like "Forbidden Paris" and "Paris X," which include such features as "strip-tease show in a typical nightclub of Pigalle [one drink included] and real 'Live Show' in a small erotic theatre." These tours cost about $110.

Upscale Paris nightclubs are *very* expensive, too. They're also private, so you won't get in unless you know someone who's a member. Hopefully your friend will be buying, because it can cost a couple of hundred dollars for a bottle of whiskey.

And All That Jazz

So what do you do when you want some after-dark entertainment that's typically French and doesn't beat up on your bank account? Parisians would probably tell you to go to one of the dozens of jazz clubs—from smoke-filled basements to rooms with concert hall acoustics—where you can hear live music, often performed by top-quality musicians.

Le Petit Journal Montparnasse (14e; 13, rue du Commandant-Mouchotte; 43-21-56-70; Montparnasse-Bienvenue Métro station) features leading French modern jazz musicians. Entrance costs from about $20 to $30, depending on who's playing.

New Morning (10e; 7–9, rue des Petites-Ecuries; 45-23-51-41; Château d'Eau Métro station) also showcases contemporary jazz, often with an African or Brazilian beat. Visiting American musicians and the best of the French bands perform at this club.

For Dixieland, go to Le Petit Journal St-Michel (5e; 71, blvd St-Michel; 43-26-28-59; Odeon Métro or St-Michel RER station).

Jazz Club Lionel Hampton, in the Hôtel Meridien (17e; 81, blvd Gouvion-St-Cyr; 40-68-43-42; Porte Maillot Métro station) has the reputation of featuring the best American jazz artists. Entrance price, which includes the first drink, is about $26.

To find out who's playing where, get a copy of *Jazz Hot* or *Jazz Magazine* at a newsstand. You don't need to read French to understand the basics; if you do need a translation, ask the concierge or someone at the front desk of your hotel. Cover charge at most jazz clubs is about $20. If there's no cover, it's a good bet that drinks are expensive, and there may be a two-drink minimum.

If you're a true jazz lover, you may want to time your visit to coincide with the "Halle That Jazz" festival in July, when top international stars perform at the Grande Halle of the Parc de la Villette and participate in jam sessions (the French call them *boeufs*). During the annual Paris Jazz Festival, held in October, leading musicians perform at clubs and concert halls throughout the city. By the way, CDs of former jazz greats like Stephane Grappelli and Django Reinhardt often cost less than CDs of any musical genre in the United States.

Though Parisians are often described as "crazy about jazz," about three dozen different kinds of music currently being played—running the gamut from grunge, punk, and power trash to disco-retro, reggae, and rai—were listed in one entertainment publication. Among the larger entertainment venues where a variety of entertainments are performed, Salle Pleyel is a popular venue for big-name musicians ranging from Oscar Peterson to the Orchestre de Paris. Pop singers, rock groups, and other stars of international stature appear at Palais Omnisports Paris (12e; 8, blvd de Bercy; 43-46-12-21; Bercy Métro station), Olympia (9e; 28, blvd des Capucines; 47-42-25-49; Madeleine Métro station), and Le Zenith (19e; 211, av Jean Jaures; 42-40-60-00). Prices vary with the event, but in most cases are no higher than those charged for comparable groups in North America.

A Potpourri of Nightclubs

A popular dance spot is the Slow Club (1er; 130, rue de Rivoli; 42-33-84-30; Louvre Métro station). According to Parisians, some of the best dancers in town show up on this big dance floor.

Another good choice if you have your dancing shoes on is the trendy Balajo (11e; 9, rue de Lappe; 47-00-07-87; Bastille Métro station).

Les Bains (3e; 7, rue du Bourg-l'Abbé; 48-87-01-80; Etienne-Marcel Métro station) is popular with fashion and show-business people. The building, as their name implies, used to be a Turkish bath, which was frequented, incidentally, by Marcel Proust, author of *Remembrance of Things Past.*

The typical cover charge at Paris clubs is about $20. Listings of current entertainment, both classical and contemporary, can be found in publications such as *Where, Paris Midnight,* and *Figaroscope.* (See chapter 13 for more information.)

As far as "gay Paree" is concerned, Queen (8e; 102, av des Champs-Elysées; 53-89-08-90; George V Métro station) is a club that's currently one of the city's most popular with gays, while the lesbian club Le New Monocle (14e; 60, blvd Edgar Quinet; 43-20-81-12; Edgar Quinet Métro station) dates back to the days of Gertrude Stein and Alice B. Toklas. There's no cover charge; drinks are expensive, but after the first one they are half price.

Gay clubs are concentrated primarily in Le Marais and the area around Les Halles. Listings of nightclubs, bars, and restaurants are printed in two publications, *Gay Pied* and *Lesbia*, sold at *tabacs* and news kiosks.

PUTTING ON THE RITZ

When talking to Parisians, often one of my questions is, "What do you do for a sort of special night out—an occasion that isn't important enough for a fancy dinner but is too important for ordinary entertainment?" One of the most frequent responses is, "Get dressed up and have a drink at an upscale bar." You, too, may find it's a great way to experience the glamour of a top Paris hotel or café without having to pony up the price of a superexpensive dinner. A sampling of places that may fill the bill without resulting in an overwhelming tab follows. Most top bars serve soft drinks, mineral water, and glasses of wine, as well as mixed drinks.

At the tiny Hemingway Bar of Hôtel Ritz (1er; 15, place Vendome; Tuileries or Opéra Métro station), it's worth the price of your drink just to watch the totally professional bartenders in action.

Le Café de la Paix (9e; 5, place de l'Opéra; Opéra Métro station) is an elegant place, with ceilings designed by Charles Garnier, architect of the nearby Opéra. Take plenty of time to soak up the atmosphere and opulent surroundings in this national historic monument.

An upscale bar not frequented by tourists is Olivia Valere (8e; 40, rue du Colesee; 42-25-11-68; St-Philippe-du-Roule Métro station).

At the 10th-floor bar of the Hôtel Hilton (15e; 18, av de Suffren; Bir-Hakeim Métro station), you don't need to pinch yourself to realize you're in Paris. Just look out the window for a terrific view of the Eiffel Tower.

Since public transport stops running at about 12:30 A.M., count on taking a taxi or walking to your hotel if you plan a late night out. Unaccompanied women should be leery of riding buses and the Métro in the late hours. Walking along main streets like the Champs-Elysées, however, is considered safe.

Special Events

Additional activities and entertainment are offered as annual events. Among those that appeal to Paris visitors as well as residents are Journée du Patrimoine, held during the third week in September. For two days of the week, some 300 historic museums and monuments are open to the public at no charge.

From October until Christmas, the Festival d'Art Sacré provides the opportunity to see religious art treasures at St-Sulpice, St-Eustache, and St-Germain-des-Pres churches.

Beginning the first of December and continuing until January, the annual Christmas illuminations light up the Grands Boulevards, Opéra, av Montaigne, the Champs-Elysées, and rue du Faubourg-St-Honoré for the holiday season.

At the Bois de Vincennes, the Faire du Trone, complete with bumper cars and *pommes frites,* is popular with Parisian families. Also at the park, on the second, third, and fourth Sunday in April, the gongs and chanting of the Buddhist New Year's celebration compete with the sounds of the fun-fair merrymakers. At Bois de Boulogne, there's also a Shakespeare Garden Festival in mid-April, when works by the Bard are presented in an outdoor setting.

On Poisson d'Avril ("April Fish," the counterpart of our April Fool's Day), pastries, cakes, and breads in the shape of fish are produced by the pâtisseries and boulangeries, and practical jokes are the order of the day.

May Day revelers (on May 1) wear sprigs of lily of the valley in their lapels and congregate in the Bastille area.

Although the day is primarily associated with labor unions, museums and public buildings are closed.

The summer solstice, June 21, is celebrated with Fête de la Music, when every kind of music is played at various venues, indoors and out, around the city.

Also watch for posters and flyers announcing events such as a Yiddish party, advertised on a poster outside Chez Jo Goldenberg restaurant on rue des Rosiers, and a dog show advertised on a kiosk near the Champs-Elysées.

CHAPTER
9

Île-de-France

Outside the Peripherique roadway that encircles Paris lie hundreds of attractions in a somewhat circular area bounded by three rivers, the Marne, the Oise, and the Seine, called Île-de-France. Within easy distance of the capital even in centuries past, the region provided favorite getaway spots for medieval kings and the nobility.

Monet, van Gogh, Pissarro, Rousseau, Millet, and Corot painted its landscapes. Though Île-de-France contains its share of faceless apartment blocks and "New Towns" like Cergy-Pontoise, it also offers a mélange of castles and châteaux, forest trails and riverside paths, historic towns and country villages.

Three Île-de-France destinations—Chartres, Versailles, and Giverny—are described in chapter 10. Until recently, most North American tourists knew little about its other attractions; lately, however, French tourism agencies have begun publicizing the region's pleasures and special places.

Although some wonderful Île-de-France destinations can be reached only by car, those that follow are but a short train ride by either the RER (Réseau Express Régional) or SNCF (Syndicat National Chemin de Fer) railways from Paris that will take you no more than an hour. This makes them great choices for a change of pace when you want to get away from city life for just a morning, afternoon, or early evening.

Only a few minutes beyond the Peripherique lies St-Denis, which was a mecca for medieval France. With a population of 95,000, the city is best known for its cathedral, a Gothic masterpiece built on the site of a fifth-century church. It has been the burial place of kings since King Dagobert was entombed there in 639. It was not exactly their final resting place, however, since during the French Revolution, the remains of 12 centuries' worth of French rulers were disinterred and thrown into a common grave (they were returned to an ossuary in St-Denis's north transept in 1817).

The basilica's collection of 12th- to 17th-century monumental tombs and statues is still intact, as are its magnificent stained-glass rose windows and the 17th-century Carmelite convent, which now houses St-Denis Musée d'Art et d'Histoire.

Also in St-Denis, Stade de France (Zac du Cornillon Nord, St-Denis; 55-93-00-00) was completed in 1998. The 80,000-seat stadium was finished in time to host the opening and final soccer matches of the 16th World Cup. One of the world's most spectacular sites for athletic competitions and major entertainments, it looks like a giant glowing satellite with its translucent, elliptical roof and dramatic lighting throughout. Eighteen monumental staircases, 22 footbridges, and a gently sloping ramp lead to seating on various levels.

In addition to about 20 athletic competitions each year, the stadium also hosts an equal number of major events such as concerts, shows, parades, and sports-related productions on its annual schedule. The Rolling Stones and John Hallyday starred in the venue's first concerts.

Within the stadium are 43 drinks bars and 14 food stands as well as year-round restaurants, including a food court called Le Planisphere. It features sporting themes and a summer terrace, and offers four types of cuisine: Trattoria serves Italian food, while Caffe Ritazza is a Viennese-style eatery. Dorius Rotisserie specializes in different styles of roasted chicken, and L'Escale themes its dishes to the season and the event—tapas, for instance, when France meets Spain in soccer matches.

Fourteen kiosks around the stadium serve as outlets for Stade de France products, and in May 1998, the largest sports shop in Europe—Decathlon—opened opposite the stadium.

Two new railroad stations serve the stadium and are linked to it by huge pedestrian tunnels. To get to St-Denis, take either the RER (line B or D) or Métro (line 13) from Gare du Nord. In summertime, you can also get to Stade de France by boat on the Canal St-Denis from La Villette. Buses also serve the stadium from Porte de la Chapelle, Porte de Clignancourt, and Porte de la Villette on the Peripherique. For ticket information, contact Consortium Stade de France, Service Billetterie, F-93216 St-Denis–La-Plaine Cedex, France.

Montfort-L'Amaury is one of the prettiest towns in the countryside around Paris. Dominated by the stolid tower of the church of St-Pierre (don't miss the magnificent stained-glass windows), the town square is a good starting point for exploring the narrow streets in the heart of town. Among the small houses you'll pass by is one in which Maurice Ravel lived when he composed "Bolero" in 1928 (Musée Ravel, La Belvedere, rue Maurice Ravel; 34-86-00-89). Admission for adults is about $4. Open Monday through Thursday 2 to 5 P.M., weekends 10 A.M. to noon and 2 to 5 P.M. To get to Montfort-L'Amaury, which is 26 miles (42 km) west of Paris, take SCNF Île-de-France from Gare Montparnasse.

Auvers-sur-Oise, in the peaceful Oise River valley 21 miles (32 km) northwest of Paris, is another pretty little town—so charming, in fact, that it attracted Pissarro, Paul Cézanne, and other artists in the last half of the 19th century. Vincent van Gogh, however, is the artist most closely associated with the village.

Van Gogh moved to Auvers in 1890 to be with his brother, Theo, and it was there that during the last 10 weeks of his life, the artist painted some 70 or so pictures before shooting himself. Plaques bearing reproductions of these works have been placed at the sites he painted, so that viewers can compare the past and present.

There are two additional spots you won't want to miss if you are fascinated by the tortured genius who painted such Île-de-France-inspired masterpieces as *L'Eglise d'Auvers* and *Mairie d'Anvers le 15 Juillet 1890*. One is Musée de l'Absinthe (Absinthe Museum; 44, rue Calle; 30-36-83-26), which chronicles the history of the drink said to have been favored by van Gogh. Absinthe was France's national drink before being banned in 1915 because of its damaging effects to the nervous system. Admission is about $5 for adults, and the museum is open Wednesday through Sunday 11 A.M. to 6 P.M., June through September; weekends only, October through May.

The other is Maison de van Gogh, formerly the inn called Auberge Ravoux, where the artist stayed during his last weeks (8, rue de la Sansome; 34-48-07-79). Open Tuesday through Sunday 10 A.M. to 6 P.M.; admission is $6 for adults. To complete your total van Gogh immersion, have lunch at the auberge, where the lace curtains and other furnishings are said to be patterned after the inn's decor when the artist stayed there.

Another attraction in Auvers, Voyage au Temps des Impressionistes (Voyage to the Times of the Impressionists; rue de Lery; 34-48-48-48), is housed in a 17th-century château. The museum provides each visitor with infrared headphones for commentary and viewing the various tableaux that depict life during the days of the impressionists. Especially impressive is the simulated train ride past impressionist scenes. Admission to the museum is about $11 for adults. The museum is open daily 10 A.M. to 8 P.M., May through October; Tuesday through Sunday 10 A.M. to 6:30 P.M., November through April. To get to Auvers, take a SNCF Île-de-France train from Gare du Nord.

An old market town, Meaux is perched on the banks of the Marne and is another of Île-de-France's pleasures. Its castle, which took more than 300 years to complete, is architecturally eclectic, to say the least. The cathedral is open daily 8 A.M. to noon and 2 to 6 P.M. A son et lumière is staged outside the cathedral on most weekend evenings in June and July (60-23-40-00). Next to the cathedral, the Bishops Palace houses Musée Bossuet, with its collection of works by France's old masters. After you've seen the sights, you might want to buy the wherewithal for a picnic beside the river—perhaps a loaf of French bread and some of the deliciously creamy Brie that's produced locally. Meaux, 25 miles (40 km) east of Paris, can be reached by a SNCF train from Gare de l'Est.

Over the Rivers

When you're on the rivers of Île-de-France, you'll see many scenes just as the impressionists saw them. Boat rentals are available at several points along Île-de-France rivers, among them Auvers-sur-Oise, Melun, and Meaux.

Commercial river tours operate out of almost every settlement of significant size located on the Oise, the Seine, or the Marne. You can cruise from Auvers to the Isle of Adam and back for about $10 per person. There's also a two-hour cruise around the islands on the Marne, beginning and ending in Nogent.

Although dinner and disco cruises are available, they're usually a good deal more expensive than those that don't include food or entertainment. (Bring your own snacks along to save even more money, because refreshments sold on sightseeing cruises are generally overpriced.)

And Through the Woods

Vast tracts of forest in various parts of Île-de-France are ideal for hiking and bicycling. The most popular are St-Germain, Fontainebleau, and Rambouillet. But don't worry about armies of thousands trudging through the woods. Though swarms of people visit the forests' centerpiece towns and châteaux each day, the wooded areas are large enough to accommodate everyone.

St-Germain-en-Laye, on a hill overlooking the Seine and surrounded by forest, is just 10 miles (16 km) west of Paris. It's an elegant city containing several well-known points of interest. Château de Monte Cristo at Port-Morly on the southern edge of St-Germain (av du President Kennedy; 30-16-49-49) is the mansion built in the 1840s by Alexandre Dumas, author of *The Count of Monte Cristo* and *The Three Musketeers*. Financed with the proceeds—real and anticipated—from his novels, the château is the epitome of overdecoration, with a facade incorporating fanciful stone carvings and pillars. Dumas wasn't able to enjoy his ostentatious home for long: He went bankrupt in 1849 and spent the rest of his life as an exile in Belgium. Admission is about $4 for adults. The château is open Tuesday through Sunday 10 A.M. to 6 P.M., April through October. Château de St-Germain, in front of the RER station, dates from the 16th and 17th centuries. To get to St-Germain, take the express Métro (RER, line A) with main stations at Etoile and Les Halles.

The castle at Fontainebleau is considered by some experts on the subject to be more opulent than Versailles. However, the gardens designed by Versailles's landscape architect, André le Notre, are not as magnificent. Highlights of the château inlcude the ballroom and a marvelous collection of painted plates. Admission to the castle is about $5.25, and guided tours of the garden cost about $4.

Despite the castle's magnificence, the main reason for anyone who loves the outdoors to visit Fontainebleau is its forest. With heather- and gorse-covered moors, rocky hills, and serene valleys, it's also a place where you'll come upon hyacinths and daffodils in spring, carnations in summer. If you know where to look, you'll find tiny wild strawberries in midsummer, and wild raspberry bushes, heavy with fruit, in late July and August.

You may not see creatures of the forest such as foxes, deer, and wild boars, since they prefer that you don't. But you will most likely catch glimpses of squirrels as they scamper up and down the trees, and of the Fontainebleau woodpecker. To get to Fontainebleau, which is about 42 miles (60 km) southeast of Paris, take RER (line D) to Fontainebleau station.

On the western edge of Fontainebleau forest, the members of the Barbizon School of painters (which included Camille Corot, Jean-François Millet, and Theodore Rousseau) lived in the village of Barbizon from the 1830s. These landscape painters, best known as the forerunners of impressionism, were at times literally starving artists and bartered their works for food.

You can see remnants of the frescoes they painted at the local inn, now Musée de l'Ecole Barbizon (Barbizon School Museum, formerly Auberge Ganne; 92, Grande Rue; 60-66-22-27). Also at the museum, you can take a short beginners' course in painting, with the canvas you've produced as a souvenir. Admission to the museum is about $4. It is open Wednesday through Monday 10 A.M. to 12:30 P.M. and 2 to 5 P.M.

Other attractions in Barbizon include former ateliers of both Rousseau (55, Grande Rue; 60-66-22-38) and Millet (27, Grande Rue), where Millet's famous work, *The Gleaners,* is on display.

To get to Barbizon, take a taxi from Fontainebleau station, which is about five miles away. Buses don't run during summer.

Though Château Rambouillet is less spectacular than Fontainebleau, its almost 50,000-acre forest is a delight, with paths through old villages, beside lakes, and along rivers. The northern part of the forest, more isolated than the rest, is especially popular with fishermen.

Rambouillet is also a destination for model-train enthusiasts. Musée Rambolitrain (4, place Jeanne-d'Arc; 34-83-15-93), which is the repository for about 4,000 models and more than 1,300 feet of track, is Frances's premier model-train museum.

Among the highlights are models of historic steam engines as well as early-day railway stations. Admission to the museum is about $3 for adults. It's open Wednesday through Sunday 10 A.M. to noon and 2 to 5:30 P.M. To get to Ramboiullet, take the SNFC Île-de-France from Gare Montparnasse.

There are many other woodlands and meadows with hiking paths within the Paris orbit. Vallée de Chevreuse, with its quiet, twisting lanes and castle ruins, is only about 20 miles (30 km) southwest, and Val-de-Marne is less than 5 miles south of the Peripherique.

WHERE TO GO? WHAT TO DO?

When you find yourself with a few unscheduled hours and want to spend them exploring the attractions and aspects of Île-de-France, here are a few ideas.

- Go riverdancing. There are still a few *guingettes* (riverside cafés) along the Marne just east of Paris, where people dance to the strains of accordion music as they did in the days of the impressionists, who captured them on canvas. It's not exactly swing-dancing, but it's fun.
- If dancing's not your thing, but rivers and canals are, go for a walk along one of them. Most towns along the Île-de-France waterways have promenades and paths to follow. You'll pass by marinas, abbeys, churches, and châteaux; small farms, villages, and riverside cafés.

  St-Mammès, named for the patron saint of boatmen, is a captivating village at the confluence of the Seine and the Loing rivers that's a favorite with meanderers (southeast of Paris via train from Gare de Lyon). Another great river-strolling town, closer to Paris, is Nogent-sur-Marne, known for its folk festivals, boat races, and charming vistas. To get to Nogent, take RER (line A) from Gare de Lyon to the Nogent station.

  You might also want to hike along the tree-shaded Canal de l'Ourcq, which goes all the way from Paris to beyond Meaux.

Railway points (trains leave from Gare du Nord) along the canal's route include Pantin, Bobigny, and Tremblay-en-France.

Conflans-Ste-Honorine, at the junction of the Seine and the Oise, is another fascinating place for water-watchers, since hundreds of barges moor there. The very best day to visit is the last Sunday in June, Feast of the Pardon, when a procession of decorated barges arrives from Paris (one of the barges bears a torch lit from the Eternal Flame under the Arc de Triomphe). Trains go from Gare St-Lazare and Gare de Lyon to Conflans-Ste-Honorine, which is northeast of Paris.

- Bask in the sun's rays at the river beach of Isle-Adam. This superbly picturesque town 22 miles (35 km) north of Paris has a sandy stretch along the river near rue de Beaumont, frequented mostly by area residents. Be sure to bring along the sunscreen. Valmondois on the SNCF Île-de-France line (catch the train at Gare du Nord) is the station that's close to Isle-Adam.
- Admire the 16th- and 17th-century Flemish and French tapestries and furniture at the Musée de la Renaissance in the little town of Ecouen. Housed in a château, the exhibits are well worth going out of your way to see (39-90-04-04). Open Wednesday through Monday 9:45 A.M. to 12:30 P.M. and 2 to 5:15 P.M. Admission is about $3.75 for adults ($2.60 on Sunday). To get to Ecouen, take an SNCF train from Gare du Nord.
- Wander the crooked streets of Senlis with no set itinerary. If you get lost, just look skyward at the Gothic cathedral spire, said to be the country's most exquisite. Though there are two commendable museums in Senlis, the town's medieval architecture is its most remarkable attraction. Senlis is about 28 miles (45 km) north of Paris.
- Tour the Musée Conde in Château de Chantilly, 23 miles north of Paris. Major works by illustrious painters such as Raphael and Fouquet, the Book of Hours of the Duc de Berry, and some gorgeous stained-glass windows are only a few of the treasures in this outstanding art repository (44-57-03-62). Open Wednesday through Monday 10 A.M. to 6 P.M., March through October; 10:30 A.M. to 12:45 P.M. and 2 to 5 P.M. the rest of the year. Admission is a little more than $5 for adults. Both Senlis and Chantilly can be reached by trains from Gare du Nord.

- Look over the 200 exhibits mirroring the history of flight at the Musée de l'Air et de l'Espace (Aerospace Museum) in le Bourget. Displays in seven buildings range from the first primitive engines used in flying machines to state-of-the-art rockets. To get to le Bourget, take an RER train (line B) from Gare du Nord.
- Marvel at artist Jean Cocteau's paintings on the walls of 12th-century Chapelle St-Blaise-des-Simples in Milly-la-Forêt. Cocteau, who lived in the town, used the theme of medicinal plants (simples) in his marvelous decorative art (the carved wood statue of the saint is wonderful, too). Milly-la-Forêt is known for herb growing and for its 15th-century covered market. To get to the town, take the train to Fontainebleau, then a bus or taxi.

Île-de-France Festivities

In addition to its picturesque villages and natural beauty spots, Île-de-France is famous for its celebrations. Though they aren't the sort of affairs you see on listings of major French festivals, to my mind they are more enjoyable, because they offer samplings of local color, history, and regional food specialties in more serene settings—and give you a chance to rub shoulders with the locals.

One of the most interesting is Fêtes Medievales of Provins in June, which features troubadors, jesters on stilts, and colorful parades of townsfolk, resplendent in costumes of Middle Ages nobility. The production involves some 1,800 people, among them about 100 horsemen.

In addition, each day from April to September, the spectacle of free-flying birds recalls the time when falconry was one of the favorite activities of the nobility. Provins, which is known for its crimson roses and remarkably well-preserved medieval town walls, also presents mini festivals called Soirées Medievals (Medieval Evenings) during summer. About 50 miles (80 km) southeast of Paris, the city is served by SNCF Île-de-France railway.

Another medieval festival—this one in Bourron-Marlotte—differs from the usual in that visitors move past the various tableaux staged in courtyards, on staircases, in gateways, and other locations at Château-Landon. The château, at the southern edge of Île-de-France, is served by train and connecting bus from Gare de Lyon.

For those interested in historical sites, Heritage Days, held on the third weekend of September, can be a real money saver. During the event, about 800 sites on Île-de-France are open to the public, many of them free. A variety of theatrical events and pageants, special guided tours of towns and villages, as well as exhibitions and concerts, also take place at venues throughout the region.

In addition to festivals, there are garden shows such as Coursin's annual Plant Day in October, with both garden and indoor plants on display in a setting of green lawns, old brick, and weathered roofs. Art shows, music festivals, and crafts fairs are other events listed in the quarterly programs of *Festivals and Events in Île-de-France*, published by the Comité Régional du Tourisme d'Île-de-France, 91, av des Champs-Elysées, 75008 Paris (56-89-38-00). Another informative publication the organization offers is *Heritage Sites in the Île-de-France*. The attractively illustrated booklet includes suggestions for nature walks in several areas of Île-de-France, as well as village strolls and visits to museums, gardens, and other points of interest.

10

Beyond Paris—Day Trips and Excursions

As far as energy saving is concerned, there's a lot to be said for staying in the same Paris hotel room every night and seeing the countryside on a series of short trips. You don't have to pack and unpack, or worry about trying to get accustomed to another bed every night or so. But perhaps best of all, if you're having a wonderful time exploring your day-trip destination, you can stay until the last train leaves for Paris, knowing you'll have a room waiting. By the same token, if it doesn't live up to your expectations—too big, too many tourists, the weather's rotten—you're not committed to stay. You can go back on the next train and find something that pleases you more.

For independent travelers, the best way to go about day-tripping is by train or rental car (taking possession of the car in the outskirts of Paris so you won't have to contend with inner-city traffic). When you plan to take two or three day trips that don't involve more than an hour's rail travel each way, you'll find that buying return rail tickets for each trip is most economical if you're traveling alone. Second-class accommodations are all you'll need for short trips, and fares are quite reasonable (there's a 50 percent discount for people 60 and over; see chapter 12). If you're planning on a couple of day trips and a longer excursion by rail, a France Railpass will be your most economical answer. Two people traveling together via France Railpass will save 25 percent of the passes' total cost (see chapter 1).

Two or more people will save money on most day trips and some longer excursions with a rental car. However, when your destination is another French city where most of the major sights are located in the heart of town, you may find that taking the train is far less of a hassle than having to contend with traffic and parking.

When you're taking trains to your day-trip destinations, it's important to go to the right railway station to catch them. Since there are seven different stations in Paris, it isn't hard to get confused. Gare du Nord serves northern France as well as traveling to and from northern Europe and to England via Calais or Boulogne. Eurostar, the new high-speed trains that go through the channel tunnel, also leave from Gare du Nord.

Gare de Lyon trains go to and from Lyons, Marseilles, and the Riviera as well as to Geneva and Italy. Trains to the Loire Valley, southwest France, and Spain originate at Gare d'Austerlitz. However, many of the TGV trains (the fast ones) go out of Gare Montparnasse.

Not only are there several train stations, but the larger ones have more than one set of quays (platforms) from which trains leave. At Gare d'Austerlitz, for example, one set of quays is identified with letters and the other with numbers. It's a good plan to arrive at the station early so you can determine your train's departure location; it may involve a fair walk. At least 30 minutes in advance, each train's number, departure time, and quay number appear on a large, prominently displayed board.

You may have noticed that I haven't mentioned anything about bus travel. Though there's great bus service in cities and the areas around them, long-distance bus travel in France is uncommon (except by tour bus), and there is no central bus depot in Paris.

If you decide to use an automobile for your trips outside Paris, you must make rental car arrangements before you leave home unless you want to pay a small fortune. Making rental arrangements through a company in the United States will cost as little as $31.50 a day (including 20.6 percent tax); it can cost you as much as $85 for the same car in Europe. You may be able to get one for less than that, but don't count on it. Therefore, if you decide to rent a car on the spur of the moment, it's worth your while to call the United States to do it. Also, when you're figuring expenses, don't forget that gasoline is very expensive; about $1 a liter, which translates to a little less than $4 a gallon.

When you're deciding on destinations, keep in mind that several major French cities—cultural centers in their own right—are within an hour or 90 minutes of Paris. Small villages with great historical or artistic significance are near at hand, too. Still other places qualify as great spots to visit simply because they're quaint, charming, or provide a change of pace from the city. Add cities like Brussels (two and a half hours away), Cologne (five hours), and London (three hours via Eurostar—a real bargain when you can buy one-way tickets for about $55)—all doable in a day—and you'll begin to appreciate the scope of your options. Since there are so many choices, I'm going to suggest a potpourri of possibilities—all of them in France.

Opulence and Ostentation

The Palace and Gardens of Versailles, the most popular of Paris day trips, are only a half hour's train ride from Paris. You can get there by train or auto (autoroute A13, then A12; parking is on place d'Armes in front of the palace). You can catch the line C RER at Left Bank stations including St-Michel and Musée d'Orsay. Main-line railroad trains that originate at Gare St-Lazare and Gare Montparnasse also stop at Versailles. The least expensive route is to take Métro line 9 to Porte Sevres, transfer to bus number 171, and get off near the palace gates (the one-way cost is three Métro tickets; if you've bought a *carnet,* this amounts to about $2.40). You'll enjoy this excursion more if you brush up on your French history in advance. You'll also have a better time if you wear comfortable shoes; the grounds cover 100 hectares (241.7 acres).

The evolution of Versailles from the simple hunting lodge of Louis XIII to the largest palace in Europe started with Louis XIV, who expanded and embellished the property during one of the longest reigns in history—72 years. His successors, Louis XV and Louis XIV, carried on, adding their own touches. The result was a palace big enough to house 20,000—members of the nobility, their servants, and 9,000 soldiers; formal gardens unequaled anywhere; a mile-long canal; a zoo; two weekend retreats (the Grand and the Petit Trianon) with their own grounds; ponds; fountains; and more than 100 statues.

Within the palace are the Grands Appartements and the Petits Appartements. The former are the most opulent, with the Hall of Mirrors—a 223-foot-long extravagance of crystal chandeliers reflected again and again through looking glasses—as the main attraction. The Petits Appartements, which were occupied by the royal family and the kings' mistresses, are almost plain by comparison.

There's so much to see at Versailles that it would take more than a day for anyone with average stamina to take it all in. Many people don't stay more than a few hours, however, because seeing too much of Versailles is rather like eating an extremely rich meal. There are separate admission charges for the château (about $6.30), Grands Appartements (about $6.30), Grand Trianon (about $3.50), and Petit Trianon (about $2.10), as well as extra charges for guided tours—necessary if you want to see the Petits Appartements. All admissions are half price on Sunday.

In summer the palace is open from 9 A.M. to 6:30 P.M.; it closes an hour earlier in winter. Grand and Petit Trianon hours are 10 A.M. to 6:30 P.M. in summer, and in winter from

10 A.M. to 12:30 P.M. and 2 to 5:30 P.M. Admission to the gardens is free. They open at 7 A.M. and close anywhere from 5:30 to 9:30 P.M., depending on the season, and are a great place for bicycling. Bicycles can be rented near the Grand Canal from 10 A.M. to 7 P.M. for about $6 an hour.

There are three-and-a-half- to five-hour commercial tours available to Versailles, which include transportation and entrance tickets but are sometimes without guided tours. Full-day tours include guided visits to the Grand Trianon, the Petit Trianon, Marie Antoinette's Hamlet—where she and her courtiers pretended to be peasants—the state apartments, queen's apartment, Reception Salons, and Hall of Mirrors. They cost about $52.

Simply Beautiful

In sharp contrast to Versailles is Giverny, where the impressionist painter Claude Monet lived from 1883 to 1926. Only about an hour from Paris, it's a favorite excursion for people who adore flowers. In 1890, Monet, after years of living off the kindness of friends, finally became successful as an artist, and he bought the pink brick house with its green shutters that he had been renting for several years and began to transform its garden. Three years later, he acquired land on the other side of the street and commenced work on his water garden: a lily pond straddled by a Japanese bridge.

After World War II, the property fell into disrepair, and restoration wasn't undertaken until 1980. Today, the garden—re-created to what it was under Monet's care—is one of the natural beauties of France. In spring, it blossoms with narcissi, tulips, azaleas, rhododendrons, lilacs, wisteria, and irises, which Monet particularly loved and planted in long, wide rows.

Next come the peonies, bellflowers, lilies, delphinium, lupine, and poppies. Summer brings morning glories, sweet peas, blanketflowers, stock, columbine, foxglove, nasturtiums, phlox, gentians, and dozens of varieties of roses. Among the autumn flowers are Japanese anemones, dahlias, sunflowers, hollyhocks, and asters.

After the garden was re-created, work began on renovating the house, also open to the public. Especially charming are the kitchen, with blue and white tiles on the walls, and the cheerful yellow dining room. Monet's collection of Japanese prints decorates the walls of the house. (None of the artist's paintings is exhibited at Giverny.) Admission to the house and garden costs about $4.90.

A treasure in the village that many visitors miss is the Museum of American Art (99, rue Claude Monet; 2-32-51-94-65), where works of American artists such as Winslow Homer and Mary Cassatt, associated with the French impressionists, are displayed. It's open Tuesday through Sunday 10 A.M. to 6 P.M; admission is about $4.90. To reach the museum, turn left after exiting the grounds and take the road that's behind Monet's house.

One couple who frequently spends summers in Paris have made a ritual of their Giverny trips. They ride the train that leaves at about 7:30 A.M. from Gare St-Lazare to Vernon, where buses wait to take passengers to the village. Upon arrival 50 minutes later, they have coffee at the café across from the museum, then tour the garden. Each visit is different, they say, because of the changing combinations of flowers.

The one-hour train ride costs about $34 for second-class round-trip. By car, Giverny is reached by taking autoroute A13 to Vernon, then D5 to Giverny. Commercial tours from Paris, which last four and a half hours and include visits to Monet's home, workshop, and garden, cost from about $50 to $70, depending on which tour company is used.

Architectural Triumphs

The majority of tourists go to Chartres to see its cathedral, and no wonder. The church, third largest in the world after

St. Peter's in Rome and Canterbury in England, dates to the 13th century, but some portions of its 12th-century front still survive. The first cathedral in which flying buttresses were used, its rib vaults soar to heights of 121 feet, and the stone carvings, both inside and out, are superb.

However, it's the cathedral's windows that are most impressive, representing the most remarkable collection of stained glass in the world. The windows, the majority of which were created during the 13th century, illustrate the Bible, the lives of the saints, and the traditional crafts of France. They're at their most magnificent in late afternoon on a sunny day.

After you've visited the cathedral, take some time to walk around Chartres, a worthwhile destination in itself. It's situated on the River Eure, which offers a series of picture-postcard views along its banks—an old mill and washhouses, a 12th-century tower, and stone buildings hundreds of years old.

To explore the old parts of the city, with their narrow cobbled streets and medieval houses, you can follow a signposted itinerary that begins at the cathedral square. Cassettes with headphones for a 60-minute, self-guided tour are available on loan from the Office de Tourisme (place de la Cathedrale).

There are several museums in town, among them the Fine Arts Museum behind the cathedral (37-36-41-39; open daily except Tuesday; free admission) and the School Museum (1, rue de 14 Juillet; 37-28-57-90; open Wednesday and by appointment).

The Agriculture and Agricultural Machinery Museum (Pont de Mainvilliers; 37-36-11-30; open daily except Saturday) is considered France's most important museum dedicated to agriculture.

While you're in Chartres, don't neglect to sample the two local delicacies, Pâté de Chartres and Mentchikoffs, the browned-almond chocolates created to celebrate the Franco-Russian alliance in 1893.

It takes 70 minutes to reach Chartres from Paris's Gare Montparnasse. Second-class rail fare is about $38 for a round-trip ticket. If you're driving, take autoroute A10 or A11. Five-hour commercial tours, which include transportation, a visit to the cathedral, and time to stroll around the old city, cost about $51. This is a case where a commercial tour may be almost the least expensive way to get to Chartres, but your time in the city will be less than three hours.

Rouen is a favorite destination of travelers who are intrigued by history. Not only is it the place where Joan of Arc was burned at the stake, but from the time of the early Vikings to the World War II invasions, this part of Normandy has figured heavily in the events of France.

It's an old city. The Cathedrale Notre Dame, consecrated in 1063, was rebuilt after the great fire of 1200. Money for building the cathedral's Tour de Beurre (Tower of Butter) came from parishioners who paid for permission to eat butter during Lent. King Richard the Lion-Hearted is buried in the Chapelle de la Vierge.

It's about a six-block walk from the cathedral to the place du Vieux-Marché (Old Marketplace), where Joan of Arc, chained to a stake, was burned alive. A bronze cross marks the stake's position; there's also a museum on the square, which chronicles the saint's life. (Open 9:30 A.M. to 6:30 P.M., May through October; 10 A.M. to noon and 2 to 6 P.M., November through April. Admission is charged.

Before you walk from the cathedral to the marketplace, stop in at the tourist office on cathedral square for a map of the city and information on various attractions. You'll find that in addition to an outstanding botanical garden, there are several museums. One of the most unusual is Musée Le Secq des Tournelles (Museum of Wrought Iron), housed in the 15th-century church of St-Laurent (rue Jacques Villon; 35-08-81-81). Ranging in style from ponderous to lacy filigree, items on display include everything from keys to kitchen utensils and jewelry to garden gates. The admission charge is minimal.

It would be easy to spend the whole day on a do-it-yourself architectural tour of the old city, wandering up and down the streets at will. Styles are more diverse than you find in equal-sized areas of Paris, since half-timbered houses, Gothic churches and public buildings, medieval towers and Belle Epoche mansions are all within steps of each other. Another option is to stroll along the Seine, with its giant cranes, plea-sure boats, and commercial vessels as well as some magnifi-cent views of the city.

The train ride from Gare St-Lazare in Paris to Rouen takes 1 hour and 10 minutes. Round-trip tickets cost about $56 for second class.

Renaissance by the River

If you have but one day and are determined to see a part of the Loire Valley—many travelers consider it a destination in itself—you can do it without spending a lot of money, espe-cially if you have done some logistical spadework in advance.

Stretching from the Atlantic to its source in the Ardeche *départment* in southeast France, the Loire is the country's longest river. Its valley, with fields, meadows, and vineyards, is made even more lovely by dozens of castlelike châteaux, built during the Renaissance by kings and members of the nobility. With turrets, towers, and opulently appointed interiors, the châteaux vary in size from huge to enormous. Each one is different, yet there's a certain fairy-tale quality about them all.

You'll be able to maximize your sight-seeing time traveling by rental car. Armed with a publication put out by the Tours Office de Tourisme, *Pays aux Châteaux*, which lists all the châteaux in the central Loire Valley that are open to the public, follow autoroute A10 from Paris to Orléans, then take route 152 (it roughly parallels A10) from Orléans to Blois and on to Tours. If you're short of time on the return trip, you can take A10 all the way back to Paris. The distance from Paris to Tours, without allowing for turnoff roads to the various châteaux, is approximately 150 miles.

The greatest concentration of châteaux and manor houses is in the Tours and Blois areas, including the two most famous—Chenonceau and Chambord (expect huge crowds at both of them). Entrance to the château and gardens of Chenonceau costs about $8, while Chambord's admission fee is about $7. You don't have to pay to go inside a few of the châteaux, but most have admission charges ranging from $2 to $6.

One-day commercial tours to the Loire Valley originating in Paris cost from about $139 to $199. The less expensive tours, which leave Paris at about 7:15 A.M. and returns at 8 P.M., include guided tours of Chenonceau and Chambord, as well as a visit to Cheverny, but don't always include lunch. The more expensive, 12- to 13½-hour tours usually feature a visit to Chambord, the Clos Luce (Leonardo da Vinci's last dwelling), a walk through the medieval streets of Amboise with an outside view of its château, a restaurant lunch, and guided tour of the château and gardens of Chenonceau.

Even if you don't want to contend with driving, you can save money by taking an early train to Tours (from Gare Montparnasse at 6:55 A.M., changing trains at the St-Pierre-des-Corps station, arriving in Tours at 8:06) or Blois (from Gare d'Austerlitz at 6:20 A.M., arriving in Blois at 8:19). Then catch one of the local tours that leave from the Office de Tourisme in Tours or the rail station in Blois. Round-trip second-class tickets to Blois cost $56, and to Tours, $102. Though the scope of the excursion is greater at Tours, the rather hefty train fare makes it less economical than the Blois option.

Tour prices out of Tours range from $20 to $32, depending on their length. The Blois tours cost from $20 to $39. The less expensive tours feature visits to Chenonceau and Chambord. The most expensive tour, which includes visits to Chenonceau, Amboise, Chaumont, and Chambord, lasts approximately 9 hours and 45 minutes. All of the tours leave at between 8:30 and 9 A.M.; in most cases, a different tour is offered each day of the week from March through October. Reservations for tours originating in Blois can be made by phoning 54-32-43-09, whereas the numbers to call for Tours-originating excursions are 47-05-46-09 (Gare SNCF tours) or 47-70-37-37 (Office de Tourisme).

Tapestries That Tell Stories

While Bayeux and Angers won't head the day-trip list for most travelers, they will for people who are interested in medieval wall hangings. The Bayeux Tapestry, most famous in the world, is displayed in a quiet town 166 miles northwest of Paris. According to legend, it was made by Mathilda, wife of William the Conqueror, but more likely it was a commissioned work produced by Saxon embroiderers.

The 20-inch-wide band of linen, which is more than 230 feet long, portrays 58 different scenes telling the story of the Norman Conquest of England. An incongruous touch is the inclusion of scenes from Aesop's Fables in the tapestry's borders. The tapestry is displayed in a glass case at Musée de la Tapisserie de Bayeux (Centre Guillaume-le-Conquerant, rue de Nesmond; 31-92-05-48). The museum is open 9 A.M. to 7 P.M., mid-May to mid-September; 9 A.M. to 12:30 P.M. and 2 to 6:30 P.M., mid-September to mid-October; 9:30 A.M. to 12:30 P.M. and 2 to 6 P.M. the rest of the year. Admission is about $5.60.

The castle at Angers contains the finest collection of medieval and Renaissance tapestries anywhere, including the world's largest medieval tapestry. Commissioned in 1375 by Louis I, duke of Anjou, this supersized work depicts the Apocalypse. The castle is open 9 A.M to 7 P.M., June through September 15; 9:30 A.M. to 12:30 P.M. and 2 to 6 P.M. the rest of the year. Admission is about $6.

Although the castle itself is a rather ugly 17-towered affair, you'll find several more aesthetically pleasing buildings nearby. Since Angers is in the western portion of the Loire.

Valley château country, you might want to visit one or two of them while you're in the area (the elegant Château de Saumur is only a half hour's train ride away).

Angers is also a wine promotion center, with a number of tasting cellars in the surrounding wine villages. Maps of the tourist route through the western Loire Valley vineyards are available at the Angers Office de Tourisme (place Kennedy; 41-88-69-93).

To get to Angers from Paris, take a train from Gare Montparnasse (the trip takes 90 minutes and costs about $116 round-trip), or drive on A11 and route 23. Bayeux is accessible from Angers by either train or bus.

A Cathedral, Champagne, and Concerts

The three major reasons for visiting Reims, 90 miles northeast of Paris, all begin with the letter *C*. First of all, there's the magnificent cathedral where all the kings of France from Louis VII in 1137 to Charles X in 1825 were crowned. Nearby, in the Palais du Tau, which was formerly the archbishop's palace, the tapestries, sculptures, and artifacts from those coronations are on display. Then there's champagne, which can only be called by that name if its grapes are grown within an 84,000-acre area, the boundaries of which are officially limited by French law. Three factors, experts say, contribute to the final product—the chalky soil where the vines are planted; the microclimates within the region, enabling wines with different characteristics to be combined; and the chalk mines, with their 90 percent humidity and constant temperature of 9 to 10.5 degrees Centigrade, where the champagne wine is "fizzed."

You can learn all about the champagne-making process and sample the finished products by visiting the various champagne houses. Mumm (34, rue du Champ de Mars; 26-49-59-70), Taittinger (9, place St-Nicaise; 26-85-45-35), Pommery (5, place du General Gouraud; 26-61-62-55), and Piper Heidsieck (51, blvd Henry Vasnier; 26-84-43-44) charge small fees (usually about $4 per person) for visits to their cellars. The other champagne makers offer visits by appointment only. The *Route Touristique du Champagne*, with lots of maps and color photos, is available at the Office de Tourisme de Reims (2, rue Guillaume de Machault; 26-77-45-25. It suggests seven different signposted auto routes to vineyards and champagne villages.

Most of the cathedral was constructed during the 13th century, and grapes have probably been grown in Reims since before that time. The third *C*, however, stands for a recent innovation. Reims's summer concerts were inaugurated in 1990. As a result, each July and August, 120 performances of folk, jazz, and classical music are presented at various venues throughout the city. Whether the music is performed at the cathedral, the Palais du Tau, or the St-Remi Basilica; in cafés, public gardens or by construction projects, most of the concerts are free.

When you're hungry, be sure to enjoy the cuisine for which the region is famous—*boudin blanc* (white sausage), local Ardenne and Reims hams, and cheese specialties including Brie de champagne, Maroilles, and Fromage de Langres. For dessert, two traditional pastries—*gateau mollet* and *galette ardennaise*—as well as Biscuits de Reims, Massepains (made of marzipan), and *pain d'epices* are specialties. The latter dates back to the 16th century, when Reims was the center of a flourishing gingerbread-making industry.

The train ride from Paris's Gare de l'Est to Reims takes about one and a half hours and costs $54 for a second-class round-trip ticket. Autoroute A4 goes between the two cities.

Four Seaside Charmers

For a complete change of pace, people who know France very well suggest day-tripping to one or more of the upper Normandy beach towns both north and south of the mouth of the Seine.

South of the Seine, Deauville has been more than socially acceptable since its founding in 1859. First it was a favorite of royalty and the nobility, then of Hollywood celebrities like Gloria Swanson. Today, it's big with the super-rich, which all makes for great people-watching. You can easily spend an afternoon looking over the rich, the famous, and the wannabes as they stroll by on the boardwalk, bet on the ponies at the town's two racetracks, or ride them at the local polo grounds. The crowd is at its most glamourous in early September, when the annual Deauville Film Festival takes place.

About a dozen miles northeast, Honfleur is the town that fits everyone's mental image of a charming fishing village. Dating to the 11th century, its most picturesque area is the Vieux Bassin (Old Harbor), with its slate-roofed houses and wooden fishing boats. You'll enjoy it more if you arrive early, before the tourist hordes descend.

North of the Seine, Fécamp's touristic centerpiece is the magnificent Benedictine distillery and museum. The old distilling chamber where the liqueur was first produced is part of the distillery tour. The museum is open daily 9:30 to 11:30 A.M. and 2 to 5:30 P.M. The admission charge is about $5.

Etretat, with its white cliffs and sea arches, is a good choice if you want to experience some spectacular hiking: It's possible to walk along the cliffs to Fécamp. Smaller than most of the towns on the upper Normandy coast, Etretat is also a place where you can sample everyday village life. Pop in at the boulangerie for a *pain au chocolat,* sit on a bench and look out at the English Channel, watch the *poste* delivery person, the butcher, and the flower seller as they go about their daily routines. All the day will cost you is your rail fare and lunch money.

If you want to make the trip to upper Normandy by train, leave from Gare St-Lazare in Paris and ride to Le Havre (90 minutes; about $54 for second-class round-trip), where you can catch a bus to your destination. Bus service between towns along the coast is frequent, so you won't have to wait long.

Traveling Farther Afield

Belle-Île, the largest of some 60 or so islands that lie off the French coast between St-Malo and La Rochelle, was a favorite of Claude Monet and Henri Matisse, as well as thousands of 19th-century Parisians. As time went by, the beautiful isle faded as a popular tourist destination, and time on the island seemingly stood still.

Now, it's again a Parisian favorite—perhaps because it still is much as it was in the days of Monet and Matisse. With standing stones that date back 5,000 years, stone crosses at the intersections of roads, and stone houses; wildflowers, wild beaches, and a wildly changing sky, the island is Brittany at its best. The locals hunt for mussels among the rocks at low tide and pick their desserts from tangles of blackberry bushes. Fishermen sell sole and scallops at portside markets, and farmers sell cheeses from roadside stalls. Eleven miles long, Belle-Île is a land of lobster traps, lighthouses, and ewes with a tendency to produce sextuplets.

Though the island is hilly, the best way to see it is on foot or by bicycle (bikes rent for around $10 a day). Guided horseback rides cost about $50 for a half day. During the annual French summer holidays, from about mid-July to the end of August, the island is crowded, so you'll probably enjoy it more at other times of the year.

To get to Belle-Île, take the TGV from Gare Montparnasse to Auray (about four hours), then a shuttle bus to the ferry quay at Quiberon. Ferries run regularly on a daily basis, and the trip takes 45 minutes. If you decide to stay overnight on the island—and you probably will—be sure to get a room with a view.

Day trips just won't do for two of Europe's most popular resort areas—the French Riviera and Biarritz—even if you travel by plane. There's just too much to see and do. Whether they call it the French Riviera, Côte d'Azur, or les Alpes Maritimes, that 120-kilometer strip of seaside real estate between St-Tropez and Menton is one of the world's premier—and priciest—vacation destinations.

No two of the Riviera sun spots are exactly alike. While Nice is France's fifth largest city, with congested traffic and a host of tourist attractions, places like Beaulieu-sur-Mer and Villefranche are known for laid-back luxury, with terrace dining, picturesque harbors, and mega-yachts anchored in the water. St-Jean-Cap-Ferrat and Cap d'Ail (Greta Garbo had a villa there) provide the seclusion that, on the Riviera, only money can buy.

Cannes is known as the glamour queen of the Côte d'Azur, in part because of the annual Cannes Film Festival, but also because of its Belle Epoche buildings. And it isn't hard to understand why artists like Picasso have been attracted to Antibes's Old Town.

From Nice to Menton, three roads parallel the sea. Basse Corniche (the low road or Corniche Inferieur) follows the shore. It passes through Beaulieu and Villefranche and by the Cap Ferrat and Cap Martin peninsulas. Moyenne Corniche, the middle road, and Grande Corniche, which climbs as high as 1,600 feet, are the view routes, although drivers need to keep their eyes on the road.

May, June, and September are the best months weatherwise, but April and October can be superb. July and August are warm, but not compared with most of North America. That's when the Riviera is most crowded, however. During the rest of the year, the climate is variable, but usually better than in most other parts of the country.

The most logical place to headquarter during your Riviera stay is Nice, since it's centrally located, with most of the accommodations as well as attractions near at hand.

Hotel rooms on the Riviera are almost as expensive as those in Paris. Prices at the Holiday Inn Nice (20, blvd Victor

Hugo; 93-16-55-00) cost about $110.60 to $189. At Hotel Sofitel Nice (2–4, parvis de l'Europe; 92-00-80-00), rates are about $133 to $168. At Sofitel's Hôtel Splendid, also in Nice (50, blvd Victor Hugo; 93-16-41-00), rooms are from approximately $138.60 to $189. Fortunately, some good deals can be found by checking around. For example, the two Sofitel hotels in Nice offer their double rooms during their "Winter Sale" and "Summer Sale" for about 40 percent off the regular rate.

If you arrive without reservations, go to the Tourist Information Office either at the main rail station in Nice, at the airport, or on Nice's Promenade de l'Anglais. Look in their brochure racks for specials. For example, when new hotels open along the Riviera, brochures advertising their special opening rates are displayed at these information centers. Promotional rates are often less than half of what the rates will be when the hotels have become established, and frequently include additional features such as complimentary breakfasts.

These offices are also sources for booklets and brochures on Côte d'Azur attractions that often include discount coupons and information on current promotions that will save you money. Also available, the bus route guide and map is invaluable if you want to cover any appreciable amount of territory. For instance, though you can walk from Nice's rail station to the water, you'll want to save some energy for strolling once you get there. After all, the Promenade de l'Anglais is five miles long. By taking a number 15 bus from the station (this bus also goes to the Marc Chagall Museum), you can ride to the promenade. While a single trip ticket costs about $1.60, you can make unlimited bus trips during one day for about $4.20.

Exploring Nice

Perhaps the most delightful way to spend a morning in Nice is by visiting its public market in the old section of town. The magic begins as you walk along cours Saleya, the street leading to the market. On one side of the street, there's a shop devoted to olive oil; on the other, a pâtisserie-confectionery called Maison Auer, whose interior of white plaster of paris moldings and medallions looks like it has been frosted with meringue. The candies, petits fours, cakes, and other delicacies on display are as tempting as any you'll find on the Riviera.

The market itself begins with the flower sellers' stalls. Pails of calendulas, lilies, poppies, carnations, crysanthemums, Dutch irises, dahlias; nosegays of violets; roses in half a dozen colors; orchids; mixed bouquets; and houseplants tempt you to spend all your time gazing at them. In the produce section, one vendor specializes in mushrooms, with more than 20 varieties. Another features herbs and spices, including several we don't usually see in North America. There are stalls with bins of dried legumes, or glacéed fruits precisely arranged; there are vendors whose eggplant and apples would win blue ribbons at any state fairs in the United States. Anyone who visits the market with a camera had better bring along two or three rolls of film.

If you bring along an appetite, however, you had better buy something to stave off your hunger, since food at the restaurants and sidewalk cafés adjacent to the market is expensive. Fruit juice or a bottle of water costs about $3.40. Coffee goes for $2 for plain decaf to $5 for Café Viennois. Breakfast, which includes a hot beverage, two pastries, a glass of fruit juice, and a small pot of jam, costs about $10.

For the best meal prices, walk along av Jean Médecin, the main shopping street. Prices at the glass-case vendors on the sidewalk are reasonable, and there's also a Prisunic *super-marché* where you can buy food for a picnic on the beach.

When you go to the beach, don't expect to lie on the sand. There just isn't any. While some of the Riviera beaches, such as those at Cannes and Antibes, are sandy, many others, including the one encircling Baie des Anges in Nice, are gravelly pebbles.

As far as sight-seeing is concerned, the most interesting of Nice's churches is the St-Nicholas orthodox church on blvd Tsarevitch. It's acknowledged to be the most beautiful Russian church ever built outside Russia. With five sparkling onion domes, it contains icons and other priceless religious artifacts.

For one of the best collections of the works of Dufy, go to Galerie-Musée Raoul-Dufy (77, quai des Etats-Unis; 93-62-31-24). The works of art, most of which were donated to the city by Dufy's widow, include 28 oils and 15 watercolors, as well as drawings and proposals for fabric designs. Admission to the museum, which can be reached by bus number 8, is free.

People who are fond of primitive art won't want to miss Musée International d'Art Naïf Anatole-Jakovsky (av Val-Marie; 93-71-78-33). Housed in the restored Château Ste-Helene, this collection was owned by Jakovsky, a leading art critic of his day. Admission is free. Buses number 9, 10, and 12 stop nearby.

Visit the Picasso and Matisse Museums only if you haven't had a chance to see their works in Paris. These two Riviera museums are small, with collections that aren't nearly as impressive as those you'll in Paris. The Chagall Museum, however, is well worth a visit to see a number of the artist's paintings based on biblical themes, such as Jacob wrestling with the angel, Moses and the burning bush, and Abraham and the three angels. The stained-glass window is particularly memorable.

Whether you stay in Nice or elsewhere else on the Côte d'Azur, you'll want to spend some time exploring the rest of the area. But sight-seeing tours are expensive—about $40 to $65 for a half-day tour, $112 to $150 for a full-day, meals not included.

You can duplicate most of these tour itineraries on your own for a fraction of the cost. For instance, instead of taking the $150 "French Riviera Tour," ride the train along nearly the same route for less than $20. Occasionally you will go through tunnels, but most of the time the views are stunning.

The entire route, from Cannes to Ventimiglia, just across the Italian border, takes about 1 hour and 20 minutes.

Although regularly scheduled bus service operates along the Riviera, the buses don't always follow the most scenic routes. Like autos, the buses have to contend with heavy traffic, so it takes at least an hour to travel the 15 miles from Nice to Menton, France's closest city to the Italian border.

Most likely you won't have time or inclination to explore all of the Riviera's beauty spots, but the following suggestions will give you a cross-sampling of what's available.

Each of the major Riviera population centers has its top tourist attractions—the palace guards in Monaco and its casino at Monte Carlo, the baroque church of St-Michel in Menton, the Villa and Gardens of Baroness Ephrussi (she was a member of the enormously wealthy Rothschild family) at Cap Ferrat, the 14th-century fortress at Cagnes-sur-Mer.

Two area attractions that appeal to children as well as adults are the Musée National de Monaco (17, av Princesse Grace) in Monte Carlo with its collection of automated puppets (open from Easter through August, 10 A.M. to 6:30 P.M.; September 1 to Easter, 10 A.M. to 12:15 P.M. and 2:30 to 6:30 P.M.) and Parc des Miniatures (blvd Impératrice Eugenie) in Nice, where hundreds of buildings at 1:25 scale illustrate the history of the city of Nice from its beginnings.

Heading for the Hills

The resort communities along the water are only a part of the area's sight-seeing options, however. The slopes of the Maritimes are dotted with interesting towns and villages. Most of the roses, jasmine, carnations, mimosa, and lavender that grow in fields on the Côte d'Azur travel either as cut flowers to the markets and shops of Paris or to the factories of Grasse, center of the perfume industry, about 15 miles west of Nice. Several of the perfume factories in Grasse offer free guided tours. If you're planning to purchase any fragrances,

THE RIVIERA IN STYLE

If you look upon your excursion to the Riviera as a once-in-a-life-time event, here's a word of advice. Pull out all the stops as far as your lodgings are concerned. Even if it means staying only two nights instead of four, reserve a hotel that's on the water, with your room looking out on the sea. You can economize in other ways. Take overnight trains from Paris to save on hotel rooms. Eat street food and supermarket picnics three meals a day. Sightsee via public buses and foot power. Anything so that you can enjoy the Mediterranean to the fullest.

The ideal is to stay at a place like La Reserve (5, blvd General Leclerc: 93-01-00-01) at Beaulieu-sur-Mer, about six miles east of Nice. The resort itself is a grande dame, with high ceilings, quietly elegant furnishings (the raw silk draperies in the dining room are stunning), and lovely fresh flower arrangements with not a petal drooping. Though it's right on one of the Riviera's main roads, once inside the hotel, you're worlds away from the madding Riviera crowds.

With only 26 rooms and suites, La Reserve is about as close as you can get to living like the very wealthy, unless you rent a villa for about $2,000 a night. Double rooms cost from about $280 to $378 per night, depending on the view, but every so often special promotions are available.

When you're not swimming in the saltwater pool or walking through the gardens, you might wander around the corner to the harbor, where fishermen moor their boats next to the stalls where their catches are sold. There's also an inviting boulangerie-pâtisserie along the way where you can stop to breakfast on freshly baked pastries.

You may choose to walk along the harbor at Villefranche, one of the prettiest on the Riviera, or you might visit Villa Kerylos in Beaulieu (rue Gustave-Eiffel; 93-01-01-44). Built in the early 1900s, it's a reproduction of a wealthy Greek's home at the time of Pericles. The mosaic floors, murals, and richly decorated interiors of the villa, along with its gardens, are intended to evoke the daily life in ancient Greece. Open 3 to 7 P.M. daily, July and August; Tuesday to Sunday 2 to 6 P.M., September through June (closed during November). Admission is about $4.

look for the brochures with discount coupons in the tourist office information racks before you leave on your excursion.

While in Grasse, you may want to visit the International Perfumery Museum (Parfumerie Fragonard; 20, blvd Fragonard; 93-36-44-65), where dispensers, bottles, and other perfume-related memorabilia are on display. It's open daily from 8:30 A.M. to 6:30 P.M., and there is no admission charge either for a tour of the perfume factory or visit to the museum.

Several of the Riviera's chapels were decorated and/or designed by major contemporary artists. Among them, Chapelle du Rosaire, in Vence, was designed and decorated by Henri Matisse. There's a mosaic by Chagall in the ancient Cathedrale de la Nativité in Vence as well.

People as diverse as Chopin's lover, George Sand, and the German philosopher Friedrich Nietzsche adored the mountain village of Eze. You probably will, too, provided your calf muscles don't give out while you're negotiating all its steps and steep, cobbled streets. Among the other villages, St-Paul-de-Vence and Mougins are popular with tourists.

While in Mougins, you may want to stop at the gift shop of chef Roger Verge's one-star restaurant Le Moulin de Mougins (Notre Dame de Vie; 93-75-78-24), where the specialty foods for sale include apricot preserves with sweet almonds, pear William jam with vanilla, sugar-candied clementine preserves, and wild blueberry jam. Despite Le Moulin's dinner prices (they start at about $100), items in the gift shop are not as expensive as you would expect.

Unless you have nerves of steel, chances are you won't want to rent a car to explore the villages. Drivers who have logged thousands of miles say that Côte d'Azur driving is especially difficult. Fortunately for people who don't want to take the expensive commercial tours, public bus transportation is available to most of the villages.

You can fly from Paris to Nice—the Riviera's population center and fifth largest city in France—in about 1 hour and 20 minutes. The train ride takes about 7 hours by TGV, and about 11 hours by conventional train transportation. Tickets cost about $256 round-trip for first class and $200 for second.

People who have no trouble sleeping on trains may want to extend their time on the Riviera by taking overnight trains to and from Paris. For example, the train that leaves Paris's Gare de Lyon at 9:03 P.M. arrives in Nice at 8:18 the next morning. Since these trains stop infrequently and the seats are comfortable (some have footrests), it's possible to get eight hours of sleep without neck cricks or leg cramps the next morning. If you've bought a first-class France Railpass, your trip will be even easier, since many nights the first-class carriages are virtually empty, and with any luck at all, you'll be able to commandeer a couple of seats and stretch out.

Of course, you can pay extra and reserve a compartment or couchette (four berths in one room), but unless there are four in your party, you'll have to share the couchette with strangers—a situation that keeps lots of us awake all night.

Atlantic Coast Charmer

Biarritz in autumn well may be my favorite spot in all of France. After the summer throngs have left, the days are still warm enough for hardy souls to swim in the Atlantic. The paths and walkways that follow the shoreline are uncrowded. The pace is relaxed.

Even in summer, Biarritz is an unpretentious place without high-powered sights to see. Its appeal comes from the quality of its surroundings—tree-lined streets to stroll, pretty gardens, smart shops, and the ocean, which, calm, choppy, or crashing, never ceases to be interesting.

Located on the Atlantic coast in the most southwesterly part of France (the Spanish border is only about 13 miles away), Biarritz is also the major city in the French Basque country. Since bus service to the villages in the nearby Pyrenees is infrequent, the best way to see them is by rental car.

While you're in Biarritz, however, a combination of walking and the excellent public bus service will get you wherever you want to go.

Because it's such a popular tourist destination, Biarritz shopping is top-drawer—Paris in microcosm, but with a Spanish Basque accent. There are boutiques—Christian Lacroix, Hermes, Kenzo, and Sonia Rykiel among them—all clustered in an easily walkable shopping area up the hill and east of the beach.

Among the specialty shops, La Fonda (27, place Clemenceau; 59-22-35-21) features decorative ceramic tiles. Helena (27, av Eduoard VII; 59-24-73-43) sells Basque bath and kitchen towels, bathrobes, and bedroom slippers in traditional striped patterns at reasonable prices.

At another Basque linen shop, Jean Vier (58, av Edouard VII; 59-22-29-36), contemporary designs are incorporated into some of the traditional weaving patterns. Among the best stores for window-shopping is Florence (10, av Edouard VII; 59-22-24-92), where the large display area contains attractive dishes and lamps, in addition to great bed and table linens.

Although the treats are expensive, it's hard to resist being enticed inside Henriet (place Clemenceau; 59-24-24-15) by the candy, *gateaux*, and pastries on display in the windows. There are giant chocolate-dipped Florentines and sheets of chocolate full of pistachios, walnuts, almonds, hazlenuts, and pine nuts. The latter costs about $25 a pound, but a $2 taste (about an ounce and a half) won't damage your budget too badly.

Maison Arosteguy (5, av Victor Hugo; 59-24-00-52) has been in business four generations, providing an astonishing array of food products from around the world—it advertises "5,000 articles from 5 continents." This is a place to restrain yourself, because you could spend hours browsing and buying out-of-the-ordinary gourmet food items.

You may decide to try your luck at the municipal casino (definitely not recommended as a money saver). The slot machine area opens at 11 A.M., and no admission is charged. If you want to play blackjack or roulette, however, you'll have to wait until 3 P.M. and pay an admission fee of about $14. The casino closes at 3 A.M.

You can reduce the cost of the casino entrance fee by using one of the coupons available at the Office de Tourisme and many of the hotels. For the coupon and $20, you will get about $10 in jetons (tokens) to use in the machines, and a free drink in addition to admission. The only catch is that the tokens are nonnegotiable and can only be used for playing the games. Therefore, you have to win back at least $4 in order to come out even with the regular entry fee.

It's far cheaper and better to visit the municipal swimming pool in the same complex, open various hours each day (but always from noon to 2:30 P.M.). You need to pay only about $2.40 ($1.20 for children) to use this state-of-the-art facility. As an exercise alternative, you might walk along the seaside promenade or through one of Biarritz's residential neighborhoods. Almost any street in town will provide you with trees, flowers, and interesting houses to admire.

The best way to explore the immediate area around Biarritz is by public bus. There are 11 different routes, which wind through various neighborhoods and also serve Bayonne.

At the confluence of the Nive and Adour rivers, Bayonne was originally a Roman garrison. Medieval Bayonne developed on the same site. The town became a flourishing port during 300 years of English rule, which came about when Eleanor of Aquitaine and Henry Plantaganet were married (their son, Richard the Lion-Hearted, married a Basque princess).

The most architecturally interesting part of Bayonne is the area around the Gothic Cathedrale St-Mary, built during the 13th and 14th centuries. The city also has a number of 17th-century stone and half-timbered houses in a style identified as Bayonne architecture.

Among the treasures at Leon Bonnat Museum (5, rue Jacques Lafitte; 59-59-08-52) are paintings, sculptures, and sketches by Goya, Durer, Michaelangelo, Rafael, Delacroix, and Constable. Other attractions include the Reptilarium (chemin St-Bernard; 59-50-11-34) with crocodiles, pythons, iguanas, and such.

While you're in Bayonne, have a cup of hot chocolate. Among the city's claims to fame is that it was the first place in France where the beverage was tasted. It seems that when the Jews, who were renowned for the manufacture of hot chocolate, fled from the Spanish Inquisition, they settled in Bayonne to resume their hot-chocolate-making endeavors.

The most fascinating side trip from Biarritz is a drive into the Basque country. Of the three Basque provinces in France (there are four more across the border in Spain), Labourd is the closest. However, Basse-Navarre, the next province, is less than an hour away, and it doesn't take much longer to get to Soule, the most mountainous of the three. If you drive high enough, you'll see stone circles and burial mounds along the passes of Bagargi and Orgambidaska, where there's also a bird-watching observatory. You'll pass through the forest of Iraty, one of the largest mountain forests in Europe.

Wherever you go in the higher reaches of the Basque country, you'll be driving through a travelogue of shepherds' stone huts, flocks of sheep, and herds of cattle in the mountain meadows, streams, canyons, and fairy-tale villages. Among the most photogenic of the villages are slate-roofed Barcus in Soule province and Sare in Labourd. Another is St-Jean-Pied-de-Porte in Basse-Navarre, where flower-decked balconies look over the Nive River.

Typically, Basque houses are built with their backs to the sea and Atlantic storms, their windows and doors on the east to take advantage of the rising sun. Most of the houses are whitewashed, with red or green timber frames and window shutters representing the Basque national colors.

To fully appreciate the country you're traveling through, stop every now and then to see what the villages have to offer besides their scenic charm. A castle-fort overlooks Mauléon, capital of Soule, where 70 percent of the espadrilles manufactured in France are made. In the Basse-Navarre village of Larressore, the famous Ainciart-Bergara makilas (walking sticks with weapons in their heads) have been made by the same family for more than 200 years. The sticks have been presented to many famous people, including Winston Churchill, Charles de Gaulle, and several popes.

La Bastide-Clairence, in Basse-Navarre, is known as the arts and crafts town of the French Basque region. Weavers, dressmakers, furniture makers, blacksmiths, enamelware craftsmen, and artists are among the people who have their studios and workshops there.

Cheese lovers should be sure to get a brochure/map called *Route du Fromage*, which shows various villages where where Basque Ossau-Iraty, Brebis-Pyrenees, and other cheeses are made.

Essential to each Basque village, regardless of province, is the architectural trinity of church, city hall, and pelota fronton. The Romans and Greeks first played *pila*, the handball game which the Basques adapted to open-air courts with high curved walls, which they call frontons. There are more than 21 variations of the game, which is played with bare hands, wooden rackets (pala), or wickerwork and leather gloves (chistera). The most spectacular variation is played on a covered court and called *cesta punta*. In North America, we know it as jai alai.

If you feel flush, during your Biarritz stay, you'll want to stay at the majestic Hôtel du Palais, built in 1855 as a summer house for Napoleon III and Empress Eugenie. Small balconies look out on the ocean and lighthouse guarding the bay. The view is exciting any time of day; at night, when spotlights play on the rocks, it is spectacular.

Although rack rates at Hôtel du Palais range from about $259 to $350 for a sea view, promotions (usually during December and March) can reduce the rates as much as 17 percent, with the price including continental breakfast and lunch or dinner. It's still expensive, but a bargain if you are interested in total luxury. If your game is golf and you're used to playing on the world's great courses, try one of the Hôtel de Palais's golf packages.

Less luxurious, but still very comfortable, the three-star hotels have rates ranging from about $50 to $164. Among them, The Windsor ($50 to $112), Plaza ($70 to $123), and Miramar (double room rates start at $157) are close to both downtown and the ocean.

To get to Biarritz from Paris, take a TGV train from Gare Montparnasse or a conventional overnight or daytime train from Gare d'Austerlitz. Round-trip, first-class fare is about $236; second-class is about $194. The trip takes 6 hours and 10 minutes.

Perhaps you will decide on other destinations—Mont-St-Michel (stay overnight so you can visit the monastery after the crowds have left), the villages of Provence, or, in wintertime, a ski excursion to the French Alps. If you decide to travel by train, a new automated system that's accessible in the United States will help you determine whether to buy a France Railpass or individual tickets for your travels. By phoning 800/4-EURAIL, you can get first- and second-class fare information, mileage between departure and destination points, and length of the one-way train journey.

Most people think of Paris as a grown-up, sophisticated place. It is. Three-star restaurants and risqué revues, they say, are for adults. And they're right. What they don't realize is that there's a childlike side to Paris as well—a side that delights in simple entertainment. As a result, activities that please the children bring pleasure to their parents, too.

Take Luxembourg Gardens. While the adults soak up the natural beauty around them, kids can float miniature sailboats on the round pond. The boats (and a long stick to push them with) rent for about $3. Or the youngsters might watch puppet shows, as French children have for 100 years. Puppet-show tickets don't cost much either.

Sounds idyllic? Sure. But that kind of family fun is possible when you put sufficient effort into planning.

Getting There

One of your big expenses will be transportation to Paris. Since prices for flight routings and children's airline tickets vary with the airline, consider the length of your flight, scheduling, and stopovers before you make any decisions. Saving 20 percent of the adult fare on a child's ticket may not be worthwhile if it involves a very long wait between connecting flights. And although children under two years usually fly free when not occupying a seat, it's safer to have a child restrained in an approved infant seat. Besides, holding a baby for eight or more hours in a crowded plane will leave you exhausted—not the best way to start a vacation.

When you reserve your seats, find out about special meals for children. Pizza, hot dogs, pasta, and other kid-pleasing foods are often available with advance notice. Airplanes usually have baby food aboard, but it's important to bring what you need in case they don't. Also, for takeoffs and landings, don't forget to have bottles or pacifiers handy, because sucking on them helps ease pressure on babies' ears.

Bedding Down

You may find that the air-and-accommodations packages will be the most economical answer to your big-ticket expenses. As I mentioned in chapter 2, however, it's not as easy to find these packages as it was just a few years ago. You'll probably do better by using the Internet. Not only will you find out what is available in your price range, but each Web site also lists specials.

One of the best promotions for families is Hôtel Sofitel's weekend promotion "Invitation Enfants," available on Friday, Saturday, and Sunday nights at all of its properties in Paris. The plan provides two rooms for the price of one, with up to two children sharing the second room. The children must be under the age of 18.

Rack rates at Sofitel's Paris hotels range from about $217 at the Sofitel Forum Rive Gauche (14e; 17, blvd St-Jacques; 40-78-79-80; Glaciere Métro station) to about $350 at Sofitel Paris Arc de Triomphe (8e; 14, rue Beaujon; 45-63-04-04; Charles-de-Gaulle-Etoile Métro station).

While this would be the least expensive way to stay at the lower-rate Sofitel hotels, it might not be at other establishments. For example, if your stay coincides with dates for their winter or summer sales mentioned in chapter 2, you might want to reserve two rooms at one of a chain's more upscale properties at 40 percent off, since the sale rates include buffet breakfast, which cut costs for a family with healthy appetites. The promotion, which has been ongoing for several years, is usually available during winter months through the first third of March and during June and July.

The current strength of the U.S. dollar will also work in your favor. For example, a double room at Libertel Croix de Malte (1e; 5, rue de Malte; 48-05-09-36; République Métro station), which cost $100 as part of an air-and-accommodations package in 1998, costs $85.50 in today's dollars. This sort of price works especially well if you're traveling with teenagers and prefer to have separate rooms.

Since most families vacation in the summer months, you'll want to look for the hotels—and there are a large number of them—where rates are at their lowest during July and August.

My vote for the best value in family accommodations goes to the Holiday Inn La Villette, across the street from Cités des Sciences et des Industries (19e; 216, av Jean Jaures; 44-84-18-18; Porte de Pantin Métro station). The hotel is only a few years old and rooms are spacious, a rare thing even for higher-priced hotels. The decor is both chic and cheerful. The rack rate is usually about $174 a double, but the "Family Great Rates" price brings the rooms down to $105 during low season and $139 in summer. This price includes free accommodations for two children or teenagers under the age of 19 sharing their parent's room. A more expensive program called "Best Breaks" (about $157 in summer) includes tax, service charges, and buffet breakfast for up to two adults and two children 12 and under sharing the room. That means you get a great breakfast with yogurt, cheese, meat, eggs, and other filling food for four people for $18. At times an additional feature—a fifth night free—has been part of the package as well.

What may seem like a drawback to some families—the 20-minute Métro ride from the hotel to the city's center—will be a plus to others. There are great play facilities at the Cités des Sciences and des Industries. A big supermarket is across the intersection from the next Métro stop, and restaurants in the neighborhood are far less expensive than those downtown.

Whatever accommodations you decide on, by all means have reservations before you leave home. Traveling to Paris with kids and without knowing where you'll stay isn't a good idea. You won't end up without a roof over your head, but you will—unless you're extremely lucky—pay a good deal more than if you had prepared in advance.

Panic-Proof Packing

Outfit each child old enough to walk steadily with a backpack—you can get them for about $7 and up at discount stores. Let the children help you decide what to put in their packs—toys, snacks, a piece of the favorite blanket that makes it easier to get to sleep in a strange bed. After you've arrived at your Paris lodgings, those backpacks can be used to carry the day's snacks or picnic lunches as well as any small purchases the children make.

When you pack the family's clothing, remember that you're not going to Paris to wash clothes in the hotel room bathtub. Bring along only enough clothing for four or five days, since you'll find Laundromats all over the city.

Be sure to include health aids, such as a few Band-Aids, children's aspirin, sunblock, and an extra toothbrush or two. They won't weigh much, but you'll save a lot of francs—not to mention time—if you don't have to buy them. Tuck in a washcloth or two also, since even the more expensive hotels often don't furnish them. And plastic cutlery plus a stack of plastic margarine tubs will come in handy when your meals come from the charcuterie or supermarket.

Whatever you do, keep your luggage light. You'll save taxi dollars if you can use public transportation or walk to your hotel. And remember, backpacks or luggage with shoulder straps will let you keep your hands free to corral straying toddlers and break up wrestling matches.

Table Matters

To be honest, it can be tough feeding a family in Paris without spending a fortune, especially if your children eat as much as adults. The prospect of dining out becomes terrifying when you realize that lunches and dinners that cost $20 to $30 are considered inexpensive in Paris.

If most of your meals are informal, though, there's no cause for alarm. You can do a great deal toward keeping everyone happy by planning a trip to the supermarket shortly after arrival—and the backpack makes it easy to carry your purchases back to the hotel. Buy a few days' supply of snacks, cheese, juices, soft drinks, and fruit, so that whenever mealtime is delayed the children will have something to tide them over.

This is a great money saver, since the inclination to stop at the first restaurant you see—whatever its prices—or at an outrageously expensive snack stand is strong when you're accompanied by cranky kids.

If breakfast isn't included in your hotel package, have fruit or juice before you leave your room in the morning, then augment it with a pastry or croissant when you see an appealing bakery. Sandwiches from a street counter or boulangerie make a filling lunch and keep costs down if you've brought your supermarket beverages along.

You may want to buy crêpes from a street vendor, but do it *after* you've eaten. If the children are hungry, it will take at least two or three to fill them up. At $2 to $3 a crêpe, that becomes expensive.

Delicious baguettes and sweet rolls from a boulangerie, produce from the supermarket, and delicatessen meats cost about the same in Paris as in North America. Supermarket cheese and cookies usually cost less. Each time you put together a simple picnic, you save a lot of money.

When it's time to sit down to a meal, you'll find a variety of restaurants with kid appeal. In addition to hamburger chains like McDonald's (be on the lookout for the "Buy a Big Mac, Get One Free" offers in coupon booklets at the tourist office racks), the less expensive brasseries and bistros are good choices. The foods they serve—especially the sausages and *pommes frites*—plus the hustle and bustle will please most children.

Dinners at the popular Chez Jenny (3e) cost about $32, but there's a special children's menu for about $16. Specialties include *choucroute garnie* (sauerkraut, pork, and sausages), shellfish, and grilled meats.

If you're in the mood for omelets, go to Le Trumilou (4e; 84, quai de l'Hôtel de Ville; 42-77-63-98; Hôtel de Ville or Pont-Marie Metro station. Set price meals start at about $13. Be sure to ask for a window table so you can watch the action on the Seine and also have a view of Notre Dame.

Perraudin (5e; 157, rue St-Jacques; 46-33-15-75; Luxembourg Métro station) is a red-and-white-checked-tablecloth kind of place, and the sort of traditional student hangout younger kids love. The lunch menu (about $12) includes such hearty fare—bowls of homemade soup, beef stew, lentils with salt pork—that you'll need only something light in the evening.

Another economical mealtime solution is to eat at ethnic restaurants. When France's former colonies gained their independence, a good number of their residents moved to Paris—often for political reasons. Through the decades, Paris has been a haven for refugees from eastern Europe. Since Belleville has traditionally been the city's immigrant area, that's where you'll find the foods of many cultures.

Among the more recent refugees have been Moroccans and Algerians—people from the former colonies in West Africa—Laotians and Vietnamese. Among the Asian restaurants you might want to try are Lao Siam (19e; 49, rue de Belleville; 40-40-09-68; Belleville Métro station), where the many-page menu lists dishes from Laos, Thailand, Vietnam, and China. Prices for the various dishes start at about $10.

At Lao Thai (20e; 34, rue de Belleville; 43-58-41-84; Belleville Métro station), lunch menus start at about $9.40 and à la carte prices begin at about $10. The Thai salads, with beef, chicken, or shrimp, are a good choice.

For North African and eastern European restaurants, walk along rue des Rosiers (4e; St-Paul Métro station) and you'll find a number of them that look inviting. The best-known restaurant on the street is Jo Goldenberg (7, rue des Rosiers; 48-87-20-16). With a yellow-and-black tile facade and joyful Jewish atmosphere, the restaurant offers Hungarian, Polish, Russian, and Yiddish specialties. Dinners cost about $30, but you may prefer to order à la carte and share, since portions are large.

Family Adventures

Family fun in Paris can come with a very big price tag—but it doesn't have to. Many museums and other attractions waive entrance fees for people under the age of 18; others charge half the adult admission. Movies and cultural performances have special rates for children and young people.

Chances are, if you haven't been to Paris as a family, you'll want to take the children on some sort of sight-seeing excursion to the major points of interest (see chapter 6). If you decide to take a bus tour, you'll probably find the hop-on and hop-off variety suits your family best. ParisBus, which makes nine stops at major attractions, costs about $20.30 for adults and $9.80 for children. Tickets are valid for two days, which makes this an especially good deal. In addition, coupons for about $1 are frequently in weekly entertainment magazines, including *Paris Midnight*.

Even less expensive on Sunday and holidays between mid-April and the third week in September is Balabus. The bus trip, which takes 75 minutes, includes drive-bys of points of interest from the Grande Arche of La Defense to the Gare de Lyon, with detours along the way. The bus stops frequently to accommodate passengers but costs only three Métro tickets (pass holders ride free and can get on and off at will).

Kids will love seeing the city by *bateaux mouche*. It's not a cheap 90 minutes as far as per-hour family entertainment goes, though. Tickets cost about $7 for adults, depending on which company you choose; about $3.50 for children (be on the lookout for $1-off coupons on adult fares). It is, however, a definitely enjoyable experience if the weather is fine.

A longer boat trip goes between the quai Anatole-France, at the foot of the Musée d'Orsay (9:30 A.M. and 2:30 P.M.) and Parc de la Villette (9:45 A.M. and 2:15 P.M.); from March 31 to mid-November, 9:30 A.M and 2:15 P.M. The trip costs about $14 for adults, $12 for young people ages 12 to 25, and $8.50 for children 6 to 11.

Another trip, from opposite the Bastille to the la Villette dock at approximately the same times, is somewhat shorter but also costs less—about $11.20 for adults and $6.50 for children under 12.

After the general sight-seeing, you'll probably want to visit some of the attractions mentioned earlier in this book. And whereas in Paris the best way to go from place to place is on foot, this can be difficult when you have youngsters along. You'll notice, however, that it's common to see children who are four or even five years old being pushed in strollers (the French call them *poussettes*). Either bring one from home or ask the concierge or reception desk personnel where they can be rented.

A Duo of Theme Parks

The ultimate family entertainment, as far as Europeans are concerned, is Disneyland Paris. About 20 miles east of Paris on the A4 autoroute (64-74-30-00), Europe's number one tourist attraction is pricey, crowded, and spectacular. The layout is much like other Disney theme parks, with a Main Street USA, Fantasyland, Discoveryland, Adventureland, and Frontierland. Many of the rides are similar, too—It's a Small World, Pirates of the Caribbean, and the Swiss Family Robinson's Treehouse, for example. A railroad with steam engines runs around the periphery, and there are Disney parades down Main Street.

But there are differences—many due to the advanced technology when the latest of the Disney wonder parks was created. Sleeping Beauty's Castle (Château de la Belle au Bois Dormant) was inspired by the Louvre and châteaux along the Loire, and somehow looks more magnificent than those in the other parks. Rides generally seem a bit more exciting, too.

The most spectacular attraction is Buffalo Bill's Wild West Show, with actors portraying Buffalo Bill, Sitting Bull, and Annie Oakley plus a cast of supporting entertainers, and live bison and longhorn cattle. One Disney buff says there's nothing that matches it, except maybe the Calgary Stampede.

In low season, the daily adult Passport costs about $23.80; it's $22 for children 3 to 11 years old (two-day passes run about $46.20 and $37.80). High-season prices are about $32.20 for adults and $25.20 for children (two-day passes, about $62.30 and $49). Dinner at the Wild West Show is about $49 for adults and $30.25 for children.

Disneyland Paris also includes six hotels, where rates for the least expensive package, "Belle Notte"—one night and two days—range from about $153 to $352 during low season, depending on which hotel is chosen. The price, which is for two adults and two children, includes accommodations, continental breakfast each morning, and two days' unlimited access to the park. There are more expensive packages as well, which include a Wild West Show option.

The park is open 9 A.M. to 11 P.M. in summer and 10 A.M. to 6 P.M. the rest of the season, except on certain Saturdays and school holidays, when it closes at 8 P.M. To get to the park by public transportation, take RER line A to the Marne-la-Vallée/Parc Disneyland station (about $16 round-trip per adult; about half that for children). From the Charles-de-Gaulle Airport, the Disneyland Paris bus leaves outside Door 1 (about $7 round-trip per person). During low season, count on spending at least $165 for public transportation and admission to the park for a family of four. Food, purchases, and the Wild West Show will more than double that amount.

Parc Asterix is themed around the comic-strip character Asterix the Gaul, who has been a favorite with French children for more than 35 years. The park, which is about 25 miles northeast of Paris on the A1 autoroute (08-36-68-30-10), isn't slick like Disneyland Paris. However, it has a Gallic sense of humor and naïveté that will appeal to families weary of glitz.

Quintessentially French, the park entrance is a street called Via Antiqua, lined with Egyptian, English, Greek, Roman, and European-style building facades. Attractions are located in six areas—Village d'Asterix, Grand Lac, Grece Antique, Cité Romaine, Domaine Lacustre, and Rue de Paris.

Many of the rides and entertainments are based on adventures of little Asterix and his huge sidekick, Obelisk, as adapted from the Asterisk book series. In one stage performance, for example, Crassus Megalus, the megalomaniac owner of the greatest chain of amphitheaters and Roman circuses, dreams of becoming emperor and presents the greatest stars of the empire in an attempt to achieve his goal.

The Rue de Paris, however, traces the history of the city from the Middle Ages. The Three Musketeers swashbuckle. Cancan dancers do their high kicks. The fables of La Fontaine come to life. Culture, history, and entertainment—as well as sidewalk cafés—make this my favorite area of the park.

Charli Encore, the unbearable all-terrain baby, goes throughout the park in his giant pram—complete with two-stroke engine and five gears. The Flying Dutchmen juggle objects while they're 13 feet above the ground on a monocycle (unicycle). Members of a roving theater troupe (from 17 countries) entertain crowds as they pass by.

Admission to Parc Asterix, which is open 10 A.M. to 6 P.M. from the second week in April to mid-October (to 7 P.M. during summer months), is about $25.90 for adults, $18.90 for children 3 to 12 years old (two-day passes run $49 and $35.70).

To reach the park by public transportation, you must first take RER line B from Chatelet or Gare du Nord station to the Charles-de-Gaulle Airport (about $14 round-trip), then transfer to the buses just outside the RER station (about $6 round-trip) for the ride to the park.

If you prefer something other than expensive, they've-done-it-all-for-you amusements, you'll find that Paris has a number of less expensive, mind-expanding attractions, too.

Parc de la Villette (Porte de Pantin or Porte de la Villette Métro station) is a 136-acre oasis in the 19th arrondissement that, as far as many children—and adults—are concerned, is the most interesting place in Paris. I agree.

In the late 1970s, a plan was conceived to convert abattoirs (places where animals are butchered and killed) in what was formerly the city's slaughterhouse district into a science center unlike any other in the world. This enormous restoration project has transformed the old buildings into state-of-the-art facilities that have been augmented by new structures. Dedicated to the promotion of learning about science and industry, as well as providing venues for musical performances, these grand structures are accented by a series of 24 contemporary, lipstick-red *folies* (follies), each of which has a different shape and function. *Folies* are usually small buildings constructed in parks or on estates for the purpose of pleasure, recreation, and leisure, such as gazebos, pool houses, and game rooms.

In one of the cubistic buildings, youngsters and adults can build structures on the black-and-white tables with big red architectural blocks. Another serves as a day-care area. There are playgrounds, too, with imaginative things to do—windmill blades that are propelled by pedaling as if on a bicycle; ground-level trampolines; undulating surfaces to run up and down. A futuristic dragon made of sheet-metal stovepipes and steel grids has a long tongue that's really a slide.

The largest of the traditional buildings is called Cités des Sciences et des Industries (40-05-70-70). In one of the structure's areas, the Explora, are all sorts of hands-on exhibits, including flight simulators that enable you to pilot a plane. Another exhibit imitates the experiences you would encounter in space travel. You can design a car, too.

The object of the "Odorama" display is to guess what smells go with the pictures projected on a screen. In the Double Perspective room, people seem larger or smaller than they actually are. There are sound dishes, plus dozens of other "learn-while-you-play" exhibits.

The Inventorium, an activity center that's also in the building, features separate areas for children 3 to 6 and 6 to 12 years old. At the Planetarium, 10,000 stars are projected onto the dome, and live images are relayed from the foremost observatories around the world. Science fiction and scientific films are shown at Cinéma Louis Lumière.

A separate structure, the Geode, is the park's most popular attraction. Made up of about 6,500 stainless-steel triangles fitted tightly together, the sphere contains a hemispheric movie screen that makes viewers feel like they're part of the action, whether you are traveling through the galaxies or scuba diving among the creatures of the sea.

The Grande Halle, a magnificent structure of wrought iron and glass, is used for special exhibitions, such as a recent retrospective of traveling fun fairs from 1850 to 1950, with more than 1,000 items from barrel organs to game stalls and carnival rides, including reconstructions of life on the midway and under the big top.

It's all open 10 A.M. to 6 P.M. Tuesday through Saturday, and 10 A.M. to 7 P.M. Sunday. Admission to the Cités is about $7 for adults and $4.90 for children. (Coupons available at Holiday

Inn La Villette and other places in the area are worth about $3 off the adult entrance fee.) Tickets to the Cités plus the Geode cost about $12.88 for adults and $11 for children. Children under the age of seven are admitted without charge.

More Fun for Everyone

Maybe all kids aren't thrilled with the thought of spending an afternoon at the museum, but the following are fairly sure to make a hit with even the most recalcitrant. (If your children have special interests, some of these facilities listed those listed in chapter 8 should appeal to them.)

Musée de la Femme et Collection d'Automates (12, rue du Centre, Neuilly; 47-45-29-40; Pont de Neuilly Métro station). This collection of automatons and clockwork dolls, which includes about three dozen automated dolls from the 19th century, has the same effect on youngsters as miniature train layouts do—they're mesmerized. Also included in the collection are items that belonged to famous French women. Open Wednesday through Monday, 2:30 to 5 P.M.

Musée de l'Air et de l'Espace (Air and Space Museum) in the suburb of Le Bourget (Aéroport du Bourget; 49-92-71-99; Le Bourget RER station) displays aircraft, including World War II Allied and Nazi planes, a V-1 rocket, the *Apollo XIII* command module, and the 1982 Soyuz capsule. More than 150 authentic aircraft and space objects make up the collection. Open in summer from 10 A.M. to 6 P.M. (in winter until 5 P.M.); admission is about $5 for adults, $3 for children.

The National Museum of Natural History at Jardin des Plantes (5e; 57, rue Cuvier; 40-79-30-00; Jussieu Métro station) and the Automobile Museum to the left of the Grande Arche at La Defense are other entertainment possibilities.

In time, the youngsters may forget what they've seen in museums, but if you take them to Fontaine Stravinsky chances are they'll remember the experience forever. Don't ask me why, but kids seem to love the collection of bizarre mechanical wonders that twist, twirl, and spray water to honor the musical compositions of Igor Stravinsky. Bright red lips, a very fat lady with a tiny head who is perched on a purple boulder, and a multicolored figure that looks something like a kachina doll—all of which might loosely be called fountains—are part of the display located at the south end of the Centre Georges Pompidou (see chapter 7).

Another unforgettable experience, as far as children are concerned, is the circus. Cirque de Paris (115, blvd Charles de Gaulle, 92390 Villenueve La Garenne; 47-99-40-40; RER line A to Nanterre-Ville station) not only puts on performances at 3 P.M. Wednesday, Sunday, and school holidays, but it also offers kids a chance to spend "Une Journée au Cirque" (A Day at the Circus). From 10:15 A.M. until show time, they're kept busy training with the performers, meeting the animals, learning to put on clowns' makeup, and even trying to walk the tightrope. They get to have lunch with the performers, too.

Going to an aquarium is not my idea of what to do in Paris, but then I'm not a kid who's crazy about fish. Those who are will want to take in the Parc Oceanique (1er; Forum des Halles; 40-26-13-78; Les Halles Métro station), a high-tech, high-priced center for marine life. The brainchild of oceanic explorer Jacques Cousteau, this aquarium lets you feel what it's like to explore a sunken ship, learn to interpret the whale's song, and like Jonah walk around in its belly.

Lots less expensive, though older and more traditional, are the Centre la Mer et des Eaux (5e; 195, rue St-Jacques; 44-32-10-70; Luxembourg RER station) and Aquarium Tropical at Musée National des Arts d'Afrique et d'Oceanie (12e; 293, av Daumesnil; 44-74-84-80; Porte Doree Métro station).

Young Shoppers' Specials

Whether money burns holes in your children's pockets or they squirrel it away, most of them like to go shopping when there's something new to look at. And Paris won't disappoint them. The following are only a few of the shops they may want to visit.

Kids may say "weird" when they see some of the wildly imaginative marionettes and automated figures at Clair de Reve (4e; 5, rue St-Louis-en-l'Île; Sully-Morland Métro station). Created by five artists, many of the marionettes are literary characters such as Cyrano de Bergerac. There are automated chefs, Spanish dons, and a marvelous mini theater with circus performers, too.

Even more exotic are the puppets and marionettes at Rigadon (6e; 13, rue Racine; 43-29-98-66; Odeon Métro station). Witches, angels, and wraithelike creatures with feathered wings, historical and music hall characters, porcelain dolls dressed for the 18th century—there's almost too much to look at in this shop, reputed to be one of the best of its kind in all of Europe.

Au Nain Bleu (The Blue Dwarf; 8e; 406–410, rue St-Honoré; 42-60-39-01; Concorde or Madeleine Métro station) has been in operation since 1836 and is a child's world of delights, with floors of marvelous wooden soldiers, model airplanes, windup toys, dolls, and hundreds of other playthings.

Le Ciel est a Tout le Monde (9e; 7, av Trudaine; 48-78-93-40; Anvers Métro station) is the place to go if your family likes to fly kites. Even if you don't, the brilliant colors and clever shapes will intrigue you.

Pain d'Epices (Gingerbread; 9e; 29–31, passage Jouffroy; 47-70-82-65; Richelieu-Drouot Metro station) specializes in miniatures with everything from dollhouse furniture to tiny tennis racquets.

Mayette Magie Moderne (5e; 8, rue des Carmes; 43-54-13-63; Maubert Mutualité Métro station), with stink bombs, whoopee cushions, and magic tricks galore, is a favorite with both practical jokers and wannabe magicians.

Bois de Rose (6e; 30, rue Dauphine; 40-46-04-24; Odeon Métro station) carries hand-smocked dresses for little girls that are one of the most incredible values in Paris. Charming and well made, many of them cost about $25.

Another shop where clothes look like they were made by someone's talented *grandmère* is Perrette (11e; 29, rue du Faubourg-St-Antoine; 53-17-13-56; Bastille Métro station). Prices, however, are a good deal higher.

Letting Off Steam

Since most kids weren't made for nonstop shopping or sight-seeing, you'll want to have some energy outlets in mind. Unfortunately, most of Paris parks aren't the kind that allow children to walk—let alone run—on the grass. But you'll find plenty of alternatives.

There are public swimming pools throughout Paris. One of the nicest is at the Forum des Halles shopping complex. Piscine des Halles (1e, place Rotonde; 42-36-98-44; Chatelet–Les Halles Métro station) is open daily. It's big—about 50 by 20 meters—clean, and convenient for most tourists.

For ice skating, there's a rink in the northeast corner of Paris (19e; 30, rue Edouard-Pailleron; 42-39-86-10; Bolivar Métro station). The rink is almost Olympic sized, and skate rentals are available.

On Sunday, automobile traffic is allowed on the Right Bank boulevards along the Seine, but long stretches of the narrower roads right next to the river are closed to traffic. They're taken over by moms, dads, kids, teenagers, and even some grand-parents on in-line skates and scooters. There are a few jog-gers, too. On Friday night at about 10 P.M., parents and older children might like to join the thousands of in-line skaters who gather near Cinéma Gaumont (13e; 40, av d'Italie; Place d'Italie Métro station) for a three-hour skate through the city, their path cleared by gendarmes on motorcycle. Several sport-ing goods stores rent in-line skates, so ask the concierge which one is nearest to your hotel.

Paris's biggest zoo, in the Bois de Vincennes (12e; 3, av de St-Maurice; 43-43-84-95; Porte Doree Métro station). One of the nicest features of the facility is that animals are kept in settings similar to their natural habitats. Open daily 9 A.M. to 6 P.M. (it closes at 5 P.M. in winter). Admission is about $7 for adults, $1.40 for children under 18.

Also at the Bois de Vincennes (Château de Vincennes Métro station), Parc Floral de Paris (40-67-90-82) has miniature golf, a miniature train, and other kiddie rides. It is open daily from 9:30 A.M. to 8 P.M. in summer, closing at 5 P.M. in winter. The attractions cost varying amounts.

At the Jardin d'Acclimatation in the Bois de Boulogne (16e; 43-43-92-95; Les Sablons Métro station), boat rides, a miniature train, a small zoo, a clockwork toys village, and a dollhouse are among the attractions for little children. For the older ones there are midway games, a house of mirrors, an archery range, and a bowling alley as well. Charges vary with the attractions.

For some free fun, if you bring along Ping-Pong paddles and balls, you'll be able to play table tennis at several of the city's neighborhood parks where tennis tables are permanent installations.

Cooling Down

To balance the physical activity, you may want some quiet time that includes entertainment especially for children. And in Paris, that means puppet shows. One of the oldest companies, Guignol du Parc Choisy (13e; 149, av de Choisy; 43-66-72-39; Place d'Italie Métro station), is also one of the best. Show times are Wednesday, Saturday, and holidays at 3:30 P.M.

Puppet shows are also a feature at most of the city's major parks, including the Tuileries and Luxembourg Gardens. Presented on Saturday, Sunday, and Wednesday afternoons (when French schoolchildren don't have classes), they're the French equivalent of Punch and Judy shows, with characters hitting each other over the head, knocking each other down, and doing all the other things that kids around the world think are uproariously funny. For information on locations, show times, and admission costs, check the entertainment publications.

There are times, too, when children and their parents need some time to themselves. That's when you call your hotel desk for names of reliable baby-sitters. Or you might talk another family into vacationing in Paris when you do and trade off baby-sitting time. And don't forget doting uncles, aunts, and grandparents—they would probably love the chance to baby-sit in Paris.

CHAPTER

12

Senior Satisfaction

It has often been said that age has its privilege. What hasn't been mentioned as frequently is that those added years change both our perspectives and our priorities. These are important when making your Paris plans, for through the years you've learned a lot about yourself—that an airline seat you bought at a discount feels just as good or even better than one that cost you full fare; that the play everyone said you ought to see and you bought the ticket for at least 25 percent off the list was a complete waste of time *and* money.

Though this chapter focuses on bargains for people who—as the French say—have reached "the third age," I realize that just because you've grown older, what may be a great deal for your neighbor isn't necessarily a bargain for you. After all, you and your contemporaries weren't cookie-cutter people 10, 25, or 50 years ago, so why should you be now? Differences in physical stamina, depth of interest, degree of emphasis on creature comforts, and travel style may be even *more* pronounced than they used to be. Not all of the advice in this chapter will apply to you, so just skip over the parts that don't.

Before You Take Off

The minute you decide Paris is the place you want to visit is when to begin considering your priorities related to saving money—whether you prefer to travel independently or with a group. One of the first things to decide is the length of your stay. If you're usually troubled by jet lag, a trip with a short turnaround time is going to be less satisfactory than one that allows you a day or two to get acclimated upon arrival. On the other hand, there's the danger of planning a visit that becomes too long if it's packed with dawn-to-after-dark activity every day.

You should also consider the question of your hotel room. There are big savings to be had by staying in a hotel without elevators and private baths—but are the savings worth contending with the stairs and the trips down the hall? In the same hotel, rooms with showers might cost less than those with baths. This can mean a major saving opportunity, plus a bonus for people for whom climbing into a European tub amounts to an Olympic event.

Then, too, there's airfare. While most U.S. airlines offer two types of discounts for seniors—discount coupon books good for four one-way flights, and discounts on individual round-trip tickets—only the latter apply to international travel. Most of the airlines listed in chapter 1 offer essentially the same discount—10 percent off the price of certain fares. This isn't applicable when fares are already heavily discounted (usually from 25 to 40 percent) but are available to everyone, regardless of age. In those situations, the promotions are almost always better bargains than the 10 percent off.

Some airlines give discounts to people who have had their 60th birthday; others start at age 62. The best of these programs allow the senior to bring along a companion of any age at the senior price.

The most attractive rates of all are often the result of promotions aimed solely at seniors, who are able to take off at times when younger people are committed to regular jobs and children are in school. These bargain tickets are available when those who predict load factors anticipate a slowdown in travel on certain routes. As a result, you may see an advertisement in a Dallas or Boston newspaper that doesn't apply to seniors anywhere else in the country.

Whenever a ticket is discounted, there may be certain restrictions, such as days of the week when you can fly, the requirement of a Saturday-night stayover, and a specified time minimum between purchase and flight. When you've amassed enough frequent flier points for Paris tickets, you might want to weigh the option of paying the lowest coach fare and using your points to upgrade to first class. The additional legroom and quiet may let you sleep when you otherwise wouldn't be able to, adding considerable value to your travels. And the extra service can't help but put you in a holiday mood.

Choosing a Tour

You won't have to concern yourself with making hotel room and airline reservations if you decide to take a package tour, but you will need to make decisions about which tour you will be happiest taking. Your choice will depend largely on your interests and physical ability. While many seniors prefer the age mix they encounter on regular tours, others find that tours designed specifically for seniors are more compatible with their needs and interests. Two groups that specialize in tours and discounts for seniors are:

Mature Outlook   800/336-6330
50+ Young at Heart Travel Program   202/783-6161

Membership in the Mature Outlook program, a Sears operation, costs $39.95 a year for the enrollee and spouse. It entitles members to 50 percent off published room rates at more than 3,000 hotels, motels, and resorts worldwide, as well as restaurants and rental car discounts, $600 in discount coupons (primarily 10 percent off) on Sears merchandise, and a subscription to the organization's magazine. The 50+Young at Heart program centers on hosteling.

You might also investigate the American Association of Retired Persons' program for independent travelers (202/434-2277). Called the Purchase Privilege Program, it offers discounts on hotels, airfare, car and RV rentals, and sight-seeing. Always remember, however, that some promotions can save you more money than senior discounts of less than 25 percent.

Penny-Pinching Packing

A penny saved is a penny earned when it comes to packing. Anyone who has ever forgotten to pack a couple of aspirin or safety pins or a small sewing kit realizes that. This is especially true when you're going to be staying in Paris, for unless you patronize stores outside tourist areas, you'll find that even little items cost a lot.

Put together a small emergency kit, with everything in it from pieces of moleskin to a small roll of transparent tape. Your kit won't weigh much, but it will enable you to take care of blisters, minor cuts, mending jobs, and even eyeglass repairs.

Speaking of eyeglasses, bring along an extra pair (or your prescription) if you wear them. You'll need sunglasses, too, if you're at all light-sensitive. Although it rarely gets cold enough to snow in Paris, days can be very windy. A head covering and extra sweater will help you feel cozy on chilly days.

If you travel during the warm-weather months, be sure to bring at least one very lightweight outfit. While you may not need it, occassionally some long, hot stretches of weather do occur during summer. Any time of year, an umbrella or light rain gear are feel-good insurance. Also, be sure to wear your heaviest clothes on the airplane—and wear a layer or more than you think necessary. When maximum de-icing is needed, the amount of heat to the cabin is reduced.

When you're packing your carry-on bag, remember any medications you may be taking. If they need refrigeration, make sure you've selected a hotel that has small refrigerators available for guests. People who don't have complete trust in baggage handlers—that includes most of us—also pack night-wear and a change of underclothing, plus essential toiletries, in their hand luggage.

Being There

Once you're in Paris, don't expect people who haven't reached "the third age" to give up their seats on a crowded bus or Métro to you just because you have. What you can expect, though, is a number of bargains in entertainment and transportation. Although there are no senior discounts on the Paris Métro or buses, anyone who has reached his or her 60th birthday is eligible for a Carte Vermeil (Silver Card, referred to as the CV). The cards, which can be purchased at any major rail station in France, come in two categories: Those that cost about $25 allow four rail trips a year at a 50 percent discount, and cards that cost about $45 are good for a year's unlimited rail travel. Both also entitle the bearer to discounted tickets at many Paris theaters and half-price admission to state museums.

If you're planning to take a long excursion or several short trips from Paris, the $25 card will result in savings. The $45 card will be economical only for those who plan to take several excursions and day trips. You'll need proof of age—a passport or photocopy of its first page will do—in order to purchase the CV, which is good from June 1 through May 31.

While you won't find senior discounts for meals very often, it doesn't hurt to ask if there are senior specials or reduced-portion meals available. Also, you might share dishes at the more informal eateries where big portions are the rule—one person ordering a salad; the other, a main course. Though you would never try this in a fancy French restaurant, in a crowded brasserie no one's going to care.

I'd wager it's virtually impossible for anyone but a teenager to eat one order of *moules* and *pommes frites* at the cafés that specialize in mussels and french fries. These are perfect places for divide-the-dish meals. If there are two of you, you might even ask to split one order. There may be a small charge for an extra plate and cutlery, however.

If you visit one of the big supermarkets in the suburbs, go on a Saturday afternoon—a busy shopping time when many of them have people giving away samples of the various products. On one trip, I sampled smoked salmon, several kinds of cheese, quiche, and ice cream, all of which were slightly different—both in taste and the way they were served—from the products at home.

Preferential Prices

It's in the area of attractions and entertainment that seniors get the best financial breaks. Most attractions mentioned in chapters 7 and 8 offer discounts to seniors, such as 50 percent off admissions to all national museums, including the Louvre and d'Orsay. Seniors are eligible for standby tickets at almost all classical music performances, too. Discount coupons on boat rides, sight-seeing buses, and the like that you'll find in tourism office and hotel racks may not amount to big money, but 5 percent here, 10 percent there eventually adds up to major savings.

EDUCATION IN THE BARGAIN

A program many seniors rave about is Elderhostel, which combines travel with learning. Several courses that meet solely in Paris, or combine Paris stops with other locales both in France and other parts of Europe, are currently being offered. Most of them last 14 or 15 days, including travel time. While the cost—including airfare—averages out to around $177.50 to $249.50 per day, this can be a real bargain when you factor in the educational value.

"Art in Paris" is an in-depth review of the evolution of paintings, architecture, and sculpture, and includes discussions of medieval and Renaissance art, classicism, impressionism, and cubism. Costs for the two-week course run from $2,830 to $3,441, depending on the gateway city and time of year. Fees cover airfare, accommodations, instruction, transportation in France, field trips and excursions, most meals, and gratuities to service personnel. Participants in the course stay in double-occupancy rooms with private baths in central Paris hotels.

Other courses include stays in Paris as well as other parts of the country. One of the most interesting courses, "The Impressionists of Normandy, the Seine, and Paris," is a two-week program that addresses the beginnings of impressionism, the lives and works of several famous artists, and the emergence of postimpressionism. Beginning inParis, the middle section of the course's lectures and discussions center on the artistic heritage of Rouen, Giverny, and Honfleur, with the works of artists Sisley, Degas, Toulouse-Lautrec, Monet, and van Gogh getting particular attention. Field trips to Barbizon and Moret-sur-Loing focus on the Barbizon School, the evolution of color design, and techniques for self-portraits and landscapes. In Paris, the emphasis is on the Musée Marmottan and the Musée d'Orsay, with its vast array of impressionist paintings. While in Paris, participants stay in typical French hotels and enjoy a concert, a Seine boat trip, a city excursion, and a stroll from the Moulin Rouge to Montmartre. Free time is also available for hostelers to pursue their individual interests ($2,485 to $ 2,869).

"Royal Splendor: Paris and the Loire Valley" is a course that moves from Paris to tours in the Loire Valley and then back to the capital, tracing the footsteps of kings, queens, and courtiers from the development of the French monarchy in Merovingian times through the end of the Bourbon dynasty. Paris streets and palaces, countryside châteaux and gardens serve as classrooms. Field trips to the Royal Quarter of the Marais, the Île de la Cité, the Louvre, Versailles, and Fontainebleau are included in the Paris portion of the course, along with a concert and Seine boat ride. From Tours, field trips take participants to the châteaux of Blois, Chenonceau, Langeais, Azay-Le-Rideau, Chambord, Cheverny, and Chenon. A Loire boat cruise, French card games, and a wine tasting are also on the itinerary. The cost of the course ranges from $2,605 to $2,820.

Another course, "Paris and St. Petersburg: Capitals, Courts and Cultures," combines a week in Paris with a week in St. Petersburg. Lectures center on such subjects as the Russian presence in Paris, Louis XIV's influence in European courts and Russia, and Russian artists and other émigrés in Paris. Parisian field trips include visits to the Russian cathedral, Orangerie, and Musée d'Orsay as well as the Jewish museum and the palace at Versailles. A special Russian dinner with Russian music and a discussion of contemporary Franco-Russian relations is also part of the experience. The course fees range from $3,995 to $4,150, depending on departure city.

CHAPTER
13

Sources and Resources

They say that it takes money to get money, but when your aim is making your francs go farther, the upfront expenditures won't amount to much—just enough to buy some postage stamps. While it's true that you can get information about Paris by phoning toll-free and 900 numbers in the United States, you obtain some of the most valuable brochures and pamphlets by writing to France.

Although there are exceptions, most French information sources publish materials in English or at least include some English text. And you'll understand more than you would have imagined from those brochures that are entirely in French. But you won't have to worry about the language barrier when you get your information from North American sources. In the United States and Canada, there are five French government tourist offices. Their addresses are:

French Government Tourist Office
444 Madison Avenue
New York, NY 10022
212/315-0888
* * *
676 N. Michigan Avenue, Suite 630
Chicago, IL 60611
312/751-7800

*   *   *

9454 Wilshire Boulevard
Beverly Hills, CA 90212-2967
310/271-7838

Maison de la France/French Government Tourist Office
1981, av McGill College
Tour Esso, Suite 490
Montreal, PQ H3A 2W9 Canada
514/288-4264

*   *   *

30 St. Patricks Street, Suite 700
Toronto, ON M5T 3A3 Canada
416/593-4723

If you call the telephone numbers listed above, in most cases you will be referred to 900/990-0040, which costs 50 cents a minute. You will, however, get a live person at the other end of the line to answer your questions and requests. Another way to get information from a live operator is by dialing the France-on-Call Hotline (202/659-7779) from 9 A.M. to 9 P.M. Eastern Standard Time to get advice, ask for brochures, or obtain specific information about French travel. When possible, it's helpful to make a personal visit to an office in addition to requesting materials by mail, since the materials there are often not the same as those mailed out. The main Paris tourist office is:

Office de Tourisme
127, av des Champs-Elysées
75008 Paris, France
49-52-53-56 (in English)

The office is open daily 9 A.M. to 8 P.M. (closed December 25 and January 1).

When you write for information, be sure to ask for a map of Paris, an explanatory brochure about the Orly or Charles-de-Gaulle Airport if you're arriving by air, and any specific requests—hotel listings, names of vegetarian restaurants, locations of public tennis courts, and so forth. Don't expect to get everything you ask for, since the French don't seem to be nearly so public-relations-oriented as many of their neighbors in Europe.

Once you arrive in Paris, you'll be able to choose from several tourist offices. In addition to the main office on the Champs-Elysées (8e; Charles-de-Gaulle-Etoile Métro station), there are offices at the Eiffel Tower (7e, Champ de Mars); Gare d'Austerlitz (*Grandes Lignes* arrivals area); Gare de l'Est (in the arrivals hall); Gare de Lyon (*Grandes Lignes* exit area); Gare Montparnasse (in the arrivals hall); and Gare du Nord (in the international arrivals hall).

Lines at all the tourist offices are fairly long anytime, and frequently impossible during summer. You'll be wise to get reams of information in advance of your trip by mail. That way, when you're in Paris, you'll only need to visit the tourist offices to scan the brochure racks for additional information and discounts. There may be charges for some of the special-interest publications, but you can expect to be told in advance if there are.

If you have enough lead time, you might consider subscribing to a travel publication, such as *International Travel News* (520 Calvados Avenue, Sacramento, CA 95815; 800/486-4968). Although information in the publication covers all parts of the world, Paris is covered frequently enough to warrant subscribing. After all, one money-saving recommendation can save you the price of a year's subscription ($16) and more.

Check, too, to see if your local library subscribes to *Consumer Reports Travel Letter*. Issues usually are 24 pages, and packed with information. Articles on Paris, or with information that can be applied to Paris, appear several times during the year. One-year subscriptions cost $39 and can be obtained by writing *Consumer Reports Travel Letter*, Subscription Department, P.O. Box 51366, Boulder CO 80321-1366. Twice a year, back issues for the preceding six months are listed and can be purchased for $5 each.

Air and Accommodations

Early in the planning process, you'll want to get in touch with a good travel agent—who should load you down with brochures and other publications that advertise hotels and air-and-accommodations packages. Start newspaper and magazine files, too, of articles about various Paris subjects—hotels among them. Whenever you read about a place that interests you, mark the information with a highlighter so that you can find it more easily when you've arrived at decision-making time.

If you're planning to reserve a hotel room in advance for your Paris stay and have decided not to purchase a package, you might want to write to a number of hotels directly. Ask the travel agent if you might look at *The Hotel and Travel Index* or some other hotel directory for ideas. You might also want to get a copy of the hotel guide that's available at the French Government Tourist Offices in New York. To get information about Paris hostels, write:

Fédération Unie des Auberges du Jeunesse (FUAJ)
27, rue Pajol
75018 Paris

Dining

Dining reviews are subjective by their very nature. However, that subjectivity can be intensified when the publication has a vested interest (translate: advertising) to say only good things in the restaurant reviews it prints. Therefore, take any review you see in a publication that carries restaurant advertising with—pardon the pun—a grain of salt.

Instead, look for reviews in newspapers and books written by restaurant critics, especially those with long track records. You can get this information by reading the authors' bios on the book jackets or covers. For example, one of the best Paris dining guides I have found is *The Food Lover's Guide to Paris* by Patricia Wells, an American who has lived in Paris for many years and is restaurant critic for the *International Herald Tribune*.

Of course, the very best recommendations are from friends who have visited Paris recently and whose culinary judgment is in sync with your own. The only problem is that they often remember the general location of a restaurant, but can't recall its name, which doesn't help a lot in a city where there are several eateries with amazingly similar names on almost every street that isn't residential.

When you plan to eat out several times, it may pay you to investigate dining club memberships. Entertainment Publications' *Paris Directory*, with 350 restaurants, bistros, and fast-food outlets, costs $53 (including postage and handling), an amount that can be easily recouped in discounted meals. The directory is available in the United States by calling 800/445-4137. In France, it can be purchased at 1 bis, rue St-Augustin in the second arrondissement (42-86-86-34; 4-Septembre Métro station) for $50. If you already have a valid Entertainment card for some other city directory, both the U.S. and the Paris offices will sell you a Paris book for half price.

The discount coupons that you find at tourist offices and hotels can mean substantial savings if they are for restaurants you would like to try. For example, Flo Tradition, a brasserie that's often reviewed, puts out a coupon worth 10 percent off the total bill, including beverages, for parties of up to four people.

To obtain a list of vegetarian restaurants that contains the names, addresses, and telephone numbers of 15 establishments, write to the Office de Tourisme on the Champs-Elysées (the complete address is on page 221).

Getting Around

If your map of Paris doesn't include a diagram of the Métro, you'll want to get one. You will also find that a map of the city bus routes and a timetable booklet will come in handy. You should be able to get these in advance from tourist offices. In Paris, they're also available at Métro stations.

Brochures put out by the various *bateaux mouche* operations are available at Paris tourist offices and in hotel information racks. You'll find information on bike rentals, commercial tours, and excursions there, too.

Museums

One of the best publications available from the French National Tourist Offices, called *Paris Museums and Monuments*, not only provides information about some 183 facilities, including opening hours and admission charges, but also designates whether they are national, municipal, private, or under the administration of other groups, and lists the museums and monuments by arrondissement as well as theme.

Shopping

Among the Paris shopping guides that I feel are most comprehensive are *Born to Shop Paris*, by Susy Gershman (1995, HarperCollins, New York), and *The Chic Shopper's Guide to Paris*, by Maribeth Ricour DeBourgies (1991, St. Martin's Press, New York). Although the latter book is a few years old, it gives a lot of good general information and tips. Since information in any guidebook can get out of date quickly, if you have specific stores in mind, it's a good idea to check the current Paris phone directory before setting out on any major shopping expedition.

Look for maps of the larger flea markets in the brochure rack of the tourist office on Champs-Elysées. The markets can be confusing to anyone unfamiliar with their layouts. Also in the brochure racks, you'll sometimes find discount coupons for clothing at various shops. Usually you have to spend a fairly large amount of money to qualify for the savings. Your purchases in one store also have to total a fairly large amount to be eligible for *détaxe* (the tax imposed by the French government on all items except food in grocery stores and markets). Any time your purchases in a store exceed $200, ask salespeople to fill out the appropriate information on *détaxe* forms, then present them at the airport or railroad station *détaxe* desk along with your unopened merchandise before you leave the country.

Sight-Seeing

Several good walking guides to Paris are currently available in North American bookstores. One of my favorites is *Walks in Hemingway's Paris: A Guide to Paris for the Literary Traveler* (1989, St. Martin's Press, New York). Not only does the book give itineraries for eight different walks, with such titles as "Montparnasse: The Expatriates" and "Gertrude Stein: The Garden and the River," but it also contains lots of anecdotes and tidbits of information that make for delightful armchair reading.

It's a good idea to buy any books you may want in North America or the British Isles, since very few books in Paris bookstores are written in English.

Gourmands may want to take a commercial tour conducted by longtime Canadian food writer Rosa Jackson. Her "Paris Market Tours" are designed to give an inside look at the French way of shopping and eating. There are both half- and full-day walking tours. For more information, write:

Paris Market Tours
84, rue du Cherche-Midi
75006, Paris
33-1-42-84-04-57

The Impressionists' Paris, by Ellen Williams (The Little Bookroom, $19.95), contains a selection of walking tour itineraries that lead to actual places depicted in impressionist masterpieces. From the cafés of Pigalle to the dance halls of Montmartre, along the grand boulevards and through narrow alleyways, the book calls attention to sites you might otherwise not notice. It not only shows you where to walk, but also includes snatches of Paris history, anecdotes, and full-color reproductions of major impressionist works.

Twenty-four different itineraries, focusing on the flora and fauna of Paris, are for sale at the Maison de la Nature in Parc Floral de Paris (Bois de Vincennes; Château de Vincennes Métro station). They cost about $1 per itinerary or about $24 for the entire two dozen. However, these "Sentiers Nature" guides are available free of charge at all Paris district town halls. Ask the concierge how to get to the town hall that's most convenient from your hotel.

Guided theme tours of neighborhood gardens, historical gardens, and the like are also available to the general public. Each tour lasts approximately two hours. For information in advance, write to one of the French tourist offices in North America (see the addresses earlier in this chapter). In Paris, you can obtain calendars of events at the Hôtel de Ville (City Hall; 4e) or the Paris tourist office on the Champs-Elysées.

Activities and Entertainment

In addition to the Ritz-Escoffier Cooking School mentioned in chapter 8, top cooking schools include Cordon Bleu (15e; 8, rue Leon-Delhomme, 75015 Paris; 53-68-22-50; Vaugirard Métro station) and La Cuisine de Marie-Blanche (7e; 18, av de la Motte-Picquet, 75007 Paris; 45-51-36-34; Ecole-Militaire Métro station).

For an extensive listing of French-language programs, consult the reference desk of your local libraries. They have brochures and directories, including *The World of Learning.*

Among the weekly and monthly activity, attractions, and entertainment publications are *Where* (monthly, in English), *l'official des Spectacles* (weekly, in French), *Pariscope* (weekly, primarily in French but with an English section), *Paris Midnight* (monthly, in English and French), *Clefs de Paris* (monthly, French and English), and *Figaroscope* (weekly, French). Before you buy these guides, check at your hotel information area and in your room for entertainment guides, since some of them are free, and those that aren't, are often furnished to guests at no charge. If they're not, you can buy a weekly guide at any news kiosk for just a few francs. *Pariscope*, for example, costs only about 60 cents.

In addition, the *Paris Free Voice* is a good, but not exhaustive, source of information on what's going on. Among the places where it's available is the American Church office (7e; 65, quai d'Orsay; 47-53-77-23; Alma Marceau Métro station). The publication is free. While you're at the office (a corridor leading to its entrance is to the right of the church door), check the bulletin board for flyers announcing various events.

If you read French, a great book available in Parisian bookstores is *Paris Pas Cher (Inexpensive Paris)* by Anne and Alain Riou. It tells you not only about cut-rate entertainment and attractions, but also about saving money on such things as haircuts and other necessities of interest to people who live in the city. Books can also be obtained by writing to BP 56, 75261 Paris, Cedex 06, France.

If you're on the lookout, you'll find discount coupons for attractions and entertainments not only in weekly publications and at the tourist centers and hotels, but in places like brasseries, bars, supermarkets, and shopping centers as well. I've found them for everything from about $1.60 off on a bottle of Pernod to $20 off on a dinner show. More usual are the $1 or $2 discounts on places like the Dome Imax at La Defense, the Paristoric multimedia presentation, and for various sight-seeing tours.

Day Trips and Excursions

When you're undecided as to which places outside Paris you would like to visit, write to tourist centers for information on various alternatives. The following list is by no means exhaustive, but will give you a number of offices to contact:

Syndicat d'Initiative (tourist office)
1, rue Bugeaud
73200 Albertville, France

Office de Tourisme d'Angers
place Kennedy
BP 2316
49023 Angers, France

Office de Tourisme de Bayeux
1, rue des Cuisiniers
14400 Bayeux, France

Office de Tourisme de Biarritz
Square d'Ixelles
64200 Biarritz, France

Office de Tourisme de Bordeaux
12 cours du 30 Juillet
33080 Bordeaux, France

Office de Tourisme de Chamonix
place du Triangle-de-l'Amitie
74402 Chamonix, France

Office de Tourisme de Chartres
3, rue de l'Etroit Degre
BP 289
28000 Chartres, France

Office de Tourisme de Lyon
place Bellecour
69002 Lyon, France

Office de Tourisme de Mont-St-Michel
Corps de Garde des Bourgeois
50116 Mont-St-Michel, France

Office de Tourisme de Nantes
place du Commerce
BP 160
44000 Nantes, France

Office du Tourisme et des Congres
2, rue Massenet
06000 Nice, France

Office de Tourisme de Orléans
place Albert 1er
45000 Orléans, France

Office de Tourisme de Reims
1 rue Jadart
51100 Reims, France

Office de Tourisme de Rouen
25, place de la Cathedrale
BP 666
76008 Rouen, France

Office de Tourisme de Tours
78, rue Bernard Palissy
37042 Tours, France

Office de Tourisme de Troyes
16, blvd Carnot
BP 4082
10014 Troyes, France

When you write, be specific about your interests. For instance, if you want to ride bicycles, ask for names and addresses of bike rental operations, costs, and information about bike trails and country roads. When you let the tourism people in areas outside Paris know what information you want, they'll do their best to get it to you—and they do have some very useful materials. For example, an especially complete publication, *Pays aux Châteaux (Château Country)* includes information on all the châteaux, monuments, and museums in the central Loire Valley that are open to the public. It also contains listings of commercial tours that originate at various population centers in the area. The 55-page brochure is primarily written in French, but there are enough subheads and occasional pieces of information in English that it's easy to figure out. The brochure is available from the Tours Office de Tourisme.

If you're interested in Eurailpasses or France Railpasses, travel agents can obtain them; or you can phone 800/4-EURAIL (800/438-7245). When you need information neither of these sources can supply, contact:

A. J. Lazarus Associates, Inc., Public Relations
1500 Broadway, #1705
New York NY 10036
212/768-2497

Paris With the Younger Generation

When you're shopping in Paris, go to museum bookstores and supermarkets for books and activities that will teach the children about French culture and history while they're having fun. You'll find activity and coloring books, as well as a series about France's favorite storybook character, Asterix.

Dining-out discount coupons for places kids like are among the easiest to find. One for the Hippopotamus chain of 15 grills distributes coupons for 10 percent off the total bill, including beverages, and two-for-one offers are frequently put out by places like McDonald's.

If visiting a theme park is high on your list of priorities, write ahead so that you can determine when your family will get the most value (considering both money spent and enjoyment):

Parc Asterix
BP 8
60128 Plailly, France

Walt Disney Company
44, av des Champs-Elysées
75008 Paris, France

Senior Strategies

Elderhostel information is available from:

Elderhostel
75 Federal Street
Boston, MA 02110

When you ask to be put on the mailing list, specify whether you're interested only in international destinations or both international and domestic.

Internet Information

During the mid-1990s, all of Paris seemed to be making arrangements by Minitel—pulling up information on museums and performances, reading the latest news, making

dinner reservations. Though Minitels still are a common convenience in Parisian hotels, homes, and businesses, the use
of the Internet has "exploded" in the new millennium, according to one longtime observer.

Parisians, he says, rarely write checks anymore, and con-
duct most of their business electronically. They're using the
Internet to find out what's playing at the cinema and to access
the French national telephone directory.

An increasing number of hotels, restaurants, museums, and
places or services of interest to tourists and residents alike
have developed their own Web pages. Most of the pages give
you a choice between French and English, but even if the
words on the Web sites are in French, you'll be able to iden-
tify times, addresses, prices, and other information without
knowing the language. If you have a rudimentary knowledge
of French, you'll be able to understand just about everything.
The following listing includes Web sites of interest to travelers. Be aware, however, that new pages are coming online
each week; check with a French tourism office for the latest.

General Information

General information on Paris http://www.bottin-gourmand.com
   (night life, expositions, restaurants)
Paris Tourist Office   http://www.paris.org
Paris—promotion   http://www.paris-promotion.fr
Pariscope (shows, spectacles, http://www.pariscope.fr
   and other entertainments)
Paris anglophone   http://www.paris-anglo.com
Eiffel Tower   http://www.tour-eiffel.fr

Paris Museums

Centre Georges Pompidou   http://www.cnac-gp.fr
City of Sciences La Villette http://www.cite-sciences.fr

National Conservatory of Arts	http://www.cnam.fr
Louvre	http://mistral.culture/fr/louvre
Museums and Monuments Pass	http://www.ubternysees.com
National Library of France	http://www.bnf.fr
National Museum of Anthropology	http://www.mnhn.fr

Dining and Accommodations

French Food and Wines	http://wwwfrenchwinesfood.com
Hotels in France	http://www.hotel-france.com
Camping in France	http://www.francecom.com/aft.camping

Newspapers

Le Monde (general information)	http://Lemonde.globeonline.com
Le Monde Diplomatique	http://www.ina.fr/CP/MondeDiplo
France Amerique	http://Franceamerique.com
Les Echos (economy, industry)	http://wwwlesechos.fr
Paris Match	http://www.Parismatch.com

Miscellaneous

ASFA (highways)	http://www.autoroutes.fr
Sytadin (traffic information)	http://www.club-internet.fr/sytadin
Driving itineraries	http://www.michelin-travel.com
Eurostar (Paris–London)	http://www.eurostar.com
Meteo France (weather)	http://www.meteo.fr

Galeries Lafayette (department store) — http://www.gl.com

Paristoric (historical tour of Paris) — http://paristoric.fit.fr

Synagogues in France — http://loubavitch.fr

Mission for the Celebration of the 21st Century — http://www.celebration2000.gouv.fr

The various departements of France have also established Web sites, which you may want to visit when deciding about day trips and excursions you may want to make. They are:

Anjou	http://www.anjou.com
Bouches du Rhône	http://www.visitprovence.com
Cantal	http://cdwww.in2p3.cr/content
Correze	http://cg19.fr
Côte d'Armor	http://www.cote-d'armor.com
Haute Savoie	http://www.cur.archamps.fr/HauteSavoie
Lot	http://www.crdi.fr/-a.lot.of.france
Morbihan	http://www.morbihan.com
Perigord-Dordogne	http://www.perigord.tm.fr

NOTES

NOTES

NOTES